100

ULSTER
SPORTING
LEGENDS

A Century of Sport in Northern Ireland

STEVEN BEACOM

BALLYHAY BOOKS

First published by Ballyhay Books,
an imprint of Laurel Cottage Ltd.
Ballyhay, Donaghadee, N. Ireland 2020.
Copyrights Reserved.
© Text Steven Beacom
© Photographs; see acknowledgments page
All rights reserved.
No part of this book may be reproduced or stored on any media
without the express written permission of the publishers.
Design & origination Laurel Cottage Ltd.
Printed & bound by GPS Colour Graphics Ltd
ISBN 978 1910657 14 0

CONTENTS

THE KICK-OFF

Northern Ireland, The North of Ireland, Ulster, the Six Counties, the different names for this little piece of land we live on reflect the divisions in the minds of its people. Divisions which, over the last century or so, have often been nurtured by some seeking to consolidate their own power bases. These divisions have seeped into many aspects of life but, through it all, one area that has been a beacon of light against division and strife is sport.

And what a beacon it has been. Brighter than 10 million lighthouses in the dead of night.

My, how we have needed our sport and our sporting heroes to break down barriers, build bridges and bring happiness to our minds, bodies and souls.

From a population only slightly larger than Dublin and way smaller than Greater Manchester it's truly extraordinary how many sporting superstars we've produced and how far above our weight we've punched.

The success has been off the charts and I love it, just like I love sport and have done since I was a little boy growing up in Fermanagh. I have taken part in many sports at one time or another and when I haven't been playing, I've been watching. Like so many, sport has been a huge part of my life.

I feel blessed to have been a sports journalist for over 25 years covering the biggest events on the planet from the Olympics to the World Cup, Wimbledon to the Ryder Cup, World title fights in boxing to European Cup finals in football and rugby as well as important sporting competitions at home and one of the biggest thrills of the job has been to report on people from here shining and seeing what that glory meant to them, their families, their communities and their supporters.

It was at the start of 2020 that I was approached by publisher Tim Johnston from Laurel Cottage about this book, with the idea to detail Northern Ireland's 100 greatest sports stars. I'd had opportunities to write books before but this one piqued my interest because it covers a subject that I'm incredibly passionate about, celebrating and paying tribute to our talented, committed and wonderful sports stars who have brought so much joy to us down the years.

I knew it was going to be a huge challenge. It actually proved to be a monumental one due to the quantity and quality of our sporting greats, which I'll explain shortly.

With any book where you are compiling a list, and I've read quite a few, terms of reference are required. So, first things first, who qualifies? Well, I felt the 100 should include people who have shone on the field, in the ring, on the track, in the water, on the roads and so on. Therefore this is about the competitors rather than coaches or managers. That's perhaps for another chapter when the exploits of people like Michael Bannon, Billy Bingham, Mickey Harte, Michael O'Neill, Brendan Rodgers, Gerry Storey and Harry Williams can be highlighted.

Along with the publisher it was agreed if you were born in Northern Ireland or deemed Northern Irish or from the North of Ireland and have competed as such for yourself, your town, your county, Ulster, Northern Ireland, Ireland or Great Britain and NI in a sporting event you were eligible. What that meant for example was that unfortunately Lurgan born Geraldine Heaney, who won a Winter Olympics gold medal in Salt Lake City in 2002, couldn't be included because while she was born here she competed for Canada. There are others in the same boat though on the flip side athletics and boxing legends Maeve Kyle and Barry McGuigan were eligible because while they were born in the South of Ireland they represented Northern Ireland in the Commonwealth Games. Hopefully this isn't too complicated or political because that's the last thing I'd want. This is about sport.

Anyway so after establishing the ground rules the task was to select a century of sporting greats. You may think that would be reasonably straightforward but after months and months of research, scouring through endless amounts of old newspaper cuttings, watching countless hours of TV footage, reading and listening to hundreds of interviews and trawling through useful websites, the short list wasn't exactly short.

I make it that Northern Ireland has produced 232 people who you could reasonably call sporting greats. Yes, 232! For such a small place that is one gigantic number and illustrates the staggering array of gifted and hard working women and men we have who have performed to super high standards in the world of sport across a multitude of disciplines.

Try getting 232 into 100. It's tough so a formula was needed and given the idea all along was to hail our sporting legends, I came up with the HAIL theory. That is H for History maker and Hero, A for Achievement and Ability, I for Inspiration and Influence and L for Longevity and Legendary status. The thought process behind it was to mix all of the above together and use the ingredients to narrow the shortlist down to 100 and then chronicle and rejoice in each and every one.

I'm all for someone who makes sporting History. Ever since I was a kid I've marvelled at the man or woman who breaks records or sets new targets. As for a Hero we all need them, someone who makes us feel proud and that all is right with the world. Achievement is about what you do in your chosen field and Ability is how you do it performing at levels others cannot reach. Inspiration is so crucial, maybe now more than ever. We need those people to look up to and aspire to and no one does that better than sports stars such as our high achieving Paralympians who have not allowed adversity to rain on their dreams. Influence is just as important. It is a requirement of society as well as sport that we have good, strong people who influence others in the right way with their actions. Longevity and staying at the top for years tells you much about a person's will to win and character while Legendary status speaks for itself relating to someone who does something out of the ordinary in their sport and has a special place in our hearts.

For instance in the book you will read about a host of Olympic medal winners and I'm comfortable with that because when someone from Northern Ireland stands on the podium at the Games, whether they are competing for Ireland or Team GB and NI, I believe, and I'm not alone in this, it puts them on a higher plane. Maybe that's the whole greatest show on earth thing or the fact that it only takes place every four years (or five if you are in the middle of a coronavirus pandemic) but what is certain is that with an Olympic medal comes special status.

Also I'm all for those who transcend their sport and sport in general, like a Joey Dunlop, George Best, Mary Peters, Rory McIlroy, Willie John

McBride or Tony McCoy and I was keen to ensure that this book wasn't just about modern heroes but about stars from the past hence why we go back to the 1920s with athlete Anton Hegarty and footballer Elisha Scott moving all the way to the present day with gymnast Rhys McClenaghan, the youngest of the 100 greats.

It was also important for me to honour those who have shone across the island if not across the world, like GAA stars. Take Peter Canavan, at one stage he was the best on the planet at what he did so he is a must for selection. If you were writing a book about America's 100 greatest sports stars, you wouldn't leave out Babe Ruth or Tom Brady, would you?

Lastly I wanted some sort of balance where our wide range of world class performers in different fields were recognised.

That's why I felt it important to talk to some fantastic people from the sporting world whose knowledge I greatly respect. I must say a huge thank you to Paul Ferguson (Sunday Life), Thomas Hawkins (Irish News) and Billy Weir (Belfast Telegraph) whose help with the book was uplifting and their wise counsel greatly appreciated. Many thanks also to Orla Bannon, Declan Bogue, Jonathan Bradley, Richard Bullick, Alastair Bushe, John Campbell, Ian Callender, Terry Crothers, John Flack, Jackie Fullerton, Marshall Gillespie, Ruth Gorman, Sammy Hamill, Graham Hamilton, Stephen Hamilton, Roy Harris, Brian Hill, Paul Kelly, Dessie McCallion, Malcolm McCausland, Alex McGreevy, Neil McKay, Colin McMullan, Alex Mills, Richard Mulligan, Mark Sidebottom and Ian Young for their time and expert insight. Thank you to two of my best friends Stephen Campbell and Ricky Beresford for their honesty during the trickiest stages of the decision making with both telling me 'whoever you choose, you won't please everyone so go with what you feel is right'.

Later in the book I will write about some of those who missed out. Just because someone is not profiled, it doesn't mean I think they aren't worthy of being labelled a great, it's simply that they didn't make this top 100.

That's the thing. For the people I'm disappointed I didn't include, I'm overjoyed with the 100 legends in this book. They are superheroes and it is a pleasure and a privilege to write about them and what they have achieved with much more to come in some cases.

What I wanted to do was celebrate them, bring back some glorious memories, enlighten you to some of our lesser well known stars and show that for a tiny spec on the earth we don't half produce spectacular sporting talent.

If debate is created that is good because it is a fundamental part of sport and one of the reasons why we love it so much.

I'd like to thank my publisher Tim Johnston for his advice, guidance and sterling work in delivering this book and also thanks to Kelvin Boyes, Philip Matthews and Presseye, the Belfast Telegraph, Billy Weir, Aaron McVitty Sr and Aaron McVitty Jr from Belfast Telegraph Archive, Fergus McAnallen from rallyretro.com, Roy Harris, Roland White, Sport NI, Malcolm McCausland, Coloursport and Pacemaker Press for providing the pictures you see in the book.

Also thank you to our magnificent sports stars because without them these pages simply wouldn't exist.

Last but by no means least some personal family thank you notes. To my Mum who continues to be there for me with her love, support and sense of fun and has forever encouraged my love of sport and to my stepdad Victor for always being there for our family. To my big brother Neil, whose enthusiasm for this book from day one was total. His exemplary research helped me out more than he will know and he looked after me just like he did in a terraced, packed and swaying Kop at Anfield when I was a lad cheering on Liverpool Football Club.

To my wonderful wife Lindsay and our beautiful children Sophia and Aaron, I wouldn't have been able to write this book without your love, support and understanding which I'm eternally grateful for. Lindsay is the love of my life, my rock and my best friend and throughout the process with her professionalism she was a great sounding board, reading through the copy and encouraging me with ideas and suggestions while Sophia and Aaron were patient and never complained as their dad worked for days and nights to complete the book. They are our pride and joy and we feel lucky to have two children who bring so much laughter and smiles into our home. Lindsay, Sophia and Aaron, you are my everything.

To the readers, I sincerely hope you enjoy the book. It's my tribute to 100 of our sporting heroes.

Yours in sport,
Steven.

GERRY ARMSTRONG

FOOTBALL: WORLD CUP
GOALSCORING HERO
B: 23/5/1954

Gerry Armstrong delivered one of the most iconic moments in Northern Ireland sporting history and sent shockwaves around the globe when he scored a World Cup winner against hosts Spain in 1982. It was a goal for the ages and a life-changing strike for the Belfast man leading to hundreds of congratulatory telegrams being sent to the team hotel with everyone from the Reverend Ian Paisley to the Irish Taoiseach Charles Haughey getting in on the act. Armstrong says: "The telegrams came from all over and what that win over Spain did was bring everyone back home together. Whether you lived in the North or South of Ireland you appreciated how hard we had battled to produce one of the biggest upsets ever in World Cup football. Knowing how happy and proud we had made people feel was the most important thing for the players and it made us realise what could be achieved through sport."

Not since 1958 had Northern Ireland played in the World Cup with Armstrong taking them to Spain after hitting the only goal of the game in qualifying against Israel at Windsor Park seven months earlier. Having drawn 0-0 with Yugoslavia in their opening group match and collected another point with Armstrong hitting the net in a 1-1 draw against Honduras, Northern Ireland knew a stunning victory in Valencia versus Spain would be required to progress to the next round.

Most feared a drubbing for the underdogs but optimistic by nature, Gerry was one of the few who sensed something special in the Spanish air and early in the second half his faith was rewarded when he smashed the ball into the net with his right foot after goalkeeper Luis Arconada dropped Billy Hamilton's cross, sparking the immortal "Arconada, Armstrong!" line from BBC commentator John Motson. Northern Ireland fans still get goosebumps thinking about it and Gerry remembers the spirit and camaraderie in the team that helped them hang on to a famous 1-0 victory despite Billy Bingham's boys playing the latter part of the contest with 10 men due to Mal Donaghy's harsh sending off.

Following his triumphant matador turn in the bristling bullring of Valencia, Armstrong didn't have much time to celebrate in the dressing room because along with team-mate Tommy Cassidy he was selected at random and whisked away for a protocol drugs test. Cassidy told me: "The pair of us were so dehydrated it took us about 90 minutes to give a sample. We just couldn't go to the toilet. We had FIFA doctors and officials in the room with us plus armed guards who no one would have messed with and we were drinking loads of water but that didn't help. We ended up drinking beer and Gerry started singing 'Danny Boy' and other songs. The armed guards were so taken with Gerry even they were smiling by the time we finally did what we needed to do before joining the rest of the lads."

A born entertainer, Gerry was the life and soul of the party in Spain and the other players loved to hear his tales after he had phoned his family in Belfast. With no internet, social media or 24 hour rolling news then, Armstrong would tease his colleagues that the only players being talked about back home were himself and Brazilian stars Socrates and Zico! After his heroics in the group games he scored again in a 4-1 defeat to France as Northern Ireland bowed out in the second phase with Armstrong named British player of the tournament.

Rarely a day goes by without Gerry being asked about the goal on June 25, 1982 that turned him into a global star, earning him a move to La Liga in 1983 with Real Mallorca which in turn set him up for a second calling as a fantastic pundit on Spanish football for over 20 years.

Gerry didn't play football until he was 16 because GAA was his first sporting love and he was exceptional at that as well, featuring for the Antrim senior team when he was only 15. He recalled: "My grandfather Joe Gallagher was the groundsman at Casement Park and when I was about four or five he used to take me to the ground in his tractor and as he worked I played with a ball on the pitch. My mum's seven brothers all played gaelic and I went on to do the same and in 1971 I played hurling and football at Croke Park. Around that time I was suspended for fighting during a gaelic match and I took up soccer."

Armstrong would whack in 35 goals in a season for local club St Paul's Swifts before turning out for Cromac Albion and Irish League side Bangor where he saw red in his first appearance for the reserves. "I came on as a substitute and scored a goal and made one, then the opposition centre-half said he was going to break my leg so I gave him a right hook in the face and I was sent off," says Armstrong, who admits he "didn't have a clue" about the laws of football in those days but boy could he play with his physical, fearless style and clinical edge in front of goal attracting scouts galore.

Just a few years after playing his first proper game Armstrong found himself moving to Tottenham in 1975 when fellow Northern Ireland man Terry Neill was in charge. He would play in defence, midfield and attack for Spurs gaining his first cap in 1977, up front alongside George Best in a 5-0 defeat in West Germany, soon becoming an established international. Gerry says: "Danny Blanchflower was the manager and the night before the Germany match he said to me 'son you are playing up front and it will be you and George' and I couldn't believe it. Not only was I winning my first cap but I was playing beside my boyhood hero. It was a dream come true."

A move to Watford arrived in 1980 with the £250,000 record signing scoring the club's first ever goal in the top flight. Armstrong enjoyed working under Watford manager Graham Taylor and partying with chairman Elton John prior to an enticing switch to Real Mallorca, where his athleticism and graft, inherited from his Fintona born dad Gerald, made him a hit. Gerry got to know Diego Maradona on and off the pitch saying: "The first time I played against Maradona's Barcelona I scored a diving header at the far post and then he took control and did things with a ball I'd never seen before and we lost 4-1. In the second leg of that tie we played in Barcelona and I had a few scoops with Diego in the hotel bar. He was a really fun character. We played Barcelona another time in the Cup and it went to penalties at the Nou Camp and I had to take the first one walking up in front of 100,000 screaming fans in a scary atmosphere. Thankfully I scored but we lost the shoot-out."

Returning to the UK in 1985 he would play for West Brom, Chesterfield, Brighton, Millwall, Glenavon and in the English non-league but it was his appearances for Northern Ireland that were most noteworthy helping the squad reach the 1986 World Cup finals, after playing an important role in British Championships successes in 1980 and 1984. Armstrong's 63rd and final cap came against Brazil in the Mexico World Cup leaving the stage with 12 Northern Ireland goals, all in competitive matches. Later Armstrong, adored for his outgoing personality and big heart, would be assistant manager twice for his country and he asked wife Debby to marry him before a game at Windsor Park, scene of so many of his dynamic performances. For some years they lived in Spain where Gerry experienced his greatest sporting moment.

JIM BAKER

BOWLS: FIRST IRISH WORLD SINGLES CHAMPION
B: 18/02/1958

When you have a stadium named after you that gives a clear indication of your status within your chosen sport and so it goes with Northern Ireland bowls legend Jim Baker who became World Champion in 1984.

Baker lost the World Indoor Bowls final to Scotland's John Watson in 1982 but when he returned to the crunch match of the tournament two years later the Belfast born player would not be denied. At the peak of his powers in Coatbridge, North Lanarkshire, Baker started off his quest to win the biggest event in bowls with victories over Australian Kenny Williams and Canadian Ron Jones before completing a quarter-final success against Jim Boyle from Scotland, then came an eagerly awaited semi-final with local hero and Scotland's defending World Champion Bob Sutherland which Baker came through 21-14. That set up a gripping final versus Englishman Nigel Smith with Baker eventually coming out on top 21-18 to achieve an ambition he had held since starting out.

For Baker it was the perfect end to a tournament in which he was the stand-out player with his nerve holding in high pressure moments and his ability to draw unlikely shots coming to the fore against Smith. It was a first world title in bowls for Ireland and watched on terrestrial television by millions with Jim telling me: "It was unbelievable to win the World Championship and with it came a lot of attention with press and TV waiting for me when I flew back into the airport in Northern Ireland. After winning at the weekend I went to work on Monday morning for Commercial Union, an insurance company, in Belfast and after getting out of the taxi to go into our office, a group of guys working about six storeys up in a high rise building shouted down to me saying 'well done Jim' and how much they had enjoyed watching the bowls. That recognition had never happened to me before but it showed what it meant to people to bring a world title home."

The success gave Baker the confidence to claim the World Outdoor Triples Championship later that year alongside countrymen Sammy Allen and Stan Espie. Not only did the double delight do wonders for Baker it also increased the popularity of bowls in Northern Ireland so much so that in September 1985 a new facility for indoor bowling opened in Newtownabbey and was called the Jim Baker Stadium. Also in 1985 he clinched the UK Singles title, one of the toughest to win on the circuit.

Ex-Boys' Model pupil Baker took up bowls at 15 playing the short mat version of the game at Helen's Bay Church where he showed potential prior to developing his game at Carr's Glen and Cliftonville Bowling clubs and becoming an international, often having to take holiday leave from his day job to play for Ireland.

It all came together in 1984 though his World Championship success didn't end there with Baker part of the triumphant Irish Fours outdoor teams in 1988 beside Sammy Allen, John McCloughlin and Rodney McCutcheon and in 2004 with Neil Booth, Noel Graham and Jonathan Ross thanks to a stunning 19-18 final win over Australia in the gold medal match. Also at the 2004 World Outdoor Bowls Championship and by now a Ballymena player, Baker claimed a silver in the pairs with Noel Graham while he brought home medals when representing Northern Ireland in the Commonwealth Games - silver in 1990 and bronze in 2002, both in the Fours events establishing himself as a big time contender over more than two decades of competition.

Supported by wife Marie and daughter Danielle it was no surprise when Baker gave up playing that this highly respected bowler became manager of the Ireland squad while the stadium named after him is home to County Antrim Indoor Bowling club and a 'Centre of Excellence' open to all bowlers, young and old, who want to play for fun or with dreams of becoming the best in the business, just like Jim.

PADDY BARNES

BOXING: HISTORY MAKING DOUBLE
OLYMPIC MEDALIST
B: 09/04/1987

Paddy Barnes is Ireland's most decorated amateur boxer, was the first fighter from the island to win medals in successive Olympic Games, made history when he defended his Commonwealth Games title and in 2010 was the first Irishman to strike gold at the European Championships for almost two decades. What makes these record breaking feats stand out even more is that the north Belfast native achieved them after losing his opening 12 fights as a boy!

In his pomp interviews with fast talking and comedy gold Paddy could often descend into laugh a minute routines which should have been on the stage, but when he spoke about boxing there was a serious edge to Barnes who refused to give the sport up despite those early beatings with his perseverance paying off.

At 11 Barnes began his boxing education in Ardglass sparring with his cousins under the watchful eye of his uncle Jimmy Linden and later would join the Holy Family gym in Belfast, where legendary trainer Gerry Storey was an inspiration. With Irish titles on his CV he was determined to prove himself on a larger scale sparking a marvellous medal run at the 2008 Olympics in Beijing, landing plenty of punches with his quick hands and a bronze in the light flyweight division after defeating Poland's Łukasz Maszczyk 11-5 in the quarter-final and while he felt the judges in his semi loss against China's Zou Shiming were way off the mark with their scoring he was pleased to come home with some treasure around his neck.

In 2010 he excelled claiming Ireland's first gold for 19 years at the notoriously tough European Amateur Championships, overcoming Azerbaijan's dangerous Elvin Mamishzade in the final, which he rated as his finest accomplishment, and later that year in Delhi, wearing a Northern Ireland vest, he won the Commonwealth Games title.

Barnes took bronze again at the London 2012 Games, losing once more to Shiming in a nailbiting semi-final, to mark himself down as the first

Irish boxer to stand on the podium in back-to-back Olympics and two years later in Glasgow, using all his ring craft and speed, he was on the top step defending his Commonwealth crown as the first Northern Ireland fighter to do so.

In between Barnes won another silver at the 2013 European Championships and there would be a third Olympics in Rio in 2016 when he carried the Irish flag in the opening ceremony but there would be no medal. He opted to move into professional boxing months later, losing a WBC world title shot at flyweight in 2018 to Cristofer Rosales from Nicaragua at Windsor Park. One of the most generous people in Irish sport with a warm and fun personality, history maker Barnes retired in 2019 after 21 years in the sport thanking his wife Mari, family and coaches for their unstinting support.

GEORGE BEST

FOOTBALL: ICON, LEGEND AND
ALL-TIME GREAT
B: 22/05/1946 – D: 25/11/2005

Look back at old black and white television footage of George Best and he will be the one playing in colour stealing your heart, capturing your soul and blowing your mind. Out of all Northern Ireland's great sporting stars the most beautiful to watch has been Bestie who played in an era when footballers were as mean as rattlesnakes and harder than steel yet he managed to float around like a butterfly in a field of moths.

One of George's most celebrated moments was the winner against Chelsea in a League Cup tie at Old Trafford in 1970, when sprinting towards goal opposition defender Ron 'Chopper' Harris tried to hack him down only for Best to somehow keep his ballet dancer style balance and glide forward on the mudheap of a pitch to round goalkeeper Peter Bonetti and calmly plant the ball in the net. The celebration was just as good with the Belfast boy sliding on his knees in front of adoring Manchester United fans and lifting his arms towards the sky. Harris would later say in the Daily Mail: "It was the opening clip on Grandstand for years and watching it over and over again I was sure I'd catch him one day! George was the one player I couldn't get near, the best I played against."

Just about every footballer Best faced in the 1960s and early 1970s would say the same. Even Pele, the iconic Brazilian and three time World Cup winner who many believe to be the finest of them all, declared that the mantle belonged to George. He was like Lionel Messi and Cristiano Ronaldo rolled into one but with his pop star, movie star and celebrity like lifestyle and those good looks, the handsome Red Devil was bigger in his day making front page and back page news on a daily basis. Best was the guy who would score goals from the gods on a Saturday afternoon and then go out with the most gorgeous girls on the planet that night and the world watched on spellbound by everything that he did. He would receive 10,000 letters from fans every week, he would be hanging out with The Beatles and The Rolling Stones and was wanted by every company in Britain to promote their products but in the background the demons of alcohol, which would ultimately cost him his life, were taking hold and he often found the attention and pressure overwhelming.

He retired on several occasions, the first time when he was just 26, and made comeback after comeback for various clubs in different countries, both stirring the emotions and leaving the feeling he hadn't made the most of his world beating talent. There are innumerable stories about Bestie, though perhaps the most famous comes from a time after his heyday on the pitch when the Northern Ireland star was in a fancy hotel suite with Miss World. They had a bottle of vintage champagne beside them on a bed covered in thousands of pounds from an earlier gambling success when a hotel waiter delivering room service entered the room to survey the scene and utter the words "Where did it all go wrong George?" It's a tale that will be told to the end of time about a sporting wizard for whom it started to go right when renowned Manchester United scout Bob Bishop saw Best play as a kid and called Old Trafford manager Matt Busby to say: "Boss, I think I've found you a genius".

Typically Bob was not wrong, although early on at United, Best suffered from homesickness and wondered if being away from mum Anne, dad Dickie, his family and the Cregagh Estate was for him. He made his debut for United in 1963 at 17 years of age and scored on his second appearance and in the next season, alongside Denis Law and Bobby Charlton, he excelled as the club won their first league championship since the 1958 Munich air crash, which tragically cut short the lives of so many United greats in their prime. The United supporters now had another magical team to cheer with Best the most breathtaking of all with his speed, skill and swerves allowing him to dribble past defenders as if they were cones on a training pitch, setting up or scoring goals that left spectators rubbing their eyes to make sure they weren't dreaming.

It's a pity all of this sorcery isn't on camera though what is on film makes us cherish it like the night in 1966, complete with the hairstyle of the day, he tore Benfica apart on their home turf in the European Cup netting twice in one of the finest individual displays ever produced in the competition as United romped to a 5-1 victory with their hero dubbed 'El Beatle' all over the continent. That night he was chased in Lisbon by someone wielding a knife and while George feared the worst, the determined Benfica fan told him all he wanted was to cut off a lock of Best's hair!

Everyone wanted a piece of George and as the goals, glorious performances and bravery in the face of savage tackles continued so did the nights out with another title coming for United in 1967 followed by European Cup success in 1968 as Busby's team became the first English side to win the trophy. Best, of course, with United playing in unfamiliar blue, was at the centre of it. The final versus Benfica at a packed Wembley was tied at 1-1 in extra-time when the number seven, who suffered rough treatment all game, anticipated a flick on to beat a defender to the ball and then waltzed around the goalkeeper before slotting the ball into an empty net with his left foot. In that instant, such was his speed of thought, he considered taking the ball to the goal-line, stooping down and heading it in from there, like he had done as a kid playing on the streets of Belfast. Instead he chose the sensible option giving his team control of a match they would win 4-1.

To this day Best remains the only footballer from Northern Ireland to have scored in a European Cup or Champions League final providing a fitting end to a spectacular season when he netted 28 league goals and was voted Football Writers' Footballer of the Year and European Footballer of the Year, where at the awards ceremony, amid all the pomp and circumstance, he made sure to have a cup of tea with Matt Busby's mother. While he would be presented with a stream of individual accolades, inducted into every football Hall of Fame possible and even have Belfast City Airport renamed in his memory, it is hard to believe that the biggest prize in club football was the last silverware he won as part of a team though the goals still flowed as did mesmeric performances such as when he struck a record breaking six times in the FA Cup against Northampton.

Problems off the field dogged his later years at United and with the holy trinity of Best, Law and Charlton broken up and Busby no longer the manager, Best grew frustrated and ill disciplined and after a few false alarms he left United in 1974 at the age of 27 with 179 goals in 474 games. In the years that followed he played for clubs in South Africa, Australia, Hong Kong and America, where for San Jose Earthquakes after outsmarting opponent after opponent he scored what the commentator described as "the greatest soccer goal ever seen". There would be other brief spells at Fulham, entertaining fans alongside close friend Rodney Marsh, Hibs, Bournemouth and others including Tobermore United in Northern Ireland. Although he was criticised for not turning up at various functions, he played in testimonials for several Irish League favourites and was the star attraction in Fivemiletown one night in the early 1980s, scoring a goal despite being man marked the entire match by my uncle Evan Condell in a seismic 90 minutes for our family who worshipped Bestie. So did every Northern Ireland fan even if he only played 37 times for his country, smashing in nine goals between 1964 and 1977.

Without question the greatest footballer never to play in the World Cup finals, there were hopes that Billy Bingham would include Best in his 1982 squad for Spain but Billy decided against it leaving the Green and White Army to memories such as when George made his international debut alongside Pat Jennings in a win over Wales in 1964 and the finest solo Northern Ireland display of all time when he tortured Scotland in a 1967 victory at Windsor Park. There was also the goal that never was when he famously clipped the ball away from England goalkeeping great Gordon Banks who was preparing to clear and ran in behind him to score with the referee disallowing it because he felt such audacity must have been against the laws of the game. Then the night in Rotterdam when he went toe-to-toe with the great Johan Cruyff and nutmegged him and other Dutch players leaving Cruyff looking on with envy, anger and admiration and Johan's team-mates laughing their socks off! Best could nutmeg a mermaid, he could dance around defenders like Fred Astaire and he could make them feel silly and dizzy with his twists, turns, twists and turns.

What perhaps is not that well known is that he could be shy, was extremely intelligent with a penchant for completing the Times crossword in minutes rather than hours and had a generous nature to him like when he gave me his time for one of his last interviews a couple of months before he passed away in November 2005. Bestie was charming speaking about modern day superstar David Beckham, revealing how he would love to be playing on perfect 21st century pitches, outlining his passion for his home country and full of fun when asked about a couple of Northern Ireland players who had been sent home for breaking curfew, saying it was right they had been expelled, adding with a chuckle: "We all like a drink but normally it is after the game!"

Sadly George liked a drink too much and tragically it would be his undoing with his death mourned across the globe as he was given what was effectively a state funeral in Northern Ireland with a service at Stormont and tens of thousands lining the streets of Belfast to say farewell. Cursed by his alcoholism, Best spent a short time in jail, went bankrupt and made big mistakes in his life, as those closest to him know better than anyone, but as he told his pal Rodney Marsh on Talksport in his final interview he wanted to be remembered for his football and as everyone knows his football was out of this world. In a pair of boots and with a ball at his feet, George truly was the Best.

RORY BEST

RUGBY: FORWARD THINKING IRISH CENTURION AND INSPIRATIONAL LEADER

B: 15/08/1982

He may have started his Ireland career with some questioning his physique but Rory Best ended it as a genuine great in green and will forever be regarded as a history making captain and an outstanding player who left everything he had out on the pitch.

Best's achievements are astounding, though, first let's reflect on an extraordinary example of his commitment to the cause from a day in November 2013 in the Aviva stadium in Dublin when Ireland were playing New Zealand. A rampant Best and the home team had started on fire with the Ulster hooker scoring a try as the Irish took a 14-0 lead only for him to fracture his arm in a tackle 15 minutes in. Best knew immediately the damage that had been done but with the Kiwis on the attack he stayed on his feet, got back into his defensive position and within seconds was throwing himself into a ruck for the good of the team. Moments later he was forced off holding his broken right arm and while the All Blacks went on to win 24-22 Best's selfless actions won respect all over the world.

In time there would be famous victories against New Zealand, with Best the inspirational skipper on the first and second occasions Ireland put the All Blacks to the sword. He would also be a double Grand Slam champion and four time Six Nations Championship winner and retire with 124 Irish caps making him the nation's most capped forward, only behind Brian O'Driscoll and Ronan O'Gara on the all-time list. He was also part of the Ulster team that clinched Celtic League glory in 2006 and while he never won any trophies for his beloved province as captain, he was the heart and soul of the side for many years helping them to the 2012 European Cup final on his way to making over 200 appearances.

Playing or talking about rugby during his career, there was an honesty to Best who was brought up on the family farm in Poyntzpass and now has one of his own just outside Gilford in County Armagh. He wasn't into bluff or spin and called a spade a spade when speaking about performances good or bad which was an admirable quality to go along with his courage, desire and ability. I remember asking him about being labelled the best hooker in the world to which he responded: "It's nice to hear things like that but those same people were saying 18 months ago that I was rubbish so you have to take it with a pinch of salt. If my wife, my mum and my dad say I'm doing okay then that's good enough for me. I also talk to my elder brother Simon because he played for Ulster and Ireland and has been there and done it."

Along with Simon and his other brother Mark, Rory played rugby on the family farm and travelled around with their grandad to watch dad John play for Banbridge Rugby Club. When Rory's own talents were coming to the fore he and his pals enjoyed a fun day out cheering Ulster to their 1999 European Cup success at Lansdowne Road. Little did Best know then or when he was studying agriculture at Newcastle University he would enjoy many more memorable days in Dublin.

Having started out at Banbridge Rugby Club and played at Portadown College, Newcastle Falcons Academy and Belfast Harlequins, Best made his Ireland debut in 2005, barely a year after first playing for Ulster, and ended up playing in four World Cups, the last of which was the 2019 tournament in Japan, and he represented the British and Irish Lions, touring in 2013 and 2017 though strangely never played in any of the Test teams.

Commitment assured, Best also brought quality and was one of the game's top scrummaging hookers who was exceptional at the breakdown and had endless reserves of energy which would see him pop up all over the pitch to aid his team-mates in defence and attack, saving countless tries and scoring 12 of them himself in an Irish shirt.

While as an all-round player Best was top class, as a captain he rates as one of the finest Ireland's ever had achieving things that even iconic previous skippers O'Driscoll and Paul O'Connell couldn't accomplish, such as leading the team to the historic 40-29 victory over World Champions New Zealand in Chicago in November 2016 and following it up a couple of years later captaining the side to a 16-9 success over the mighty All Blacks amid a frenzied atmosphere at the Aviva stadium.

Best was skipper on 38 occasions including throughout an incredible period when Ireland beat the Kiwis, South Africa and Australia in the same year for the first time ever with Rory winning his 100th cap against the Wallabies in the 2016 victory. He received a standing ovation as he left the field late in the game that day which showed the fondness, regard and love the Irish public had for him. It would not be the last memorable reception for the player whose wife Jodie and their children were constantly by his side.

The Middlesbrough fan has been a crucial part of so many glorious one off occasions for Ireland but his consistency and durability through 14 memorable years as an international outlined how Best became the reliable, lead by example guy who was always there, fighting for his team, influencing in the dressing room and on the park having overcome doubts raised early in his international career by some about his fitness and weight. Best won the Six Nations Championship in 2009, 2014, 2015 and 2018 claiming Grand Slams in the first and last of those successes. The Ulsterman was the skipper for the Slam in 2018 when it was completed at Twickenham against England on St Patrick's Day and in that year Ireland hit the number one ranking in world rugby. Though he was not one for blowing his own trumpet his retirement in 2019 brought numerous warm tributes from home and around the globe to a wonderful player and magnificent leader.

DANNY BLANCHFLOWER

FOOTBALL: WORLD CUP CAPTAIN
FANTASTIC AND DOUBLE WINNER
B: 10/02/1926 - D: 09/12/1993

There really was only one Danny Blanchflower, a footballer before his time and a class apart who was the original captain fantastic in Northern Ireland sport leading where others would follow. Blanchflower was skipper for his country in their first World Cup finals in 1958 and for the best ever

Tottenham side that won the League championship and FA Cup double in 1961 and became the first British team to succeed in Europe when they lifted the European Cup Winners' Cup in 1963.

Blanchflower was one for style and substance and walked the walk in terms of both and he could talk the talk like no one else, coming out with worthy, visionary, humorous and cutting remarks that are still amongst the most iconic in football. Perhaps his most striking was: "The great fallacy is that the game is first and last about winning. It's nothing of the kind. The game is about glory. It is about doing things in style, with a flourish, about going out and beating the other lot, not waiting for them to die of boredom."

Viewed as a man for all seasons and any situation, his former Northern Ireland team-mate Harry Gregg used to tell me that with Danny's intellect and sharp brain he could turn his hand to anything and was generally better at it than anyone else. The only thing Danny didn't fancy doing was appearing on hugely popular TV show This is Your Life. When host Eamonn Andrews appeared in 1961 with the big red book ahead of what was going to be a celebration of Blanchflower's life, the Spurs legend was the first person to refuse to appear on the programme after a year earlier being the first footballer to appear on radio show Desert Island Discs choosing golf clubs and balls as his luxury castaway items in a nod to his other sporting passion.

Born in the Bloomfield area of east Belfast, he grew up idolising Northern Ireland player Peter Doherty not thinking at the time that the pair would become one of the country's most celebrated double acts as captain and manager of the national team in the 1958 World Cup. Danny, whose younger brother Jackie played at international level and for Manchester United prior to suffering injuries in the Munich air disaster that ended his career, couldn't get enough of football as a youngster playing three times on Saturdays ending with a night game for his local team having played for his school and the Boys Brigade in the morning and afternoon. With his mum a fine player herself, he even formed a football club called Bloomfield United when he was just 15 before lying about his age to join the RAF in 1943, taking part in training courses in Scotland and Canada in the middle of the Second World War.

Returning to Belfast he joined Glentoran in 1946 and played in two losing Irish Cup finals for the Oval outfit before asking for a transfer which saw him join Barnsley and then move to Aston Villa, playing over 150 games for the midlands side though he was no fan of their training methods or brand of football. In 1954, and already an influential Northern Ireland player, Blanchflower's next transfer changed his life and the history of Spurs, who beat off Arsenal's interest with a £30,000 deal for the then 28-year-old midfielder. The early years for Blanchflower at White Hart Lane were far from what he had envisaged as the team struggled and he, in his role as captain, became frustrated at managerial decisions from Jimmy Anderson and even when the great Bill Nicholson took charge in 1958 there were issues as Danny was dropped and talked about leaving the club.

When Nicholson restored Blanchflower to the starting line-up and made him skipper again everything clicked with the Belfast man conducting sweet music from the middle of the park leading to an historic campaign in 1960-61 when Spurs cruised to their first league title in a decade and became the first team in the century to double up by winning the FA Cup. There was further FA Cup glory in 1962 with Tottenham's greatest player netting a penalty in the 3-1 final victory over Burnley at Wembley.

Producing a tactical masterclass in midfield despite a knee problem, Danny was also on hand to raise the European Cup Winners' Cup following a brilliant 5-1 final success over Atletico Madrid in 1963 when two goals were scored by Jimmy Greaves, who told the official Spurs website: "Danny Blanchflower was the brain. He was a brilliant player, a brilliant captain and had a brilliant mind. He was a real leader."

The charismatic Blanchflower retired at 38 in 1964 having won 56 caps for Northern Ireland, and 45 as captain, with a hero status at home that led to reverential treatment. He first played for his country in 1949 and didn't take long to emerge as a powerful figure, with team-mates suggesting he had swallowed the blarney stone yet at the same time listening to every word as he held court on football and other subjects. What gained him respect initially was his quality on the field and how he was calm in possession and an excellent communicator to those around him which was telling as Northern Ireland qualified for the 1958 World Cup finals. Blanchflower rose to the occasion in Sweden as Doherty's team reached the quarter-finals and three years later he was the first Northern Ireland player to win 50 caps, rightly regarded as one of the most accomplished ever to wear a green shirt.

After he quit playing he was a thoughtful and candid newspaper columnist, managed Chelsea for a short spell and Northern Ireland for three years with his first game in charge the epic 1976 Johan Cruyff v George Best showdown when Holland took on Northern Ireland in Rotterdam and a classic contest, much to football romantic Blanchflower's liking, finished 2-2. In his latter days, Alzheimer's Disease took hold and he died in 1993, aged 67, with football left in mourning at the passing of a true great who won the Football Writers' Footballer of the Year award in 1958 and 1961 and played himself in a 1983 movie called 'Those Glory Glory Days' relating to Tottenham's historic double, the title of which he thoroughly approved.

RALPH BRYANS

MOTORCYCLING: WORLD
CHAMPION WHO LED THE WAY
B: 07/03/1942 - D: 06/08/2014

Ralph Bryans was Northern Ireland's first motorcycling World Champion starting out on the road to glory as a teenager when he forged his mother's signature on the entry form to compete at the 1959 Tandragee 100 on a borrowed bike. The next year Bryans, who could fix bikes as well as he could ride them, won the Irish 200cc Championship and with a steely determination the Belfast man rose up the ranks to become the number one rider on the planet in the 50cc class.

It wasn't just on the smaller machines that Bryans impressed, performing well at the Ulster Grand Prix on 350cc and 500cc bikes in the early 1960s making influential people in the industry sit up and take notice and at the same time gaining vital experience against the top road racers of the era. In 1964 came the all important offer he had been waiting for from a Honda works team allowing him to enter the 50cc World Championship and in his first year he created shockwaves by winning Grand Prix races in the Netherlands, Belgium and Germany finishing second in the standings to New Zealand great Hugh Anderson.

Fast learner Bryans used the knowledge gained from 1964 to finish as top dog in 1965 coming home first in Germany, France and Holland and being well placed in other races throughout the season, which proved crucial as he beat Anderson and Switzerland's Luigi Taveri by four points to become the World 50cc lightweight Champion. To put in context what Bryans achieved in 1965, the World Championship he raced in later morphed into Moto GP which today is considered the premier motorcycle racing World Championship.

In the same year Bryans was eighth in the 125cc World Championship and in 1966 moved up to third in that category and was close to retaining his 50cc crown, losing out by just two points though he gained immense satisfaction from winning at the Isle of Man TT. In 1967 Bryans showed his class at 350cc claiming a brilliant victory at Monza as he finished third overall and there were successes in Germany and Japan in the 250cc class on his way to fourth in the standings which were topped by his close friend and multiple World Champion Mike Hailwood. Coming home in front in Japan meant much to Bryans because it proved to be his last race victory in the World Championship and his 10th at that level in a high risk sport that he took up at the age of 16 riding a BSA Bantam when serving as an apprentice fitter at Chambers Motors in Belfast.

Ralph retired in 1970, having won the 250cc race at the North West 200, and living in Ayrshire in Scotland he established a successful business, enjoyed meeting up with old pals and rivals at vintage motorcycling events and played a range of sports including ten-pin bowling, never losing his competitive nature, until he died in 2014 suffering from cancer, having created a pathway that other Northern Ireland motorcycling World Champions Joey Dunlop, Brian Reid and Jonathan Rea would follow.

MIKE BULL

ATHLETICS: DECATHLON AND POLE
VAULT CHAMPION
B: 11/09/1946

Mike Bull is the best all round male track and field star to hail from Northern Ireland and created history by winning Commonwealth Games gold in two different events, the decathlon and pole vault.

A legendary figure in British Athletics circles, Bull was one of the best pole vaulters of his generation and got there thanks to some rather unique training methods when he was a student in the 1960s using old mattresses from refitted ships in a shed close to the famous Harland & Wolff shipyard in Belfast. At lunchtime the Bangor man would have an audience with hundreds of shipyard workers interested to see how high he could go. "We located mattresses from the ships that were being refitted, it was a good soft landing and people were eating their packed lunches with flat caps on their laps and cheering. Every session was like a major competition for me," recalled Bull in the Belfast Telegraph.

Encouraged by his father to take part in sport, a teenage Bull represented Ireland in swimming when he was known as 'Tarzan' prior to turning to athletics and initially the pole vault, coming up with his own practice ideas due to a lack of proper facilities. At 17 and still attending St Malachy's College, Belfast, his natural talent took him to victory in the Irish Pole Vaulting Championship and the next year he was in a Great Britain vest for the first time.

Bull set a UK record of of 15ft 6 inches in the 1966 Commonwealth Games in Jamaica as he claimed a surprise silver medal for Northern Ireland in the pole vault which was followed by his first appearance at the Olympic Games in 1968, making the final, and then a brilliant gold medal record breaking performance at the Commonwealth Games in Edinburgh in 1970 when he was also in the 4x100m Northern Ireland relay team that reached the final.

At his peak and seen as one of the finest vaulters in the world, only for a serious ankle injury sustained preparing for the 1972 Olympics in Munich he could have struck gold in Germany but two years later in emotional circumstances he was back on the top step again in the Commonwealth Games, though not in the pole vault. Coach Buster McShane had seen enough in Bull's all round ability to suggest he could shine in the decathlon so rather than specialising in one event he now had to compete hard in 10. Inspired by the memory of McShane, who had tragically died in a car accident nine months earlier, heroically Bull, in hospital just a week before with a back injury, won the 1974 decathlon in Christchurch and even managed to grab a silver in the pole vault.

Bull is the only athlete to have first places in pole vaulting and the decathlon at the Commonwealth Games, and still had enough left in the tank to take part in the 1978 Commonwealth Games pole vault and decathlon won by a certain Daley Thompson.

Mike claimed 69 British international caps, a record which stood for decades until hurdler Colin Jackson broke it. He would go on to open a gym and be the Head Fitness Coach for the Ulster and Ireland rugby teams but still enjoyed doing some heavy lifting himself winning the Northern Ireland and Ireland Pole Vaulting Championships at the age of 44 and the World Masters Championship for over 40s in 1991. Today he holds the NI Pole Vault record of 5.25m set back in 1973 and won a new set of fans in 1985 when he was triumphant in the popular Superstars TV programme. The indefatigable Bull co-founded the sports charity Sparks Northern Ireland, raising money for children suffering from crippling illnesses and in 2012 was honoured with an MBE for services to sport and charity.

JOHN CALDWELL

BOXING: OLYMPIC TEENAGE STAR
AND WORLD CHAMPION
B: 07/05/1938 - D: 10/07/2009

John Caldwell won an Olympic medal at 18 years of age, became World Champion in sensational style, was involved in one of the most talked about fights in the history of the King's Hall and for decades the mere mention of his name in gyms around Belfast evoked unforgettable memories in old timers and nods of appreciation from younger souls aware of his status in the sport.

After learning his trade as a kid at the Immaculata Boxing Club, collecting Irish amateur titles at a rate of knots, he was known as the baby of the Ireland Olympic squad that would enjoy a successful trip to Melbourne in 1956. Caldwell, blown away by the pomp and scale of the opening ceremony, had plenty of faith in his ability but even though he breezed past his first opponent few thought he had a chance against Aussie favourite Warren Batchelor in the quarter-finals. The boy from west Belfast shook up the flyweight division with a well deserved points win though found Romanian Mircea Dobrescu a tougher nut to crack in the semis, having to settle for a bronze, one of four medals the Irish boxers brought home from Down Under.

In his later years Caldwell fondly remembered the warm homecoming receptions in Dublin and Belfast but most of all cherished his return to the place where he grew up, Cyprus Street close to the Falls Road, which was swamped with family, friends and adoring fans.

Working as a plumber he stayed an amateur until 1958 before moving to Glasgow with his wife when a career on the professional scene beckoned. There were few more dedicated or disciplined fighters around than Caldwell who would go to mass at 6.30am each morning prior to running up hills and working on his technique leading to the then Celtic manager Jimmy McGrory, the club's all time top goalscorer, inviting the boxer into training sessions to improve the fitness of his players. Caldwell even joined in when the Celtic stars were playing matches in training though they weren't allowed to tackle him!

Rules were different in the ring but in those early professional days Caldwell's foes found it difficult getting near him as he marched from one victory to another claiming the British flyweight title in 1960. The following year Caldwell was given his chance to become Champion of the World having moved up to bantamweight and he wasn't going to let it pass him by, beating France's Alphonse Halimi on points in London, with a final round knockdown helping his cause, earning the Immaculata man a European and World title.

Caldwell would dominate his next three battles, including a Wembley rematch against Halimi, before losing the crown in a unification bout amid a raucous and intimidating atmosphere in Sao Paulo against Brazilian bantamweight legend Eder Jofre and 25,000 screaming fans. It was his first defeat as a pro but it was another loss in 1962 that will forever be regarded as one of the most iconic fights in boxing history when Caldwell came up against fellow Belfast native Freddie Gilroy in front of a packed King's Hall with a contest against Jofre the prize. It was a bruising, bloody, all action battle that engrossed the crowd with underdog Gilroy winning when Caldwell was forced out at the end of the ninth round because of a cut eye.

While Gilroy would retire following that titanic tussle, Caldwell continued claiming Commonwealth and British bantamweight titles in 1964 ahead of calling it quits at the age of 27 the next year and going back to his plumbing job after a career to be proud of in which it is reckoned he contested 275 fights as an amateur and professional, winning the lot bar 10. Family man Caldwell, courageous and one of the Ireland's most skilled fighters, would sadly pass away in 2009 after a long battle with cancer seven years before Belfast City Council unveiled a much merited statute in his honour in West Belfast's Dunville Park where he played as a child.

DAVID CALVERT

SHOOTING: RECORD BREAKER
ALWAYS ON TARGET
B: 24/03/1951

David Calvert is Northern Ireland's most successful shooter, a history maker, a World Champion and a Commonwealth Games legend who incredibly has managed to stay at the top of his game for 40 years. The ace marksman has competed for his country in every Commonwealth Games since 1978 meaning he has taken part in the multi-sport extravaganza on a record 11 occasions and when you consider there have been 21 of these events, starting with the 1930 British Empire Games, that amounts to Calvert being involved in more than half of them!

He doesn't just turn up for the uniform, he brings home the bacon having won four gold and four bronze medals and yet he admits that he doesn't even have the best eyesight. Regarded as one of the finest Full Bore shooters in the world, Belfast man Calvert has been on target since first taking up arms almost 50 years ago at Campbell College in the RAF section of the Cadet Force. He says: "I first shot with the Cadet Force in 1965 and got selected for the All-Ireland team in the Home Internationals in 1968 the year before I left school and it went on from there."

It is a scarcely believable statistic to note that Calvert has represented Ireland in the Home International series every year since his debut performance. As a teenager he left home for England to become a pilot in the RAF and when he wasn't flying through the clouds he was establishing himself on firmer ground on the shooting circuit.

It was 1982 in Brisbane where Calvert first made the Commonwealth Games podium in third place in the pairs alongside partner Hazel McIntosh with the first gold coming in the Full Bore Individual competition in Victoria 1994. Four years later in Kuala Lumpur, Calvert and Martin Millar claimed pairs gold and they repeated the trick in the 2002 Manchester Games, when the shooting events took place at the National Shooting Centre in Bisley. Calvert clinched Northern Ireland's other gold medal in Manchester all on his own in the individual category with his proud family watching every shot while in 2010 he picked up his last Commonwealth Games medal to date grabbing a bronze in Delhi in the Full Bore singles.

If the Comber Rifle club member is renowned for his marvellous record in the 'Friendly Games' what he has achieved at Bisley in The Queen's Prize - shooting's most iconic competition - in the modern era is bewildering too having won it a record equalling three times in 2010, 2015 and 2016. Only four shooters since the event started in 1860 have enjoyed a hat-trick of triumphs putting Calvert's victories into perspective. There have been numerous other successes around the globe including six golds and two silvers with Great Britain in the eight team World Championships and individual wins in a host of countries such as South Africa, Canada, Namibia, Malaysia and the West Indies.

True gentleman Calvert may have retired from his job as a pilot to teach students in the Air Squadron at Cambridge University how to fly, but he has no plans to stop shooting and with his ability and experience he will be firing at the highest level for as long as he sees fit.

ALAN
CAMPBELL

ROWING: OLYMPIC HERO
OUT ON HIS OWN
B: 09/05/1983

Tears of joy flowed down rower Alan Campbell's face as he was presented with his Olympic medal at the London 2012 Games and as the giant of a man wept uncontrollably his parents Jennifer and William and wife Jules beamed with pride in the stands at Eton Dorney. Moments earlier Coleraine native Campbell had produced a gutsy, gritty and gallant performance to earn bronze, becoming the first British Olympic medalist since 1928 in the men's single sculls, a gruelling event of gladiatorial proportions where unlike other disciplines in the sport you are on your own in the boat.

Four years later in Rio, Campbell, a charismatic character, would create further history as the first Northern Ireland sports star to compete in the Olympics four times and this after in primary school insisting he wanted to be a farmer or minister!

Attending Coleraine Academical Institution, he tried every sport going before taking up rowing and being coached by the late great Bobby Platt at Bann Rowing club, giving up a potential army career and position at the prestigious Sandhurst Academy in 2003 to follow his dream. That same year, Campbell, part of the Tideway Scullers club in London, first rowed for Great Britain in the World U23 Championships in the single sculls, making his Olympics bow in Athens the next year in the quadruple sculls and helping GB claim a first World Cup medal in that discipline in 2005.

From 2006 he focused on the single sculls winning the overall World Cup title, recovering from a knee injury to take fifth in the 2008 Beijing Olympics and claiming a hard earned silver and two bronze medals in the 2009, 2010 and 2011 World Championships. For context Campbell was up against the two greatest single scullers ever, five time World Champion and double Olympic champion Mahe Drysdale from New Zealand and the Czech Republic's Ondrej Synek, also a five time World Champion and three time Olympic medalist.

It was that pair Campbell finished behind in the London Olympics using every ounce of strength he had and the roars of 30,000 home fans to pass Sweden's Lassi Karonen in a spine tingling final 100 metres to grab the place on the podium he so desired. Campbell had been offered the chance to row as part of a team in 2012 but wanted to deliver in the most physically demanding race of all and was so shattered after putting his body through what he described as "a world of pain" he could hardly get out of the boat in time for the medal ceremony.

When he did Alan provided some of the most emotional and endearing images of the Games as he cried thinking about sacrifices made by his family. While there were more World Cup medals to come, preparation for Rio 2016 was hampered by illness and injury and a bout of vertigo meant his last race came in the semi-finals.

With head held high the motivational speaker on sport and business retired, swapping the Team GB tracksuit for a shirt and tie and becoming a London banker in 2017 having graduated with a business studies degree from the Open University, doing so after winning Olympic bronze and being a three time World Championship medalist in the toughest era in history for single sculling.

PETER CANAVAN

GAELIC FOOTBALL: PURE CLASS AND TYRONE'S ALL-IRELAND KING
B: 09/04/1971

Peter Canavan is known as 'Peter the Great' in his home county of Tyrone though perhaps 'Peter the Greatest' is more appropriate because many believe he is the finest GAA player to hail from Ulster and up there with the best ever. It is hard to argue as Canavan was the man who gave the Red Hand county hope when they had none and drove the team on with his ability and attitude to end decades of heartache and become All-Ireland champions.

Some going for a boy from the townland of Glencull close to Ballygawley who was sometimes left out of teams as a youngster because he was deemed too small leaving him to steel himself to be better than anyone else, if not bigger. Size did not matter to hard as nails Canavan who would take anyone on whether they towered over him or had muscles like The Incredible Hulk. In the forward line he could pull rabbits out of a hat when Tyrone needed magic, would use his street smarts, skills and speed to score the most unlikely points and goals and took team-mates to places they thought were beyond them lifting them in mind and body, eventually to an historic All-Ireland victory in 2003.

Growing up in a GAA mad home Canavan, who has a photographic memory which has helped him thrive in his post playing career role as a television pundit, practiced with family members and friends in a nearby field and kicked a ball on to his roof trying to catch it on the way down, but due to a fall-out and split at his local club, he had to be content playing in challenge matches rather than competitive encounters, though there was little doubt regardless of the nature of games that the young Peter had something about him.

As the years passed it became clear to all that the St Ciaran's High School pupil had everything, playing his first match in Croke Park for Tyrone Vocational Schools in 1988 when he took grass home from the pitch just in case he never performed there again! The trips to the fabled stadium would become frequent as would honours like double All-Ireland Under-21 success thanks to his prolific scoring. There was also a 1993 triumph with Errigal Ciaran after the club row was resolved in his parish with Canavan influential in a first Ulster Club Championship victory for the Tyrone side as Downpatrick were defeated in the final. It may seem hard to believe now with all he achieved but in an interview with Orla Bannon for BBC NI, Canavan said he entered that club final with "a point to prove" feeling that he was being doubted in his early days as a Tyrone senior player. Any doubts disappeared as Canavan helped deliver Ulster Championship and National League glory for Tyrone, enjoyed multiple Railway Cup wins with his province and produced star turns for Ireland in the International Rules series against Australia.

Throughout all of the above what asthmatic Canavan wanted most though was for the Tyrone senior side to be crowned All-Ireland Champions and from the moment he played alongside his brother Pascal in the team in 1989 it was an epic mountain climb that would not be complete until the summit was scaled.

In 1995 Canavan was the catalyst behind Tyrone reaching the All-Ireland decider yet despite scoring 11 out of his side's 12 points he would be heartbroken at the final whistle as the game was lost narrowly to Dublin. Canavan would continue to deliver majestic performances but to no avail with some dubbing him the greatest player never to win the All-Ireland.

Mickey Harte took charge of Tyrone in late 2002 and naming Canavan captain it was as if fate had intervened to set 'Peter the Great' on the path to the destination he craved, starting out in the first round of the Ulster Championship when he scored in the dying seconds to earn Tyrone a draw against Derry, who were easily despatched in the replay with Canavan scoring eight points. They would move on to reach the Ulster final against Down, with Canavan admitting that his "head was all over the place" following the death of his father Sean a week before. A blockbuster game ended in a draw with Canavan scoring one goal and six points before grabbing 11 in the replay as Harte's men cruised home.

In 2003 the first all Ulster All-Ireland final versus Armagh beckoned for the Red Hands after beating Fermanagh and then Kerry, following which Tyrone's style of play was controversially labelled 'puke football' by pundit and ex-Kerry great Pat Spillane but if Tyrone were irked by those negative comments more worrying was that Canavan picked up an ankle injury leaving him a severe doubt for the final.

Nowhere near 100% fit he played in the first half, as always coming up trumps scoring five points, to give his side a lead they would not relinquish. Interviewed for the GAA oral history project, PE teacher Canavan said: "I stayed in the dressing-room after half-time and missed the first 10 minutes of the second-half while I was getting the ankle sorted. That was a surreal experience because you're in a stadium with 80,000 people and you can imagine the noise and excitement generated by that, but I couldn't hear a thing because the treatment room I was in was sound-proofed. You could hear nothing, so I hadn't a clue what was going on in the biggest game of my life."

To an ear-splitting reception Canavan would re-enter the fray in the last 10 minutes with his leadership and experience seeing out a 12 points to nine win. Fitting that he was on the pitch at the end, as captain he would lift the Sam Maguire trophy and deliver an impassioned and emotive speech on the steps of the Hogan Stand with the joy, relief and pain of previous disappointments flowing out of him ending his nine minute address with "I think I've said enough, it's time to take Sam to Tyrone!"

At the age of 35 Canavan would win another All-Ireland in 2005 though beset with injury problems the genius from Ballygawley was used more sparingly in a dramatic trip to glory. Red carded a minute after coming on in the Ulster final replay defeat to Armagh, he won his appeal for the dismissal and in the All-Ireland semi-final against the same opposition, substitute Canavan hit the winning point in injury time. Peter the Great would have one more glorious final say scoring a goal in the decider with Kerry that was first about his anticipation and awareness and last his unerring ability to make the right decision in monster moments, coolly passing the ball into the net with his left foot. The goal turned the game in Tyrone's favour and they went on to win a firecracker of a contest 1-16 to 2-10 with Canavan opting to retire from the county scene as a two time All-Ireland winner with six All Stars and content that he had finally taken his beloved county to the top of the hill.

PETER CHAMBERS

ROWING: WORLD CHAMPION AND LONDON 2012 MEDAL MAN

B: 14/03/1990

Peter Chambers is the European Champion and World Champion rower who was centimetres away from winning an Olympic gold medal at London 2012 and opted to retire at the age of 29 to coach future stars of the sport. Growing up as a member of Bann Rowing Club in Coleraine, Chambers had big shoes to fill given that his older brother Richard had already shown serious talent on the water, but far from feeling overawed Peter was inspired to follow in his sibling's footsteps.

In his teenage years he displayed an acute knowledge in the boat and a will to win, which was enhanced by coach Seamus Reynolds, leaving the impression amongst rowing aficionados in the area that here was a boy ahead of his time. It was a quality that would help lift him to great heights at world level, winning a bronze medal for the British team in the men's lightweight quadruple sculls at the World Under-23 Championships when he was just 19. Others may have had more experience and a bigger build at that time but Chambers had a quiet determination and natural talent that made a difference.

The following year, outlining his versatility, he landed a silver in the same Championships in the men's lightweight single sculls and then came gold at the event in 2011 coming home first in the men's lightweight double sculls with Kieren Emery. On the crest of a wave, Chambers and Emery teamed up again one month later at Lake Bled in Slovenia in the senior

World Championships in the men's lightweight pair to deliver a unique double success. Third at the halfway point of the race, they surged to lead with 500 metres left and were strong enough to see it home ahead of Italy and Germany. At just 21 the quietly spoken Chambers was on top of the world.

Chambers entered the 2012 Olympics in good heart and in the lightweight men's four alongside his brother Richard, Rob Williams and Chris Bartley there were high hopes going into the final at a packed Eton Dorney, where 30,000 fans were cheering the Team GB quartet on in what turned out to be one of the races of the Games, with the younger Chambers and his pals finishing in the silver medal position just behind South Africa, whose time was 6 minutes 2.84 seconds compared with 6 minutes 3.09 seconds for the GB boat. There was pride on the podium tinged with a little disappointment but the latter didn't stop Chambers racking up more medals at the top regattas including a bronze with his brother in the 2013 World Championships in the men's lightweight double sculls and 2015 European Championship gold with fellow Bann Rowing club member Joel Cassells in the lightweight men's pair.

There were also silvers at European level in 2014 and 2016 and bronze and silver at the World Championships in 2014 and 2017 plus an appearance at the 2016 Rio Olympics, all before this world class rower, who is also an accomplished furniture maker, retired in 2019 to start coaching with a glittering decade of competition behind him.

RICHARD CHAMBERS

ROWING: WORLD CHAMPION AND
LONDON 2012 MEDAL MAN

B:10/06/1985

To have one world class sportsperson in a family is exceptional but the Chambers clan from Coleraine had double that with Richard leading the way for younger brother Peter as both ruled the waves to become rowing World Champions. By the time older sibling Richard had retired from competing in 2016 to become a coach with Cambridge University Boat Club he was regarded as one of the finest lightweight rowers of his generation.

Starting out as a 15-year-old at Bann Rowing Club under coach Bobby Platt, Chambers was encouraged by parents Gillian and Eric to follow his dream which was to study construction management at university and as fate would have it his chosen seat of learning was Oxford Brookes which was a high performance centre for the sport he would excel in. During his first week at the rowing club he found the going tough but rather than wilt under the workload and fierce competition Chambers relished the challenge, grafted hard, enhanced his technique and progressed so quickly that a month before his 20th birthday he won a silver medal in the lightweight quadruple sculls at the 2005 World U23 Championships in Amsterdam.

The following year he went one better in the same competition clinching gold for Great Britain alongside Chris Bartley in the pairs and from there the senior World Championships beckoned as did history with the then 22-year-old Chambers, in his first season in the Olympic class lightweight four, helping Team GB to their first victory in that category at the World Championships in 2007.

There was further elation in the 2010 World Championships when the Coleraine man surged to another lightweight four gold in one of the greatest finals the sport has seen with the British boat beating Australia, China and Germany by millimetres in a sensational finish.

Chambers made a habit of being involved in classic big time races and famously along with his brother Peter, Rob Williams and Chris Bartley they were 0.25 seconds away from coming home first in the final of the 2012 Olympic lightweight four decider. While agonisingly close to the top step, Chambers, who also competed at the Games in 2008 and 2016, was proud to land silver at the greatest show on earth taking heart that the whole of Northern Ireland was cheering him and Peter on.

Consistent throughout his impressive career with World Cup success and podium places at the European Championships, Richard won another silver and three more bronze medals at the World Championships before deciding to hang up his oars with memories to savour and an endearing humility that is a family trait. After his retirement, he said: "I had a career in rowing much greater than I could have ever dreamed and it shows what can be done with hard work, effort, application and great support. Winning the World Championships was incredible and in London I won an Olympic medal with my brother Peter which was such a special moment for our family."

DARREN CLARKE

GOLF: ONE OF THE MOST POPULAR
OPEN WINNERS EVER
B: 14/08/1968

It was 6.30am on Thursday morning on July 18, 2019 with the stands around the first tee at Royal Portrush packed to capacity and thousands lining the fairway, all waiting to greet Darren Clarke, who a few minutes later was set to hit the first shot of the 148th Open Championship as the historic tournament returned to Northern Ireland for the first time since 1951. The loud roars for Clarke's arrival could be heard around the course and all the way to Barry's Amusements and beyond. It was a sign of the esteem in which Clarke is held in in this part of the world and recognition of what he has done for golf and Northern Ireland sport.

For Clarke it was an emotional moment in a career that has seen quite a few, though he managed to hold himself together to make a birdie putt on the green where cheers once again echoed all over the famous links. Eight years previously Clarke, at the age of 42, enjoyed the highlight of his golfing life when he won The Open at Royal St George's and gave one of the best acceptance speeches of any major tournament victor. As a boy he practiced holing out to lift the Claret Jug and at his 20th attempt he pulled it off in sensational style to record one of the most popular triumphs in 21st century sport.

Clarke played rugby, football, tennis and squash when he was young but opted to focus on golf at Dungannon Golf Club, representing Royal School Dungannon and playing collegiate golf at Wake Forest University in the United States. The boy had much to offer in the game as he proved with a rousing victory over Paul McGinley in the North of Ireland Championship at Royal Portrush in 1990 and after turning professional he won his first European Tour event in 1993 at the Alfred Dunhill Open in Belgium showing bottle to see off Nick Faldo and Vijay Singh.

There would be more victories and a series of strong performances in the decade that followed with his most impressive coming in 2000 when he defeated Tiger Woods in the final of a World Golf Championship Matchplay event before another WGC success three years later. In between, while living in Sunningdale in England, Darren's wife Heather was diagnosed with breast cancer and so began a brave battle that sadly ended in 2006 when Heather passed away at just 39 years of age. It was a heartbreaking time for the golfer and children Tyrone and Conor who were only eight and five with Darren saying in a statement: "Heather's courage and bravery throughout the last two years when she was diagnosed with secondary breast cancer has been an inspiration. She never complained once throughout her ordeal and we will all miss her greatly. She was a wonderful and enormously supportive wife, mother and friend."

Six weeks later Clarke found it within himself to play for Europe in the Ryder Cup at the K Club in Dublin and amid emotional scenes the Ulsterman was the inspirational force behind a fantastic victory over the USA winning all three of his matches having been a wild card pick for captain Ian Woosnam. From the moment he was cheered by all and sundry on the opening morning to breaking down in tears on the final day, after beating Zach Johnson in the singles, it was an intense period and telling that the American players were as pleased for Clarke as his European team-mates offering an insight into the warm feelings for him around the globe.

There were wins in Asia and Europe in 2008 but disappointment too when Clarke was controversially left out of Nick Faldo's European Ryder Cup team leading to suggestions that the Northern Ireland man's best days were behind him though what happened in 2011 blew that theory to pieces when the fan of fast cars, known to enjoy a drink and a smoke making him even more of a favourite with fans, scorched to his greatest glory.

Before a shot was played at Royal St George's in Sandwich, Kent, Clarke, who by now was based in Portrush with his sons, was 125/1 to win with some bookmakers but he kept the faith with intelligent golf in the first three rounds carding 68, 68 and 69 on the par 70 course to top the leaderboard though even then with Americans Phil Mickelson and Dustin Johnson on his tail many felt he wouldn't be there at the end. Despite the pressure, Clarke stayed calm, brilliantly navigated his way round the course with his experience and knowhow to the fore and knocked in crucial putts at vital times smiling his way through the 18 holes for a level par round and five under par total to win by three shots and be hailed as the oldest Open champion since 1967.

When he reached the final fairway the tournament had all but been won and the ovation he received walking up the last was something to behold, hugging his mum Hetty, dad Godfrey and fiancée Alison Campbell when his round was complete. Clarke had become the country's second Open winner after Fred Daly and made it a remarkable three majors out of six for his homeland following US Open triumphs for compatriots Rory McIlroy and Graeme McDowell.

In a heartfelt speech Darren told the adoring crowd: "I've tried for 20 years to make this speech. It's been a long bumpy road but I've had so much support from so many people. As you know I'm fond of a little beverage now and again and with the R & A's permission there might be lots of nice Irish black stuff in this trophy this evening. I want to thank my mum and dad and my whole family and Alison for their neverending support and as you may know there is someone up there watching down as well. To the support I've had this past four days I can't thank you enough."

The following year Clarke would marry former Miss Northern Ireland Alison, the owner of successful agency ACA Models and in 2016 he captained the European Ryder Cup team having made five appearances as a player. Darren continues to raise awareness and money for breast cancer through his Foundation and charity work as well as play on tour. Clarke, a winner all over the world, also loves to fish, not least in the Bahamas, knowing full well that in golfing terms he landed the biggest catch of all in 2011.

MICHAEL CONLAN

BOXER: TOP OF THE WORLD FIGHTING MACHINE

B: 19/11/1991

With the wonderful array of talent over the years it is extraordinary to think that an Irish male boxer didn't win a senior World Amateur Championship title until 2015 though perhaps it is no surprise that the man who did it was the majestic Michael Conlan.

The Belfast fighter entered the Championships in Doha high in confidence having previously claimed Commonwealth and European titles and fiercely determined to achieve something nobody from north or south had done before. He made his fast hands and fast feet count to reach the bantamweight final where he faced Uzbekistan's Murodjon Akhmadaliev with Conlan strong in the first round, dominant in the second and in control in the third until he was knocked down in the final minute, though even with that shock to the system the judges gave the Irish team captain a unanimous points decision and a place in the record books.

It would prove to be the highlight of a sensational amateur career for Conlan who was originally drawn to boxing because of his fighting brothers Brendan and Jamie and while the former moved away from the sport the

45

latter stayed in it, challenging for a world title and becoming renowned for his all action contests and being one of the nicest guys in the game.

That was clear when Jamie and Michael were supposed to fight in an Ulster senior flyweight final in 2009 but the elder sibling decided to forfeit the bout and turn pro leaving Michael as the champion. Ulster and Irish titles were welcome but the St John Bosco boxer really wanted to deliver on the world stage and he did just that as an underdog at the 2012 Olympics reaching the semi-finals and earning a bronze medal at flyweight.

The following year it was silver at the European Championships and having moved to bantamweight he won gold at the 2014 Commonwealth Games in Glasgow, overcoming cuts throughout the competition which ended with a final success against England's Qais Ashfaq and a big hug in the corner from his proud dad John, the tactically astute coach of the Northern Ireland boxing team that year.

In Scotland Conlan, who has said his positive thinking comes from mum Teresa, impressed with his slick footwork and ability to switch styles and when he was victorious at the 2015 European Championships, where he was voted Boxer of the tournament, ahead of taking the World Amateur Championships by storm, glory at the 2016 Olympics seemed on the cards. Controversy raged though when he was dubiously defeated on points in the quarter-finals by Russia's Vladimir Nikitin leaving the Belfast man fuming and accusing amateur boxing officials of corruption in a no holds barred interview on RTE moments after the decision.

A few days later, as he sat on Copacabana Beach in Rio, Conlan told me that he cried his heart out in the dressing room knowing that his Olympic dream was over. For this supremely gifted boxer, however, the ambition to be a World Champion in the paid ranks is well and truly on following a blistering start in the pro ranks and it seems a matter of when not if he will have a world title belt around his waist, completing a unique amateur and professional double.

Fred Daly

Golf: Made the big major
breakthrough
B: 11/10/1911 - D: 18/11/1990

Long before Rory McIlroy, Graeme McDowell and Darren Clarke made 'Northern Ireland the golfing capital of the world', Portrush native Fred Daly became the country's first major winner when he won The Open Championship in 1947 at the Royal Liverpool Golf Club, Hoylake earning £150 in prize money. It would take another 60 years for an Irishman, in the shape of Padraig Harrington, to claim Open glory and a further three years for Northern Ireland to have a second major champion thanks to McDowell.

Daly's story is fairytale stuff from being a youthful caddie at Royal Portrush who never took golf lessons to becoming one of the most appreciated players during his era leading the great America star Sam Snead to comment: "Fred's one of the finest long iron players in the game and could knock your hat off with a one iron at 220 yards". The first victory of note for Daly came in 1936 in the Ulster Professional Championship and led to the first of many outings for Ireland. He became a prolific winner of the same event during the Second World War and was successful in the Irish Professional Championship building his reputation across the island and further afield.

The youngest of six children and son to a blacksmith, Daly worked as a pro at Mahee Island Golf Club, Lurgan and City of Derry before in 1944 moving to Balmoral where he stayed for the rest of his life. A year after the War ended in 1945 Daly impressed in a host of tournaments and clinched the Irish Open at Portmarnock beating off the challenge of the revered Bobby Locke. If 1946 was good, 1947 was great with Daly in fine form at the start of the year and the highlight coming at Hoylake in July with his historic triumph in the biggest tournament of them all. On a difficult course a first round 73 and second round 70 eased Daly into a four shot lead at the halfway mark but he had a difficult third round culminating in a 78 which brought him level with three others. In those days the final two rounds were played on the same day so the Portrush man had to quickly re-focus and with fierce determination a strong back nine moved him ahead until on the 17th hole he suffered a double bogey meaning a birdie was required at the last to put himself in prime position to lift the Claret Jug. The pressure was on but Daly revelled in it holing out on the final green from 10 feet for a 72 and a one shot victory. It was a popular win with the crowd who had taken the Ulsterman to their hearts and laughed during his acceptance speech when he said he hoped by taking the trophy home to Northern Ireland the change of air would help it!

Later that year Daly won the prestigious British Matchplay event and became the first Irishman to play in the Ryder Cup, making the first of four appearances, while in 1948 he was also a multi-tournament winner and runner-up in The Open. He was unlucky not to win it a second time, finishing third in 1950 and 1952 and fourth in the year in between when it was staged at Royal Portrush. There was more success, however, in the British Matchplay most notably in 1952 when on his way to victory he overcame Alan Poulton at the 12th extra hole after a marathon match lasting over five hours and put a young Peter Alliss to the sword. It was to prove his last notable success across the water though he continued to dominate the Ulster Professional Championship showing style on the course and wit and charm off it with an array of stories that kept friends and fans entertained. Long past his best, Daly played a handful of occasions in his beloved Open Championship in the 1970s and was awarded an MBE in the 1984 New Year Honours 'for services to golf', passing away in 1990, aged 79, at the time Northern Ireland's only major champion.

STEVEN DAVIS

FOOTBALL: EURO STAR
ADORED BY THE FANS
B: 01/01/1985

If I was selecting my dream five-a-side team for Northern Ireland it would be Pat Jennings, Danny Blanchflower, Steven Davis, David Healy and George Best and Davis would be the captain. Yes, even ahead of that glorious general Blanchflower. That's how I feel about Steven.

You cannot exaggerate the influence Davis has had on the Northern Ireland side since winning his first cap in 2005. He has carried the team and without him the Green and White Army would not have had the chance to savour the experience of major tournament football in the 21st century. For me he deserves to be mentioned in the same breath as Bestie and Pat when discussing the country's all-time greats.

Davis isn't just Northern Ireland's finest modern day footballer, he's the most capped British outfield player of all time and from the moment he first played a senior international, a month on from his 20th birthday, it was clear he had it in him to be a Windsor Park hero standing head and shoulders above his team-mates in a 1-0 friendly defeat at home to Canada. Seven months later, already established in the side, it was his delicious pass that set up David Healy to score a famous winner against England. Fans in the Kop still sing about how Davis outperformed Steven Gerrard and Frank Lampard in a majestic midfield display that has been a hallmark of his career in a green shirt.

As a kid in Cullybackey, Davis, a product of St Andrews Boys club, idolised Paul Gascoigne and like his hero always seemed to be the most talented player on the pitch. After Aston Villa won the race to sign him, he made his first team bow in 2004 and with his ability to create and score goals from midfield the following season he swept the board at the club's annual awards ceremony ahead of a transfer to Fulham and then a dream move to his boyhood team Rangers in 2008, playing a key role as they reached the UEFA Cup final that year - the club's first European final since their 1972 Cup Winners' Cup success.

Davis excelled at Ibrox winning three league titles, both domestic cup competitions multiple times and was renowned for five star displays in big games, often making the difference in Old Firm derbies versus Celtic. He joined Southampton in 2012 and enhancing his status at the top level of English football, he captained the Saints to the 2017 League Cup final prior to a Rangers return in 2019 with Gerrard the manager.

Throughout his club career he has delivered for Northern Ireland, constantly turning up to play when others couldn't be bothered as the side went through difficult times and being the vital cog in the machine that qualified for the Euro 2016 finals. Davis ran the show for manager Michael O'Neill, oozing authority and calm.

It is no coincidence that the only group match O'Neill's side lost was with Davis injured and when an understrength team needed their skipper most, with qualification on the line at home to Greece in October 2015, he came up with one of the best individual displays by a Northern Ireland player, scoring twice in a 3-1 victory to take the country to their first major tournament since the 1986 World Cup. After breaking the deadlock he looked to the heavens, dedicating his goals post match to his mum and 'biggest fan' Laura who had passed away from cancer seven years earlier. Leading the team to the knockout stages of the Euro 2016 finals, Davis wrote a superb column for the Belfast Telegraph during the competition and without fanfare donated his fee to cancer charity Myeloma UK in a classy gesture typical of the man.

Married to childhood sweetheart Tracy and devoted to their children Chloe, Kaia and Cobi, the midfielder became his nation's youngest modern day skipper in 2006, has been permanent captain since 2011, reached a century of caps in 2017 and in October 2020, in a dramatic winning penalty shoot out against Bosnia in the Euro 2020 play-off semi-final, Davis, with 12 international goals to his name, won his 120th cap overtaking fellow legend Jennings to move to the top of the all-time appearance list for Northern Ireland.

Humble Steven has always down played his immense contribution. It is telling that all his team-mates, past and present, laud him as one of Northern Ireland's greatest players. They are not wrong. Davis says: "I've always seen it as an honour to play for Northern Ireland and our fans." The honour has been all ours.

ROBIN DIXON

BOBSLEIGH: WINTER OLYMPICS
GREAT WHO BROKE THE ICE

B: 21/04/1935

On the bobsleigh track at Innsbruck in 1964, after being granted leave from the Army, Robin Dixon won a gold medal at the Winter Olympics with his close friend Tony Nash and they followed that unlikely success up a year later by becoming World Champions. It was a stunning double that would never have occurred for Dixon but for a chance meeting with his second cousin, the infamous Lord Lucan. Dixon, or Lord Glentoran as he is known, is the eldest child of Northern Ireland politician 2nd Baron Glentoran, inheriting the title when his father died in 1995. Although born in London, with the given name Thomas Robin Valerian Dixon, he is very much a Northern Ireland man and resides in Ballyclare having held a number of leading roles in organisations such as the Northern Ireland Tall Ships Council and Positively Belfast. He has also been a Conservative Party Shadow Minister, an active member of the House of Lords and the High Sheriff of Antrim.

What sets him apart, though, is that historic two man bobsleigh Olympic gold medal which came in the middle of his service with the Grenadier Guards after he was educated in Eton and Grenoble in France. Dixon, an excellent sprinter in his youth, didn't have a clue about the sport until speaking to his relative John Bingham in 1957 while on holiday in the exclusive St Moritz resort in Switzerland. Bingham, who would become Lord Lucan, talked about the thrills of bobsleigh in the morning and by the afternoon Dixon tried it and was hooked. In an interview with the Belfast Telegraph, he recalled: "I told him I had never even heard of bobsleigh but I was willing to give it a go. I'd been a boxer in the Army and a fairly good sprinter and wanted to try something different. It was more dangerous in those days as the tracks were not as well manicured and people were dying every year. I don't think I'd ever seen a bobsleigh when I climbed into the back of it and didn't look at the course on the way down but when we stopped I realised I quite enjoyed it."

After initially being involved with four man teams for Great Britain he teamed up with Nash, a former motor racing driver with poor eyesight, and as the pair learnt to work together at breakneck speed with Dixon as brake man they began to make an impression, finishing sixth in the 1961 World Championships in their first major race as a duo. A bronze medal was secured at the World Championships two years later at the opening of the Innsbruck Olympic track setting themselves up for a shot at Games glory in 1964 in Austria where they downed whiskey the night before competition started. Dixon and Nash led after day one but their hopes looked over when they discovered a rear axle bolt had broken off their sled after dropping to second on the opening run of day two and they were without a spare. In a wonderful act of sportsmanship legendary Italian racer Eugenio Monti, who was in contention to win, offered to lend the British pair one of his bolts and fully functional they roared down the artificial ice with the fastest time in the final run to strike gold, just 0.12 seconds ahead of Italy's Sergio Zardini and Romano Bonagura with the gallant and generous Monti and Sergio Siorpaes in third.

With Dixon back in uniform at his barracks in England later that week he and Nash savoured the celebrations and champagne knowing they had come a long way from starting out together when their families and friends raised money so they could drive around the Alps in an old Land Rover in order to compete. Proving their Olympic victory was no fluke, Dixon and driver Nash, who have a corner named after them at the St Moritz Olympic Bobrun, were victorious at the 1965 World Championships and claimed bronze at the same competition the next year. To this day they remain Team GB's only Winter Olympics bobsleigh winners. Dixon says: "I'm immensely proud of the gold medal. It makes you a member of a very exclusive club, not just in Northern Ireland but also worldwide."

PADDY DOHERTY

GAELIC FOOTBALL: DOWN

FAVOURITE KNEW THE SCORE

B: 28/03/1934

Paddy Doherty is a three time All-Ireland winner with Down and one of the most dangerous forwards Gaelic football has ever known. From Ballykinlar, Doherty was a dominant force for his county when they brought home the Sam Maguire trophy in 1960, 1961 and 1968 though the sporting life of the man known as Paddy Mo could have been so different.

Having progressed from the minor to senior ranks with Down, Doherty was already considered an excellent GAA player when the chance came along in 1957 to have a trial with English Football League Division Two side (or Championship in modern terms) Lincoln City who had heard about his goalscoring prowess when he netted five times against an Army Select team for Downpatrick side Rathkeltair. Doherty scored four in his trial and was immediately handed a contract with Lincoln thinking they had signed a prolific striker who could take them to the next level but the Down man suffered from homesickness and left England after just eight weeks.

For playing 'a foreign game' the GAA suspended Doherty for a year, which was reduced to six months, but he continued to hit the target as an amateur soccer player with Ballyclare Comrades scoring a remarkable 33 goals in half a season in the B division. What he wanted to do more than anything, however, was deliver for Down and with a left foot to die for he would return to play for the Mournemen and make a mighty contribution during the greatest period in the county's history.

In the 1960 All-Ireland semi-final versus Offaly at Croke Park, Doherty hit 1-7 in what he said was his 'best ever game' in the superbly detailed 'The Making of Paddy Mo' memoir by Tony Bagnall. Trailing for most of the match Doherty was instrumental in the comeback scoring a penalty and all of his side's points bar three to earn a replay which Down won to reach the final where they overwhelmed Kerry with Doherty once again on the spot with a brilliantly taken penalty in a 2-10 to 0-8 victory to take the Sam Maguire trophy to the North for the first time.

Proving conclusively that they were the best team in the land Down were back at Croke Park the following year for another All-Ireland decider with Doherty in the role of inspirational captain as well as phenomenal scorer in a magical forward line alongside fellow greats Sean O'Neill and James McCartan. This time Offaly were Down's final victims with Doherty as proud as punch to lift 'Sam' after a dramatic 3-6 to 2-8 win. If the back to back triumphs were spectacular perhaps the 1968 All-Ireland final glory for Down over Kerry was even more impressive with the majestic Doherty scoring five points in a 2-12 to 1-13 victory. Paddy was 34 then but still as deadly as ever with his natural ability to score at will.

According to Bagnall, in total Doherty hit 962 points at county level breaking records year on year, ending up as the top scorer in the Ulster Championship on four occasions and finishing with a landmark 15 goals and 159 points in the competition which included six goals and 41 points in Ulster finals. Doherty won seven Ulster Championships, the same amount of Railway Cups and earned three National League medals and this master marksman landed more than 4000 points in club football.

The 'Paddy Mo' nickname came from his godfather Malachy Doherty who was a fan of gifted American tennis star Maureen 'Mo' Connolly, known for her nimbleness, balance and ability to hit winning points from seemingly impossible angles which the darling of Down himself did for years.

PETER DOHERTY

FOOTBALL: LEAGUE WINNER, CUP
WINNER AND REVERED BY ALL
B: 05/05/1913 - D 06/04/1990

Peter Doherty is renowned for being the manager who guided Northern Ireland to the last eight of the 1958 World Cup finals but before that he was a magnificent, maverick footballer who is rightly regarded as one of the finest the country has ever produced. Held in high esteem by some of the biggest names of his time, the iconic Harry Gregg described Doherty as 'Peter the Great' and often placed him on a higher level than George Best, Liverpool's legendary manager Bill Shankly viewed Doherty as one of the most talented to ever play the game and former England hero Len Shackleton said he was "the genius among geniuses".

Ahead of inspiring Manchester City to their first league title in 1937 and scoring in an FA Cup final success for Derby County nine years later, flame-haired Magherafelt man Doherty worked as an apprentice on a building site and as a bus conductor. His football career started in the Irish League with Coleraine and then Glentoran, who he helped win the Irish Cup in 1933 prior to moving to Blackpool later that year at the age of 19 for a bargain price of £1,900.

Dazzling at inside left Doherty became a favourite with the fans in the seaside town with his skills earning a move to Manchester City early in 1936 for what was then a club record fee of £10,000 and while his early games weren't anything to write home about his performances in his first full season with the Blues were spectacular. Playing like modern City greats Sergio Aguero and David Silva rolled into one, class apart Doherty scored 30 goals lifting the Manchester side to their first league championship in the 1936-37 campaign, a feat still celebrated at the club today despite all their recent achievements.

That summer City went to Nazi Germany and played in front of 70,000 spectators at Berlin's Olympic stadium with Adolf Hitler determined to use the tour as propaganda for his leadership. In later years Doherty, always his own man, recalled: "We were expected to give the Nazi salute before the match started but we decided to merely stand to attention. When the German national anthem was played only 11 arms went up instead of the expected 22!"

During the second World War, Doherty served in the RAF but he continued to play for Manchester City and make guest appearances for many other clubs including Liverpool and Manchester United. He also played alongside the legendary Stanley Matthews on occasions for a highly entertaining service team.

Following the war, Doherty moved to Derby County and as he and Raich Carter tortured and tormented defences in a dynamic double act the Rams roared to FA Cup glory in 1946 with the Northern Ireland native scoring a goal in a 4-1 Wembley final victory over Charlton. Doherty, whose endeavour was as impressive as his elusiveness on the ball, would later shine for Huddersfield Town and Doncaster Rovers and won 16 caps at international level, netting three goals between 1935 and 1950 exciting crowds wherever he played.

Amongst the first group of players to be inducted into English football's Hall of Fame, Doherty would go on to become a huge hit as the Northern Ireland manager taking the country to the quarter-finals of the 1958 World Cup finals in Sweden which was the first time the nation had ever reached a major tournament. Regarded as a visionary there are some suggestions that the phrase 'the beautiful game' was coined in appreciation of Doherty's footballing ability. What is widely accepted is that it was he who invented the two-touch or passing penalty, first carried out by Danny Blanchflower and Jimmy McIlroy for Northern Ireland in 1957 which superstars such as Johan Cruyff, Lionel Messi and Thierry Henry would later try and emulate. As well as being a fabulous player Doherty was a man who stood up for others and was never afraid to air his views about how clubs treated players, writing a hard-hitting book called 'Spotlight on Football'. A man ahead of his time, 'the genius among geniuses' passed away in 1990.

JOEY DUNLOP

MOTORCYCLING: MULTIPLE WORLD CHAMPION AND KING OF THE ROADS

B: 25/02/1952 - D: 02/07/2000

Affectionately known as 'Yer Maun', Joey Dunlop was also our man, his own man, an everyman, a family man, a quiet man, a down to earth man, a humble man, a generous man, a charitable man and in motorcycling he was THE Man - a five time World Champion, Isle of Man TT history maker, King of the Roads and more popular in Northern Ireland than an Ulster Fry.

Like so many people who followed his career and even those who didn't I can still remember where I was when I heard the news about his fatal crash which happened when he was racing in Estonia. Covering the European Championships in 2000, I was sitting beside the great sports journalist Malcolm Brodie in the De Kuip stadium in Rotterdam waiting for the post match press conference to start following France's dramatic golden goal victory over Italy when my mum phoned to tell me that Joey had died. The news shocked and saddened Malcolm and I to the core and those same emotions were felt across Northern Ireland and further afield because Joey just wasn't a local hero, he was a legend all over the world.

There's the story about a traffic policeman in Queensland, Australia stopping a rider at full throttle and saying to him as he approached "Who do you think you are, Joey Dunlop?" only to be stunned to find when a yellow helmet was removed it really was Joey Dunlop leaving the star-struck copper not knowing whether to book him or ask for an autograph! Motorcycling is a dangerous sport and those entering it know the risks but maybe because he was revered so much there was a view that Joey was invincible, hence the disbelief on July 2, 2000 when details of his passing were released.

The respect and appreciation of this ordinary bloke capable of extraordinary things on a bike brought over 50,000 people to his funeral in his hometown of Ballymoney with mourners coming from all parts of Ireland and the UK plus countries like Australia, New Zealand, America, South Africa and Japan. For Joey's devastated family there was some comfort that their husband, father, son and brother had enriched so many lives. Sadly there would be more tragedy for the Dunlop family when Joey's brother Robert died in 2008 and Robert's son William passed away in 2018 competing in the sport.

Fifteen years after Joey's death, to mark the 20th anniversary of the Belfast Telegraph Sports Awards, I organised a poll for the readers to vote for Northern Ireland's greatest sports star with 20 legends, all written about in this book, included in the vote and to underline Joey's popularity he came out on top ahead of George Best and Rory McIlroy. It was wonderful to have Joey's wife Linda and their children there to collect his award that night and while understandably it became emotional on stage everyone in the audience was with them every step of the way, just like everyone had been behind Joey all those years before.

Born William Joseph Dunlop and educated at Ballymoney High School, he bought his first motorbike as a teenager and had his first race in 1969 on a short circuit at the Maghaberry airfield circuit close to Moira and soon he was making an impression on more experienced riders, becoming part of county Antrim's 'Armoy Armada', along with Frank Kennedy, Mervyn Robinson and his brother Jim Dunlop taking on the famed 'Dromara Destroyers' from county Down, Ray McCullough, Brian Reid, Ian McGregor and Trevor Steele in an intense rivalry that had fans flocking to see it. Joey had talent and John Rea, grandfather of another multiple World Champion Jonathan Rea, recognised it and began a sponsorship deal that would lead to Dunlop, with the Rea Racing Yahama, earning his opening Isle of Man TT success in the 1977 Jubilee Classic. Though a man of few words, when his dear friend and loyal backer John Rea passed away, Joey gave a glowing tribute with late motorcycling writer Harold Crooks once recalling: "At John Rea's funeral Joey Dunlop, whom we talk about not being able to interview, took it upon himself to go into the pulpit and paid a tribute to John that would have brought tears to a stone."

After being signed in 1981 by Honda, with the Japanese manufacturers having to come to terms with Joey wanting to work on his own bikes, Dunlop's number of victory laps moved up several gears as he took racing by storm winning an astonishing FIVE Formula One World Championship titles in a row from 1982 to 1986. The first was the tightest of all edging out fellow Honda rider Ron Haslam in a Championship that offered points all over Europe, at home at the Ulster Grand Prix and at the Isle of Man TT where Dunlop began to rack up first place finishes.

The world famous 37.73 mile mountain course between the hedges started becoming Joey's own personal playground in 1985 when he claimed his first hat-trick at the meeting triumphing in the Formula One, Junior 250cc and Senior classes but what made this remarkable feat the stuff of legend was that Dunlop, his brother Robert, fellow World Champion Brian Reid and others nearly died on their way to the island. The Tornamona, a large fishing boat, was ferrying riders and their bikes across but in the early hours of the morning the boat struck rocks at the entrance to Strangford Lough and sank. Only for the quick thinking of Joey, who raised the alarm, and his calm authority taking control in the middle of a crisis in dark and scary waters, lives would have been lost before the 13 passengers and crew were rescued by a RNLI lifeboat.

Somehow, after the near death experience, Dunlop managed a treble and he would do it again in 1988, minus the boating drama, with more success following in the 1990s including hitting the top of the all time TT winners list passing the legendary Mike Hailwood who claimed 14 victories. Dunlop won at least one race in 1992, 1993, 1994, 1995, 1996, 1997 and 1998 excelling on the Lightweight 125cc and 250cc bikes ending the decade on 23 wins at the mecca of road racing. This amazing man was far from finished because in 2000 at the age of 48 he would savour another three wins to complete an historic hat-trick of hat-tricks. Every one was special but the most stunning conquest of all was in the Formula One class given that some critics had suggested he would never be the top rider on big bikes again. Having won that he clinched the Lightweight 250cc and Ultra Lightweight 125cc races too taking his overall TT tally to 26.

Compassionate he was but this was a man who was also seriously competitive and using all his experience and knowledge it was a week to relish beating younger, cockier bucks at the place he knew better than anyone with his legion of fans revelling in all his glory not knowing that a month later events in Estonia would leave them heartbroken. Dunlop's staggering winning record on the island between 1977 and 2000 is well worth recording with the victory sheet reading: seven TT F1, six Lightweight, five Ultra Lightweight, four Senior, two Junior, one Classic and one Jubilee. Two decades on, next on the list is England's John McGuinness, who idolised Joey, on 23 and today the most successful rider at the TT is presented with a trophy bearing Dunlop's name. He was also prolific at the Ulster Grand Prix, topping the podium on a record 24 occasions, beating David Jefferies in a breathtaking Superbike duel in 1999 for his final win at the Dundrod meeting, and at the North West 200 where he won 13 times between 1979 and 1988 including multiple Superbike wins. The roars greeting him as he whizzed by on his machines complete with that famous number three, like his own personal coat of arms, were a show of love as well as admiration.

He did it all by modest means, with friends saying he would happily live out of a van on his travels eating beans and avoiding the limelight. Through the years he suffered serious injuries, ranging from a broken leg and fractured ribs to a cracked pelvis and losing the tip of his wedding ring finger and worse he lost close friends to the racing game. What he always maintained was devotion to his family and a sense of decency which led to a series of humanitarian visits to the Balkans and other countries, some of which people knew about and some that they didn't because Joey wasn't doing it for publicity but for people who needed help. Learning about the conditions in places like Romanian orphanages, Dunlop packed his van with food, clothes, nappies, toys and other items and ventured off on his own to deliver the goods in selfless acts of heroism that few others would even have contemplated let alone do given the dangers in those nations at the time. He received royal approval for his work abroad with an OBE in 1996 a decade after being appointed MBE for his services to motorcycling. 'Yer Maun' was also awarded the Freedom of Ballymoney and many other honours that he never sought or craved. Adored now as much as he was when he was the best racer around, to the people of Northern Ireland the peerless Joey Dunlop will always be King of the Roads.

MICHAEL DUNLOP

MOTORCYCLING: TT SPEED
SENSATION AND A MAN APART

B: 10/04/1989

As fascinating as he is fast, Michael Dunlop is a modern day road racing great who stands third in the all time list for Isle of Man TT victories, has set some of the most historic lap records in his sport and draws attention like he draws crowds. Michael is part of the iconic Dunlop dynasty of motorcycling that transcends two wheels and has suffered deep family tragedy over the years. Michael's brother William, dad Robert and uncle Joey have all lost their lives to racing and while some question how Michael copes and why he continues to ride the title of his acclaimed autobiography 'Road Racer It's In My Blood' provides an answer.

Prior to the publication of that book in 2017, I interviewed Michael and what sets him apart from so many of today's sports stars is that he doesn't care how people view him and in a world where most well-known personalities want to feel loved there's something to be said for having that kind of take me or leave me attitude. Mavericks tend to be electrifying to watch and even those who think of Dunlop as an abrasive character will admit he is a tremendous talent whose aggressive attitude in competition combined with his racing skills take him to a different level.

There have been countless big moments in Dunlop's career but perhaps the first time the wider public started to become aware of his incredible inner strength, inherited from his father, was in 2008 when he won an emotionally charged race just two days after his dad's death in practice for the North West 200. Both Michael, then 19, and his older brother William showed their intentions to ride in the 250cc race by putting their machines on the start line and even though officials ruled they should not compete, there was no stopping them until a problem with William's bike halted him from taking part.

Michael, though, went ahead with tens of thousands of fans around the course in shock and awe as he raced past them on the roads where Robert had excelled. Battling it out with Christian Elkin in an exhilarating race, there was an eruption of noise all around the county Antrim coastline when Dunlop passed the English rider on the final lap and the cheers increased as he sped through the finish line for his first North West victory. In tears, the winner dedicated the remarkable victory to his father and in an interview almost a decade later, with scores more big time successes under his belt, he told me: "I wouldn't be where I am if it wasn't for my dad. Before my dad passed away he put me in a position to be someone and to do something. If it wasn't for him I wouldn't be doing what I'm doing. My dad was a big inspiration for me. He was my idol. When I win races I wish he was still around to see it but at the end of the day that's not the case."

Nineteen of those wins have come at the Isle of Man TT leaving him just four behind John McGuinness and seven adrift of his uncle Joey on the island. Number 19 arrived in 2019 almost a year on from the heartbreak of his brother William dying at the age of 32 following a crash at the Skerries 100 in Dublin.

Michael claimed his first TT victory in a Supersport race in 2009 and to date he has seven wins in that class on the mountain course, four in Superbikes, three Senior TT triumphs, three Superstocks and a double in the Lightweight Supertwin events for a host of different manufacturers, becoming the first man to have four TT race wins in successive years in 2013 and 2014. The Ballymoney man says: "The Isle of Man to me is the pinnacle. I suppose I see winning a race at the TT like winning a gold medal at the Olympics." Throughout a career in which he has suffered serious injuries Dunlop has delivered multiple wins at the North West 200, Ulster Grand Prix and Southern 100 meetings plus a whole lot more and set numerous records along the way. Amongst his historic bests, he was the first rider to lap the Isle of Man course in under 17 minutes and in 2016 set the outright lap record for the North West. Like other Dunlops before him Michael has pure talent and the ability to captivate bike fans any time he starts his engine.

ROBERT DUNLOP

MOTORCYCLING: SUPREME RACER
WITH DETERMINATION TO MATCH
B: 25/11/1960 - D: 15/05/2008

When you reflect on all that Robert Dunlop achieved in motorcycling before his tragic death in 2008 and how he did it, you find a man with racing expertise, immense character and a competitive spirit that everyone else in this book would admire. He entered a world where his older brother was King yet became one of the best in the business himself and after sustaining life changing injuries in a crash at the 1994 Isle of Man TT, that were supposed to finish his career, he bravely fought back to become a winner again.

After the crash he could only race smaller bikes but before it he was one of those riders who could turn his hand to any machine. If you had given him one of those Flicker Scooters that children whizz around in today and put an engine in it, he probably would have nabbed a podium place!

Different to his famous brother Joey in that he was comfortable when a microphone was stuck in front of him and his gregarious nature flowed out, old footage will show he could pull off wearing a stetson just about better than anyone in the country, fitting really given that for years he was the fastest gun in the North West. What a record he had around Portrush securing 15 victories between 1986 and 2006 topping the all-time list until 2016 when Carrick's Alastair Seeley overtook him.

Robert's opening win at the North West was on a 350cc four years before the first of his four hat-tricks in 1990 when he blitzed to two Superbike successes on the legendary JPS Norton and a 125cc victory. It was as if Robert owned the coast roads in those days landing more trebles in 1991 and 1993 with fans lapping up his brilliance and when he claimed another hat-trick in 1994, including a Superbike double, he was on top of the world.

Less than a month later he travelled to the Isle of Man intent on more glory which would enhance his status amongst the greats. Following a 130mph crash in the Formula 1 race, however, when the rear wheel of his

Honda RC45 collapsed, Dunlop suffered a broken right arm and broken right leg with doctors declaring that he would never compete again because of restricted movement due to nerve and tendon damage. As tenacious as they came Robert refused to give up, undergoing numerous operations and going through the pain of intensive rehab in a bid to return to what he loved and against all the odds in a miraculous comeback he made it to the start grid in 1996 at the Cookstown 100, where he had previously excelled.

Unable to close his hand fully, he also had a shortened leg and was badly restricted but to even sit on a bike was a triumph over adversity and here was this remarkable man ready to go out and race one. Dunlop, detailed in his preparation and professional alongside mentor, mechanic and dear friend Liam Beckett, felt the TT crash prevented him from having a shot at becoming a World Champion. He had a point because he had been at the peak of his powers in the years before enjoying a Macau Grand Prix triumph and his first TT win in 1989, beating World Formula One Champion Carl Fogarty in two Superbike races during his first North West treble in 1990, overcoming challenges in 1991 from his brother Joey and Phillip McCallen to take a 125cc/250cc double at the TT and in the same year he became British Champion in the 125cc class prior to continuing his domination at the North West. He was back at the TT in 1997 and a year later, with a modified braking system, he was winning again, capturing a fifth success on the island on the 125 bike, sending fans crazy in the evening when at the presentation he flung his crutch, which he was using as a walking aid, into the crowd.

Devastated by the death of his brother Joey in 2000 in a racing accident in Estonia, four years later Robert, who was a winner at the Ulster Grand Prix on nine occasions, announced he would be retiring before returning to action in 2005 and in 2006 he won his 15th and final race at the North West 200 at the age of 45 catching England's Michael Wilcox on the last lap and powering home for an emotional victory.

Focusing on helping sons William and Michael with their blossoming motorcycling careers, Robert was set to compete at the North West with them in 2008, when he suffered a fatal crash in practice leaving wife Louise, their boys William, Daniel and Michael, the wider Dunlop family and the Northern Ireland public heartbroken. Ten years later Robert's son William, a gentleman and fantastic racer, died following a crash at the Skerries 100 in county Dublin. At Robert's funeral at Garryduff Presbyterian Church near his hometown Ballymoney, Rev John Kirkpatrick, chaplain of the Motorcycle Union of Ireland, summed up the racing hero, saying: "We live in a world where not many people finish what they start, not all persevere in adversity or push themselves to their potential and this makes those such as Robert stand out from the crowd." That he did.

RICHARD DUNWOODY

HORSE RACING: NATIONAL TREASURE WHO WENT WEST TO WIN

B: 18/01/1964

Before the great Tony McCoy came along, the most successful jump jockey of them all was Northern Ireland's Richard Dunwoody who won 1,874 races and 1,699 of them in Britain including the Grand National twice, the Cheltenham Gold Cup and formed a fabulous winning double act with the popular grey Desert Orchid. With both his grandfather and father respected trainers Dunwoody was comfortable with horses from the moment he could walk and was destined to go into racing, once recounting how he knew he wanted to be a jockey at the age of five declaring it was "a natural decision". The family decided to leave their Comber home in 1972 because of the Troubles and living in Newmarket, Dunwoody's obsession with horse racing was in full flow before he entered his teens.

By 1982 he was riding as an amateur and after enjoying some eye-catching successes turned professional two years later when he continued to make people sit up and take notice, consistently being in contention and passing the post in front almost 50 times in his first season, most notably on a mount called West Tip at the Cheltenham Festival. It was a relationship that would prosper and in their first Grand National together weeks later, with Dunwoody just 21, they were leading until falling at Becher's Brook.

Far from being discouraged, Dunwoody was spurred on and showing strong character that was a feature of his career he and West Tip returned to Aintree in 1986 and won the most talked about race around.

Dunwoody finished second on West Tip in 1989 but would not be denied a National double romping home eight years after his initial triumph on Minnehoma, owned by comedian Freddie Starr, and with the victory arriving 12 months after the famous race had been voided the cheers were loud and proud as horse and jockey made their way into the winners enclosure.

In between in 1988 Dunwoody was delighted to fly to Cheltenham Gold Cup success on Charter Party and in 1990 deliver the goods in the Champion Hurdle aboard Kribensis while with Desert Orchid, the best horse he ever rode, there were back to back wins in the King George VI Chase in 1989 and 1990 and an Irish Grand National success. Dunwoody had another King George double in 1995 and 1996 with One Man.

He wasn't just a master at the big meetings, he was consistent too and was crowned Champion jockey from 1993 to 1995, edging an exciting and tense battle with Adrian Maguire 197-194 in 1994. When a neck injury forced him to retire in 1999 Dunwoody had amassed more jump jockey victories than anyone else as he left behind a brilliant career and a tough fitness regime to make his racing weight. What Dunwoody has done since retiring from the saddle is even more impressive and tells you much about his desire to take on the next challenge and raise hundreds of thousands of pounds for charity such as when he embarked on a 680 mile and 48 day trek to the South Pole, describing it as his greatest achievement. This remarkable individual has also completed a cross country ski race to the Magnetic North Pole, a 1000 mile walking challenge in Newmarket and a walk across Japan all for good causes. It doesn't end there for motivational speaker and one time Strictly Come Dancing contestant Dunwoody, who is a hugely talented photographer earning rave reviews for his exhibitions and striking images which have been published all over the world.

SAMUEL FERRIS

ATHLETICS: MARATHON MAN WITH
A SILVER LINING
B: 29/08/1900 - D: 21/03/1980

There will be many reading this book who until now have never heard of Samuel Ferris, but his is a story worth telling, having suffered family tragedy as a young boy living in County Down, served in the first and second World Wars and won an Olympic silver medal in the longest race of them all.

Born in Magherabeg, near Dromore in 1900, Sam's mum died when he was a young boy with him and his dad moving to Scotland before they returned home. Like his mother, Ferris loved to run but thoughts of taking part in races were put on hold when at the end of the First World War he joined the Royal Flying Corps, which would become the Royal Air Force, and was posted to India. Coming back to Dromore he indulged in his passion finishing first in many local races prior to re-joining the RAF in 1923 and taking part in a cross country race when stationed in Uxbridge. It was there that a gentleman called Bill Thomas from the Herne Hill Harriers club spotted Sam's talent encouraging him to try the marathon.

Building his way up to the 26 miles, 385 yards Ferris ran his first marathon in the 1924 Olympic trials, doing remarkably well to finish second out of 80 to earn himself a place in the British team for the Games that year in Paris, where in exhausting, hot conditions and on the cobbled streets of the French capital the Dromore man ended up in an impressive fifth. He was back for another go at the Olympics in 1928 dropping to eighth in Amsterdam before the most eventful race of his life at the 1932 Games in Los Angeles.

As the wonderfully detailed Dromore and District Local Historical Group Journal report on Ferris, written by Trevor Martin, points out Sam was hindered by not knowing the course unlike competitors and when his British running vest turned up it was far too long to race in. Martin writes: "Sam tried to redesign his vest cutting some 18 inches off but this was to prove catastrophic during the race. After a distance into the race the vest began to ride up Sam's back exposing the kidney area to the wind and causing it to chill. He stopped several times during the race to adjust the vest eventually holding it down using the safety pins that held up his number."

For all that Ferris was strongly motivated by an Olympic medal, preferably gold, and ran magnificently only to be given dubious tactical advice in the closing stages meaning Juan Carlos Zabala, years later named Argentina's track and field athlete of the century, crossed the line in front with Sam in the silver medal position as the pair of them broke the previous world record.

Ferris, a diligent trainer, was viewed as one of the best marathon runners of his generation, winning countless races across the globe, smashing course records and earning a second place at the first Empire Games in 1930 ahead of serving in the Second World War in various places including Dieppe in the Normandy region of northern France, when in 1940 he was in charge of evacuation. Ferris Park in Dromore, which stages a host of sports for children and adults, is named after this marathon man and awesome athlete.

STEPHEN FERRIS

RUGBY: SUPERPOWER FOR ULSTER AND IRELAND
B: 02/08/1985

On the rugby field Grand Slam winner Stephen Ferris was like a missile trained on a target and once this rocket of a player launched and hit his mark it was like the opponent had been smashed into a different stratosphere. Just ask Australian scrum half Will Genia who felt the full force of the Ulsterman's power in the first half when Ireland defeated the Tri-Nations champions 15-6 in the 2011 World Cup at Eden Park in

Auckland. Collecting the ball at a scrum Genia was tackled immediately by number six green with Ferris picking him up as if he was lifting a beach ball, driving him back 15 metres in an electrifying piece of action that led to Ireland winning a scrum in an attacking position.

Talk about setting a tone and setting standards, though that's what the flanker did regularly in an explosive career which was punctuated by injuries and unfortunately cut short by a serious ankle problem bringing about his retirement at 28 in 2014. Even so in the years before he packed enough in to be remembered as a special talent and from a personal point of view was the Ulster player I loved watching more than any other at Ravenhill before it became the Kingspan stadium.

Ferris, who won 35 Irish caps, was the guy who wanted to make things happen, and generally did, and he got the crowd going like no one else with a crunching collision or a rampaging run that would end in a score, often looking like a high class full-back or winger with his turn of pace. There was a time he was the best back row forward in the world providing a physicality for Ulster and Ireland that has been rarely matched in a white or green shirt.

In 2010 he took on New Zealand at their own game in Dublin, scoring a fabulous try leaving the great Richie McCaw in his wake as he touched down, a year after a superb showing in the Six Nations when Ireland delivered only the second Grand Slam in their history and their first since 1948. Ferris was an ever present in Declan Kidney's side in nailbiting home wins over France and England and on the road victories against Italy, Scotland and Wales. The man from Maghaberry in county Antrim was a huge influence in the perfect campaign in 2009 and is one of the few from Northern Ireland who can say he started every game for Ireland in a Grand Slam season.

That year Ferris was selected for the British and Irish Lions tour of South Africa and was sensational when he played in early games, running the length of the field to score a classic try versus Golden Lions, only for injury to intervene ruling him out of a Test Series good judges felt sure he would dominate.

Frustrated when on the sidelines, Ferris made up for it when he was on the park coming back a number of times to produce dynamite efforts, such as shoving Ulster hard with brute force and brilliance on their way to the Heineken Cup final in 2012 at Twickenham where they would lose to

Leinster with Stephen, who played 106 matches for his province, suffering another injury. He could catch anything on the field of play, be it the ball or an opposing back, but he couldn't catch a break though when he published his must read autobiography Man and Ball he told me he had "no regrets" about his career.

In his book Ferris offered a moving account of a heartbreaking time for his mum Linda and dad Rab after their son Andrew died in a car accident, aged four, before Stephen was born. He's also open and honest as one of the best rugby pundits on television, so good at it that like some other top sports commentators, they can be known for that rather than their playing exploits. No one, though, should forget how fantastic Ferris was from making his Ulster debut in 2005 and his first Ireland start in 2006, after working as a labourer and in a gelatine factory in his teenage years, to those big hits, inspirational moments and making a lasting impact in more ways than one.

BETHANY FIRTH

SWIMMING: PARALYMPIAN GOLDEN GIRL MAKING WAVES
B: 14/02/1996

Bethany Firth has won Paralympic swimming gold medals for Ireland and Great Britain, is a world champion and world record holder, was named in the top 100 inspiring and influential women around the world in 2019 and is a wonderful ambassador for Northern Ireland. Bethany Firth is also a brave lady because all of the above only happened after she overcame a fear of water, having fallen into an adult pool as a four-year-old on holiday in Australia.

When she started lessons at Longstone Special School in Dundonald, teachers could see she had an aptitude for swimming and with strong family backing and under the guidance of Ards Swimming Club coach Nelson Lindsay, the Seaforde woman, who has learning difficulties which causes her to have short term memory loss, has become a sensation in the water.

Firth's rise up the ranks was as swift as her strokes competing in able bodied and disability competitions in her teenage years and making a massive breakthrough at the London 2012 Paralympic Games when, despite a shoulder injury, she won a gold medal for Ireland in the 100m backstroke S14 final at the age of 16. There would be a hat-trick of silver medals at the IPC Swimming World Championships the next year and at the end of 2013 a switch to Great Britain for "personal reasons" with her mum Lindsey explaining that Team GB had other S14 swimmers with whom her daughter was friendly with and socially it was the right call to make.

The move didn't halt Firth's progress as she hit new marks of excellence competing for Northern Ireland in multiple events at the Glasgow Commonwealth Games in 2014 before breaking a host of world records ahead of the 2015 IPC World Championships though a fractured wrist would unfortunately rule her out of the event. While disappointed by that, Firth was not disheartened claiming European titles before going to the 2016 Paralympics in Rio where she would rule the waves retaining her S14 100m backstroke title in record time and adding the 200m medley and 200m freestyle golds plus silver in the 100m breaststroke for good measure, making her Team GB's most decorated athlete in Brazil.

With as much humility as talent Bethany was quick to pay tribute to everyone who helped her, not least her parents who moved house so she could be nearer the pool for training. There have been plenty of sacrifices from dedicated Firth waking up at 4.15am ahead of intense daily sessions to keep her at the top in a sport that transformed her life.

"Swimming gave me confidence, it gave me new friends, it allowed me to travel and it changed who I was and I just hope that I can inspire people to get into sport because it was somewhere I could shine," she said to me weeks after coming home from the Rio Paralympics, having upstaged Sex and the City star Kim Cattrall on her arrival at Belfast City Airport. The actress is used to having photographers taking pictures of her but this time around as both walked through the airport it was Bethany the snappers wanted with gracious Kim congratulating the younger star on her success which has continued at pace.

In 2018 at the European Para Swimming Championships in Dublin the Ards Swimming club member won six medals including four golds and in the 2019 World Para Championships in London she claimed double gold plus two silvers. Firth was also proud to hear she had been included in the BBC's 100 Women list of inspiring and influential women around the world for 2019 alongside other sporting stars and women in science, politics, law, the arts and other areas.

CARL FRAMPTON

BOXING: MULTI-WEIGHT WORLD CHAMP AND FAN FAVOURITE

B: 21/02/1987

Even though he can hold a tune better than most sports stars, it's nothing to do with his singing why Carl Frampton has the X-Factor. It's his World Champion boxing prowess at different weights, exhilarating fighting style, charisma, charm, a personality that can sparkle in conversation with a Prince or pauper and an eloquent yet straight talking way about him that makes the Tiger's Bay man such a favourite with the Northern Ireland public.

A month after Frampton lost his World featherweight title to Leo Santa Cruz in January 2017, he was invited to a glittering awards ceremony in Belfast to pick up a prize and still bruised in mind and body he could have easily swerved it with no questions asked. Instead he turned up suited and booted and once he entered the room you could sense the feelgood factor start to flow around the tables. That's the thing, there's something about Carl and the public know it and love him for it and that night he posed for pictures, signed autographs and spoke to whoever wanted to have a chat well beyond midnight. The positive vibes probably did him good after the crushing disappointment of the loss to Mexican Cruz in Las Vegas, but what was a sure thing it made the evening of those who came into contact with him and enhanced their feelings towards the fighter. They would have discovered that Frampton was not one to stand on ceremony, that he had a fun, playful side and that he still held the respectful values he was taught by his parents and at Midland Boxing Club as a boy.

Mum Flo and dad Craig have been in Carl's corner from day one with Flo detailing in a 2016 Belfast Telegraph interview how he was destined to follow one path. She said: "From a child Carl was very much into sports. He started boxing aged seven and it is something that was born into him. He has worked very hard, we're really proud of him and are all delighted with how well he is doing but it hasn't changed us or Carl at all. We are still the same. Carl's exactly the same. He is very grounded and will always stop to say hello to people. His fans always come first."

Under the watchful and genial gaze of coach Billy McKee at the Midland Boxing club in Tiger's Bay close to his house, Frampton learnt the ropes and while other youngsters would come and go, the Crusaders fan was dedicated putting in the hours and putting in the work leading to Ulster and Irish senior titles and a silver medal in the 2007 European Union Championships during a noteworthy amateur career. The professional game beckoned in 2009 with Frampton confident and classy enough to beat anyone put in his way, impressing Academy award winner Daniel Day Lewis who was at the Ulster Hall to see one demolition job, and becoming Commonwealth Champion at super-bantamweight in his 11th fight.

The buzz was growing around Frampton and as the opponents became stronger so did the Belfast man's displays sending his rapidly expanding support into a frenzy with a fantastic win over Spain's Kiko Martinez at an atmospheric Odyssey Arena in 2013 to claim European title success. Knockout shows from 'the Jackal' against France's Jeremy Parodi and Hugo Cazares from Mexico in Belfast followed setting up a world title shot against Martinez on September 6, 2014. By now Frampton was one of the biggest names in Northern Ireland sport and Pied Piper like in that wherever he went everyone, regardless of religion, wanted to follow. They didn't just love his fearless, attacking nature that made for an entertaining watch and a great night out in the Jackal's Den, they loved the backstory of the humble working class boy made good who came from the Protestant streets of Tiger's Bay and married the love of his life, Christine Dorrian from the Catholic area of Poleglass, having met years before in Kelly's nightclub in Portrush.

Christine would be at ringside with an estimated 16,000 fans roaring her man on at the Titanic Quarter in Belfast in a bespoke venue put together for the night and put together for a champ as Frampton grabbed the IBF super-bantamweight belt with a punishing performance to beat Martinez on points after 12 pulsating rounds. Frampton's title dream had come true and the adulation across the country was at a level few sporting heroes had ever felt.

After a couple of successful defences, Frampton was way better than England's Scott Quigg in a Battle of Britain clash in Manchester adding the WBA Super-bantamweight belt to the IBF version when his raucous fans took over the arena on Quigg's home patch. If that contest didn't live up to expectation, the next one in July 2016 most certainly did when the unbeaten Frampton became King of New York and Northern Ireland's first two-weight World Champion overcoming Santa Cruz in an epic featherweight battle, deservedly landing a majority decision after 12 gripping rounds and inflicting a first loss on the Mexican's previously unblemished record. It was a victory that didn't just put Frampton on a different plane in terms of home country achievement but turned him into one of the most talked about boxers on earth, being awarded the coveted title of The Ring Magazine Fighter of the Year for 2016.

In the first month of 2017 Frampton lost the re-match with Santa Cruz in another belter and later that year after separating from manager Barry McGuigan he was back on the winning trail and then fulfilled his ambition to fight and win at Windsor Park in 2018 against Australian opponent Luke Jackson amid a cacophony of noise before losing a World featherweight title fight to Josh Warrington from Leeds. Proud father to Carla and Rossa and strong advocate of integrated education Frampton is determined to become Ireland's first three weight World Champion and with his will, work ethic, ability and backing from his loyal support there is every chance, which would surely make him the island's greatest ever to step into a ring.

KELLY GALLAGHER

SKIING: SNOW QUEEN WINNER AT
WINTER GAMES
B: 18/05/1985

Kelly Gallagher is the history making skier from Bangor who became a household name in 2014 when she won Team GB's first ever gold medal at the Paralympic Winter Games. Visually impaired Gallagher claimed victory in the Super-G event in Sochi in Russia alongside her sighted guide, Charlotte Evans from Kent, thanks to a dynamic display of racing and bravery that captured the imagination across the globe and led to royalty, politicians and celebrities including Victoria Beckham sending their congratulations. For Gallagher, who suffers from a condition called oculocutaneous albinism which affects the pigment in her hair, skin and eyes, it was a stunning triumph and reward for all the hard work she had put in on the slopes since falling in love with skiing as a 17-year-old on a family holiday in Andorra.

Bitten by the bug, Gallagher grew in confidence and in speed competing in her first international race in 2009, winning the giant slalom at the New Zealand Winter Games and going close to a medal one year later as the first Northern Ireland athlete to take part in the Winter Paralympics. Improving her technique rapidly, and just months into a new partnership with Evans, Gallagher finished second in the slalom and third in the giant slalom in the 2011 World Championships and followed that up with a haul of four more medals (two silver and two bronze) in the 2013 event.

Though pleased with her efforts she craved another colour and with the University of Bath mathematics graduate counting the days until a golden moment it duly arrived in Sochi on March 10, 2014. Having disappointed in the downhill a few days before, Gallagher upped the ante in the Super G clocking a time of one minute 28.72 seconds to set the rest a testing target and with nerves shredded the Bangor woman watched as one by one her competitors failed to beat her time meaning she would forever be the UK's first Winter Paralympics champion.

The response to her success was overwhelming with the relationship and trust between Gallagher and Evans hailed for the way they communicated down slopes via bluetooth headsets, travelling at speeds of up to 80km/h. This wasn't just huge for the then 28-year-old Kelly Gallagher, who played with a skiing Barbie as a child, it opened up a whole new world to people whose knowledge of the Winter Paralympics was limited or zero and it inspired many youngsters to give skiing a go, making the Sochi champion immensely proud.

Gallagher was determined to savour further Games glory but in 2017, training in Italy and working with new guide Gary Smith, she suffered a horror crash fracturing three ribs and dislocating her elbow ruling her out of the World Championships and while she was a late entry for the 2018 Winter Paralympics her best finish was fifth place. Others may have decided to call it quits but not Gallagher who returned to the rostrum in 2019 at the World Para Alpine Skiing Championships claiming three medals in two days with a silver alongside Smith in the downhill and two bronzes in the Super G and Combined disciplines taking her number of medals at World level to nine. An even happier event occurred during the coronavirus pandemic in 2020 when she gave birth to her first child Brigid, with husband Gerard, who had proposed on Christmas Day four years previously.

MIKE GIBSON

RUGBY: GENIUS FOR IRELAND AND THE LIONS
B: 03/12/1942

New Zealand rugby stars are notoriously hard to impress so when former All Blacks captain and all-time Kiwi great Sir Colin Meads said "he was as near the perfect rugby player as I have seen in any position" when talking about Mike Gibson it gives an illustration just how good the Belfast man was. Modest Gibson is someone who prefers to engage with others about their lives rather than chat about himself but thankfully over the years plenty have been willing to wax lyrical about one of the finest the sport of rugby has ever seen. Interviewing modern day Ireland legend Brian O'Driscoll I recall how he smiled in appreciation when Gibson's name was mentioned describing him as a "shining light, magnificent player and a true ambassador for the game." The doyen of rugby commentators Bill McLaren labelled Gibson the most complete player ever adding in his own inimitable style: "He had everything. He had a forest animal's instinct for what was on and he could sniff a score quicker than anybody."

To watch, play with or play against Gibson was an experience to behold though intriguingly his first sporting love was football - his grandfather played for Bury and his uncle was a star turn for Belfast Celtic and Glenavon, who a young Gibson used to watch on a regular basis with his mum and dad. It was when the boy christened Cameron Michael Henderson Gibson started attending Campbell College, where football was not played, that his rugby talent began to flourish. To improve all aspects of his play there were games when he would only kick with his left foot and in others he would use his right while constantly striving to perfect taking and delivering passes. As he turned out for North, Ulster and Cambridge University, where he studied law admitting it was "frightening" on his first day, natural ability oozed out of him with a strong work ethic evident too. Then there was his rugby brain which, when it came to high intensity international battles, put him those vital steps ahead of everyone else, instinctively knowing what opponents would do even before they did.

On his debut in green as a 21-year-old in 1964 against an England team that Ireland had not beaten in London since their Grand Slam year in 1948, Gibson's skill set, vision and quick thinking inspired the visitors, creating tries and taking control like he was an established performer rather than a rookie to earn a thumping 18-5 victory at Twickenham. A star was born and Gibson would only improve as the years whizzed by with the Ulsterman playing on the wing, at out-half and centre for Ireland carving defences apart and producing scores that ended up on rugby highlights reels season after season. In 1974 he would play a crucial role as Ireland won the Five Nations Championship outright for the first time in 23 years scoring two tries in a 26-21 success over England.

When drinking and smoking were commonplace in his sport, Gibson did neither, with lemonade and lime his tipple, and he trained with athletes to increase his fitness and speed. If his stellar Ireland career, amassing a then record 69 caps over 15 years and ending with an influential role in a victory in Australia at the age of 36, was one to savour his performances for the British and Irish Lions often saw him take the game to new levels as he played with better players and glided over the grass. An individual talent but a team man to his bones, outlined by playing for his club North for 22 seasons, Gibson featured on FIVE Lions tours saving his best for trips to New Zealand. He excelled in a losing Lions squad against the All Blacks in 1966 and in 1971 alongside JPR Williams, Gerald Davies, John Dawes, David Duckham, Barry John and Gareth Edwards in one of the greatest back lines ever assembled he was the King of Kings in what remains the only time a Lions side won a Test series in New Zealand. In total Gibson, who had as much courage as class, played 68 times for the Lions, one of which during the 1968 tour of South Africa saw him become rugby's first ever substitute.

A private, golf-loving family man and well respected solicitor, Gibson is not prone to interviews though one he gave in 2016 with the Sunday Independent's Paul Kimmage offered an invaluable insight displaying deep emotions when speaking about his parents and positive influences in his life. Hilariously he told how he can never live down taking his wife Moyra to the cinema to see the War movie 'The Guns of Navarone' on their first date as teenagers. He also questioned whether he would want to be a professional today though Gibson would have stood out in any era and having been fortunate to spend time with this Hall of Fame great at the Belfast Telegraph Sports Awards, it is worth pointing out, given Michael would never say so himself, he is a gentleman, scholar and charming company as well as one of the best rugby players in the history of the game.

FREDDIE GILROY

BOXING: DYNAMITE, DARING
OLYMPIC MEDAL PERFORMER
B: 07/03/1936 - D: 28/06/2016

Liam Neeson is not only one of the finest actors in the movie business, he also has a serious knowledge of boxing and it says much about the qualities of Freddie Gilroy that the Belfast fighter was the Hollywood star's childhood hero. There are many others who felt the same about the Olympic medalist, Commonwealth and European champion and winner of one of the most memorable contests ever staged in Northern Ireland.

Freddie was reared in the Ardoyne area of Belfast and it didn't take long to get himself noticed in the ring when he joined the St John Bosco Club as a boy. In Gilroy's obituary in the Irish Times the newspaper reported how the Bosco club raised £600 for his fare to Melbourne for the 1956 Olympics when he was a late addition to the Ireland team. It proved to be money well spent as in his first bout 18-year-old bantamweight Gilroy left those inside the arena gasping after he delivered a knockout blow to the Soviet Union's Boris Stepanov in the third round before pulling off another big performance to overcome Mario Sitri from Italy. On the verge of a shock final place he was defeated by Germany's Wolfgang Behrendt on points in an intriguing battle ending up with a bronze medal, the same colour claimed by another teenager from Belfast on that trip, John Caldwell.

Following the Games, Gilroy turned professional and was good enough to claim British, Commonwealth and European titles. Along the way he became the first Irishman to claim the Lonsdale belt, the oldest championship belt in the sport, though unfortunately the belt went missing in the mid-1980s and Freddie never had it returned.

Adored in his homeland, Gilroy drew huge crowds for his boxing matches with his fans sure he would become World Champion only to lose to France's Alphonse Halimi on points in 1960 with the title on the line. Caldwell had beaten Halimi to take the World Bantamweight title and then lost it to Brazilian bantamweight legend Eder Jofre which set him and

Gilroy on a collision course for a night to remember at the King's Hall in 1962 in front of 16,000 spectators with the victor due to fight Jofre.

The world title may not have been at stake but it was a world class struggle between the two Belfast warriors which left the fans in a state of frenzy after every round with Gilroy winning at the end of the ninth and claiming British and Empire titles when Caldwell had to concede defeat due to a cut eye. The world title shot against Jofre never took place with Gilroy retiring after slugging it out with Caldwell, later revealing that he had not wanted the fight to take place because they had been close friends from their youth.

Gilroy's boxing career was relatively short but in keeping with his style he packed a lot in and left long lasting memories for those who saw him in the flesh. In later life Gilroy emigrated to Australia before returning home to Belfast where he passed away at the age of 80, acknowledged as one of the country's boxing superstars.

JANET GRAY

WATER-SKIING: BLIND AND BRAVE
MULTIPLE WORLD CHAMPION
B: 16/08/1962

The story of Janet Gray is one of the most stirring in Northern Ireland sport taking her from the depths of despair to multiple world titles as a blind water-skier followed by a near death experience before becoming the best on the planet all over again. It should be made into a heartrending film starting off with Gray as a sporty young girl swimming in the Grove Leisure Centre in Belfast laughing and joking with her family as she loved to do. Tragedy struck when she was four and her dad John lost his sight due to a rare eye disease and worse was to follow when Janet's brother Ian also went blind with the hereditary condition when he was 12. There was hope that Janet would be spared but at the age of 21 she too lost her sight, telling the News Letter she went from an "outgoing, confident young woman to someone who felt isolated, vulnerable and lacking in self-belief. Those were very dark days."

Janet dropped to below six stone in weight and even broke off her engagement to childhood sweetheart Paul because "I didn't want him to feel pity for me" though thankfully Paul stuck around and they stayed together and married in 1984. Learning to travel on a bus to go shopping and slowly gaining confidence, Gray felt her sporting days were over but that all changed when along with Paul, a fine water-skier himself, she was taken to a lake by his uncle. Initially Janet was a spectator but when asked to give it a go, she skied alongside her husband and loved it, telling the Belfast Telegraph in 2019: "It was a wonderful, exhilarating experience. It was out on the water where I found the freedom that I didn't have on land. That's what turned my whole life around."

In 1994 Gray and her husband joined the Meteor Water Ski club in Boardmills, near Lisburn, where despite being the only blind member she wanted to be treated like everyone else and improved at such a rapid rate she was soon competing in national and European competitions leading to qualification for the 1997 World Disabled Water Ski Championships in Florida and a bronze medal in the slalom.

Two years later in London she won her first World Championship after finishing first in all three disciplines – slalom, tricks and jump – beating sighted skiers in the process. There were more world titles in 2001 and 2003, when she broke numerous world records, but in 2004 disaster struck when she collided with a jump ramp at high speed while training in Florida.

Airlifted to Tampa General Hospital her blood loss and injuries were so severe that doctors feared she would not pull through. Unconscious for almost a month, she had broken and dislocated her left elbow, foot and ankle, snapped her thumb tendons, broken and dislocated her right hip and pelvis, broken her patella, crushed her ribs, smashed her nose, eye sockets and jaw as well as losing part of her skull. Back home in Northern Ireland, Paul had been informed by doctors to get in touch with undertakers before flying out to America.

Janet would later reveal: "I was resuscitated four times and told that with the injuries I sustained, it was possible that I'd never walk again. I may have lost my sight but I never lost my vision. I was damned if I was going to be blind and in a wheelchair and be totally dependent again."

So began another battle for this remarkable woman who was determined to get back on her feet knowing if she did there was a slim possibility she may compete again. Incredibly she was representing Great Britain and Northern Ireland at the 2007 World Disabled Water Ski Championships in Australia and sent shockwaves around the sport with her outstanding performances.

"Against all the odds, I regained all my titles, bringing home five gold medals to Northern Ireland. I think that would be my proudest moment," said Janet, who has learned to play the piano and clarinet by ear. After retiring from water-skiing Gray, a founder member of Disability Sport NI, fought hard for disabled rights, worked for a number of charities, became a DUP councillor and is a motivational speaker telling her story which is one of staggering courage, spirit and hope.

HARRY GREGG

FOOTBALL: GOALKEEPING HERO ON AND OFF THE PITCH

B: 27/10/1932 - D: 16/02/2020

Harry Gregg was honest, modest, frank, fearless, fun and as hard as nails with a heart of gold and in his heyday he was the best goalkeeper in the world. He was also a reluctant hero who in a remarkable selfless act of courage saved the lives of Manchester United team-mates and strangers in the aftermath of the 1958 Munich air disaster.

Henry Gregg of 34 Windsor Avenue, as he called himself using his given name, preferred to talk about football than his bravery and he loved playing what he saw as a simple game. In the 1958 World Cup finals he played so well for Northern Ireland that in a poll 478 journalists voted him as the top goalkeeper with Russian legend Lev Yashin next on 122. Gregg relished commanding his area and in Northern Ireland's first major tournament produced spectacular and defiant performances, keeping a clean sheet in a 1-0 group victory over Czechoslovakia before making countless saves in a 2-2 draw with West Germany which led the great Uwe Seeler to say that Harry had "sprung like a panther" throughout the game to deny his team.

Gregg had fitness issues prior to the finals and his heroics versus the Germans led to an injury which was enough to keep him out of a play-off win over the Czechs in which deputy Norman Uprichard stepped up superbly though he suffered injury too meaning Gregg, who had been using a walking stick, returned to the side as Northern Ireland were knocked out in the last eight by France.

Before the tournament the then church going Gregg had spoken to a minister about his moral dilemma relating to playing on a Sunday which was not the done thing in those days and as Evan Marshall uncovered when making his 'Spirit of '58' documentary some at the Irish FA didn't want the team to take part in the finals as games were scheduled for the Sabbath!

With the World Cup just a few months after the Munich air disaster, Gregg travelled to Sweden for the competition by boat and rail. At that stage he was the world's most expensive goalkeeper after joining Manchester United from Doncaster in December 1957 for a fee of £23,500 with Red Devils boss Matt Busby convinced Gregg would make a difference. Born in Tobermore, Gregg played for Linfield Swifts and Coleraine ahead of a transfer when he was 18 to Doncaster, who were managed by Harry's hero Peter Doherty, the man who took Northern Ireland to the 1958 World Cup. Gregg dislocated his elbow on his Doncaster debut but while that ruled him out for weeks, he would become a big favourite with Rovers fans, once turning out with a broken finger.

That character combined with his ability between the sticks attracted United and at 25 he became part of the Busby Babes. Two months later on February 6 tragedy struck with United returning from a European Cup match in Belgrade when the plane they were travelling in crashed while attempting to take off on the slush-covered runway at Munich-Riem Airport. Gregg pulled team-mates Bobby Charlton, Jackie Blanchflower and Dennis Viollet out of a burning plane, helped rescue boss Busby and pregnant passenger Vera Lukic and her two year old daughter Vesna. The crash resulted in 23 fatalities, including United players and staff, crew members and journalists though it would have been more but for Harry who played in United's first match after the disaster two weeks later helping the club reach the FA Cup final where they lost to Bolton.

It's odd to think that with injury ruling him out of the 1963 FA Cup final success against Leicester, not playing enough games in the title winning 1964-65 campaign and being sold during the successful 1966/67 championship season Gregg never won anything at United, but to all connected with the club he has a medal of honour in their hearts. When Harry passed away in February 2020, Sir Bobby Charlton, Sir Alex Ferguson and Denis Law made the trip to Coleraine for his funeral underlining what the goalkeeping great meant to everyone at Old Trafford and in another nod of respect Ferguson brought over a star-studded United side to play in a testimonial for Gregg at Windsor Park in 2012 just days after they lost the league in the final seconds to Manchester City.

Leaving United in 1966, Gregg joined Stoke and after retirement managed Shrewsbury, Swansea, Crewe and Carlisle as well as having a stint as goalkeeping coach with his beloved Red Devils. He eventually returned home where he would work with Coleraine FC, enjoy spending time with his family, write poems and indulge in long walks on the beach and he was immensely proud to set up the Harry Gregg Foundation, giving children opportunities that would otherwise not have been available to them.

Gregg played at international level for nine years winning 25 caps, the first of which came in 1954 and the year before his World Cup starring role he stood out in a memorable 3-2 victory over England at Wembley. There would be many individual honours bestowed on Harry in his later years which he would dedicate to his old United team-mates, Peter Doherty plus wife Carolyn and his family who he was devoted to. Fiercely loyal, champion of the underdog and never afraid to say his piece Henry Gregg was a true great, a true hero and forever true to himself.

DAVID HEALY

FOOTBALL: RECORD GOALSCORER
WHO SLAYED THE ENGLISH

B: 05/08/1979

David Healy scored one of the most celebrated goals in the history of Northern Ireland football when he smacked the ball into the net against England at Windsor Park on the iconic night of September 7, 2005. Think of Northern Ireland 1 England 0 and magical memories come flooding back to anyone who was cheering on the team in the stadium or at home as they watched the World Cup qualifier on television. From the eruption of noise when Healy scored to the joyous scenes on and off the pitch when the final whistle blew it remains an evening that sends shivers down the spine of Northern Ireland fans.

Unlike the decade that followed, the 2000s was not a time when Northern Ireland enjoyed great success on a global sporting scale but that night Healy bucked the trend providing the nation with some much needed pride, becoming a national hero in the process. Before kick-off in Belfast all the talk was about the team labelled England's 'Golden Generation' which included superstars David Beckham, Steven Gerrard, Frank Lampard, Wayne Rooney, Michael Owen, Ashley Cole and John Terry but post match Healy was the name on everyone's lips having collected a classy pass from Steven Davis he raced clear of the visiting defence to fire the ball into the net in front of disbelieving and delirious spectators in the Kop stand. It wasn't just a goal to win the game, it was a goal that brought the country together with people revelling in Healy's matchwinner and England's embarrassment. As post match analysis was conducted in a BBC studio at Windsor the shock victory for Northern Ireland rendered pundit Ian Wright speechless. An impressive feat in itself!

Healy described that goal like scoring the winner in a World Cup final and for Northern Ireland supporters, starved off success since the 1980s when Billy Bingham's side qualified for back to back World Cup finals, they experienced similar emotions. So how did Healy celebrate? Well, because he was on an early morning flight the next day back to his club Leeds

United he sat in his room in the Hilton Hotel in Templepatrick watching a special re-run of the entire game on local television eating chicken and mayonnaise sandwiches and drinking a pint of lemonade he had ordered from room service. If the goal against England is regarded as Healy's most famous moment representing Northern Ireland there were plenty more highlights in what turned out to be a spectacular international career.

Almost 12 months after the success over England Healy did go out on the town with several team-mates following another match at Windsor Park – a gut-wrenching 3-0 loss to Iceland – and due to the manner of the defeat some newspaper headlines were not positive, scathing in their belief that the players would have been better served staying in. Healy was fuming with what had been written feeling that his commitment to the cause had been questioned and driven from an early age to prove doubters wrong, a couple of nights later he produced the greatest display of his life scoring a stunning hat-trick to defeat Spain 3-2 in a Euro qualifier.

The final and decisive goal from Healy was one of the most delightful ever seen in Belfast as he lobbed Real Madrid goalkeeper Iker Casillas from 30 yards to pull off an even bigger shock result than against England. For the record, the Spanish team contained world class players Sergio Ramos, Carles Puyol, Cesc Fabregas, Xavi, Xabi Alonso, Fernando Torres, David Villa and Raul. Healy didn't just beat a phenomenal Spanish side that night, he changed international football because following their humbling loss at Windsor, Spain decided to drop the legendary Raul and build the team around Xavi and Andres Iniesta, who was on the bench against Northern Ireland. Spain would go on to win Euro 2008 and 2012 and the 2010 World Cup!

Growing up in Killyleagh the people in the County Down village knew Healy was special. He scored for fun as a kid with Crossgar Youth and Lisburn Youth and learnt some tough lessons playing in a handful of games as a teenager for his home town in the Amateur League when take no prisoner defenders kicked lumps out of the young whippersnapper with an eye for goal. Healy became a target for Manchester United with the legendary Sir Alex Ferguson particularly taken by the mannerly kid who signed as a professional for the club in 1999. He played a few first team games for the Red Devils and hit the woodwork as a substitute on his Premier League debut but chances for the youngster were few and far between at Old Trafford with the exceptional forward talent at the club leading to loan spells at Port Vale and Preston before signing for the latter where he performed well under David Moyes.

Later there would be further loan spells at Norwich City, a move to Leeds, then Fulham and Sunderland. More loan spells at Ipswich and Doncaster followed prior to a dream switch to his boyhood club Rangers, where he won the Scottish Premiership title. Healy ended his playing career at Bury, aged 34, admitting that injuries had taken their toll and he had become a little disillusioned with the sport he loved. In club football Healy enjoyed some bright spots but it was in the Northern Ireland shirt where he shone like a beacon hitting the target on his senior international debut in 2000 against Luxembourg and three years later ending Northern Ireland's record breaking barren run of 1298 minutes with a goal when he scored in a 4-1 home defeat to Norway. In 2004 he passed the long standing scoring record for the nation which had been 13 and by the time he was finished he had 36 goals to his name from 95 caps.

In the Euro 2008 qualifying campaign, Healy hit a record 13 goals including that epic hat-trick versus Spain, a majestic double against Sweden and the most wonderful chip in the pouring rain to beat Denmark. From 2005 to 2007 he was one of the most dangerous strikers in international football as fans showed up at Windsor Park expecting heroics and were rarely let down by the striker with Northern Ireland never having a more clinical finisher. Healy has warmth in his personality but with a green shirt on he was as cool as ice and has a ruthless streak that has seen him become a huge success as manager of Linfield.

He may have deserved it but unfortunately Healy never got the chance to play in a major tournament though his final international goal proved vital in his country doing just that four years later. On a cold November night in 2012, Healy returned to Windsor having been left out of prior squads and came off the bench with Northern Ireland losing 1-0 at home to Azerbaijan with the atmosphere turning hostile towards manager Michael O'Neill and his players. A humiliating defeat was on the cards until Healy whacked in a 96th minute equaliser from a free-kick which helped keep O'Neill in a job and build belief, spirit and discipline which led Northern Ireland to qualify for the Euro 2016 finals. Healy may not have been there but in France the Green and White Army did not forget the man who gave them hope and happiness. Throughout the tournament the fans sang about the current stars and two past greats with George Best being one and David Healy, the country's greatest ever goalscorer, the other.

ANTON HEGARTY

ATHLETICS: COUNTRY STAR WITH
OLYMPIC HIT

B: 14/12/1892 - D: 10/08/1944

Trailblazing Derry athlete Anton Hegarty has been a forgotten Olympic hero for decades but he deserves to be remembered and I'm happy to include him in this book. Hegarty won a silver medal at the 1920 Antwerp Olympics and according to a register of names on SportNI.net he was the first person in a list of NI Olympians and Paralympians to stand on the podium at the Games.

With partition between North and South not until 1921 and Ireland not sending a team to the Antwerp Olympics, Hegarty competed and excelled for the British team in the cross country event. There was no sense of destiny from an early age about this, however, because it wasn't until Anton left school and was stationed in India, after joining the Royal Inniskilling Fusiliers, that he realised he was an exceptional runner. Writing for Derry Track Club in 2020, journalist Malcolm McCausland revealed that Hegarty led "the Skins 1st battalion to success in inter-regiment competitions in 1913 and 1914" though World War I interrupted any thoughts of racing in major competitions. It was only when Hegarty was wounded at Sulva Bay in the battle for Gallipoli in 1915 that he was discharged from the Army, returned home and enjoyed the chance to run again.

In 1919 he was a co-founder of the City of Derry Harriers and the same year he won the mile in the Celtic Sports in Glasgow. The Celtic Sports and the Rangers Sports were two of the superior running meetings of the time.

Selected to compete for Ireland in the 1920 International Cross Country Championships, he helped the team to silver in Belvoir Forest in Belfast.

Thanks to impressive performances and long strides that could eat up the ground, a place at the Olympics was on the horizon and with Ireland not eligible to send a team to Antwerp in Belgium, Hegarty was invited to take part in the British Olympic team trials in England performing well enough to secure his selection as part of the British team.

In the cross-country race in the 1920 Games, Hegarty finished fifth in the individual event but crucially the points he scored took the British team to second place overall and a silver medal.

The other British squad members who like Hegarty scored points counting towards the team score were James Wilson and Alfred Nichols, with Finland, led by middle distance and long distance icon Paavo Nurmi, claiming gold. Known as Anton in Derry, and given that name in the extremely well researched 'Lion for a Day' book by Irish News athletics writer McCausland detailing Hegarty's life and times, he is called Frank Hegarty in the official Olympic results and elsewhere he has been labelled Francis Anthony Hegarty. What is clear is he represented Ireland again in 1921 and used to race against a pony in the Brandywell in Derry, which must have been a sight to see. This Olympic medal winning star from Derry would go on to live in Rugby in England where he was sadly killed in an accident in 1944.

ALEX HIGGINS

SNOOKER: WORLD CHAMPION, PEOPLE'S CHAMPION, NATURAL TALENT
B: 18/03/1949 - D: 24/07/2010

Alex Higgins didn't just play snooker, he made snooker, transforming it from an obscure game with a fuddy-duddy persona into an enthralling sport gripping millions of television viewers, becoming a two time World Champion, the people's Champion and the most talked about sportsperson in the UK along the way. When the Hurricane blew the snooker establishment apart to win his first world title in 1972 he took home £480 and a decade later collected a winning purse of £25,000 as he famously lifted the trophy a second time with the sporting public transfixed by his outrageous skills on the table and an unpredictable personality off it.

At his breathtaking best Higgins pulled off scintillating shots other professionals couldn't even imagine but at his aggressive worst he was a nightmare for fellow players, referees and officials making for a dangerous but unmissable cocktail that huge TV audiences tuned in to see. The 2020 World Snooker Champion Ronnie O'Sullivan put a cheque of £500,000 in his pocket and it is no stretch to say without Higgins making the sport so popular in the 1970s and 80s such a figure would have been impossible.

Higgins was never shy in telling anyone who would listen about his importance to the game once replying when asked if he could live without snooker "could snooker live without me?" It was quite the boast though the greats of the green baize from Steve Davis to O'Sullivan will openly say they owe the Belfast native big time for his influence on their sport.

Speaking to me after Higgins had passed away in 2010, seven-time World Champion Stephen Hendry, viewed in some quarters as the greatest player of them all, revealed why he made the trip to Belfast for the Hurricane's funeral, stating: "Everyone knows that Alex was a Jekyll and Hyde character but there is no doubt about it, snooker would not be where it is without him and that was one of the reasons I came to Belfast for the funeral. I think it was only right for me as a snooker player to be there and pay my respects to Alex, one of the legends of the game because I realise what he did for snooker."

As a kid, young Alexander Higgins, known as Sandy to his family, harboured hopes of being a jockey rather than a snooker star despite showing immense potential with a cue in his hand at the legendary Jampot club in the Sandy Row area of south Belfast. He left home at 15 moving to England where he was an apprentice jockey at Eddie Reavey's stable and while disappointed to be too tall to make it in that field he lapped up the experience.

Returning home destiny drew him back to playing snooker and when he won the 1968 Northern Ireland Amateur Championship, Higgins knew with his natural ability there was much more to come, turning professional at the age of 22 and winning the World Championship the first time he entered it in 1972. He had to go through qualifying before beating countryman Jackie Rea, John Pulman and Rex Williams on the way to the final at the British Legion in Birmingham where he was too good for reigning champion John Spencer defeating the Englishman 37-32 to create history as snooker's youngest World Champion.

Here was a working class hero potting balls from crazy angles and playing with a speed that made those watching dizzy, firing in century breaks quicker than it took to boil an egg. The more the growing audiences enjoyed it, at tournaments or exhibitions, the more Higgins revelled in the adulation and the more snooker benefited though had he taken greater care rather than playing to the crowd he could have claimed further World titles losing in the 1976 and 1980 finals.

On the upside he clinched Masters final victories in 1978 and 1981 versus Cliff Thorburn and Terry Griffiths respectively but his off the table antics were gaining as much attention as his sorcery on it due to an increasing number of run-ins with authority and tales of nights out that became the stuff of legend such as when he and his movie star pal Oliver Reed ended a raucous evening with a sword fight!

Then there was the 1982 World Championships with fedora wearing Higgins considered a dark horse in a tournament world number one Steve Davis was supposed to win but when the Hurricane's fiercest rival exited early on, the Ulsterman went to work overcoming Jim Meadowbank, Doug Mountjoy and Willie Thorne to set up a classic semi-final with his protege Jimmy 'Whirlwind' White. Trailing 15-14 in the best of 31 frames match, Higgins was 59-0 down when he produced the finest high pressure break of all time, knocking in balls from all over the place including one staggering blue to make 69 and take the contest into a final frame decider which he duly won. The compelling final against Ray Reardon finished with Higgins compiling a magical 135 to close out the match by an 18-15 margin though it is best remembered for a tearful Alex waving his then wife Lynn and baby Lauren on to the Crucible stage in Sheffield so that he could hold his darling little girl as well as the trophy.

If that was the golden moment in one of sport's most eventful and controversial careers there were other notable highlights such as coming from 7-0 down to beat Davis 16-15 in an epic 1983 UK Championship final completing snooker's coveted triple crown, winning the World Doubles title with best mate White in 1984 and somehow triumphing in the 1989 Irish Masters final 9-8 against Hendry amid an incredible atmosphere in county Kildare when he was limping around the table having fallen 25 feet from a flat weeks earlier in one of many stormy episodes in his private life.

While Higgins could hit a cue ball like nobody else, too often he would hit the self destruct button losing money through drinking and gambling and losing respect with his behaviour which included head-butting a tournament director, punching a snooker official and threatening to have compatriot Dennis Taylor shot when they were playing for the same side at the 1990 team World Cup, an event which the pair alongside Eugene Hughes won three times for Ireland. Higgins retired from the professional game in 1997 though continued to play exhibitions and would take on all comers for a fiver in clubs around Northern Ireland. Diagnosed with throat cancer in 1998 in the years that followed his weight dropped dramatically. After intensive radiotherapy for the cancer he lost his teeth which prevented him from eating solid food. Family and friends, including loyal pal White, did what they could for Higgins and money was raised for him to have dental surgery but he was too frail and passed away aged 61 from multiple causes in 2010, so ending the life of a troubled maverick who thrilled and captivated with his audacious shot making and unique style, changing the sport he began playing as a boy in Belfast.

THELMA HOPKINS

ATHLETICS: MADE A GIANT LEAP
FOR HISTORY
B: 16/03/1936

Thelma Hopkins is one of the greatest athletes to represent Northern Ireland and was at the peak of her powers in the 1950s when she broke an historic world record, claimed an Olympic medal and struck gold in the Commonwealth Games in the High Jump event. Although born in Hull, Hopkins grew up in Belfast after her family moved to Northern Ireland when she was nine months old and loved playing sport with her elder sister Moira. Thelma was a natural at everything she tried but proved to be world class at the High Jump and her precocious talent took her to the 1952 Olympics in Finland with the Great Britain team at the age of 16. While everyone else was impressed by her fourth place finish at such a young age, Hopkins was disappointed in Helsinki though the teenager was smart enough to learn from the experience at that level.

Coached by Austrian Franz Stampfl, who inspired Roger Bannister to become the first man to run a mile in under four minutes, Queen's University graduate Hopkins went from strength to strength winning High Jump gold medals in 1954 at the European Championships in Berne and the British Empire and Commonwealth Games in Vancouver, where illustrating her versatility she also took home silver from the Long Jump.

Two years on the sporting status of Hopkins soared to new heights as she became the first person to break an athletics world record in Ireland. On May 5 on a warm day in Belfast's Cherryvale Park at an intervarsity competition against Manchester University, Hopkins cemented her place in history leaping 1.74 metres (five feet eight and a half inches) in the High Jump surpassing the previous mark of 1.73 metres set by the USSR's Aleksandra Chudina two years earlier. The new record would only last two months but the achievement is commemorated forever in the shape of a plaque in Cherryvale playing fields.

Also in 1956 Hopkins travelled to Melbourne for the Olympics becoming the first Northern Ireland female to earn a medal at the Games claiming a silver and only beaten to gold by American Mildred McDaniel, whose world record jump took her to the top of the podium. All rounder Thelma continued to shine and set British records in the five discipline pentathlon inspiring the great Mary Peters and many others with her all round ability which saw her excel at hockey and squash in internationals for Ireland. Hopkins played 42 times for Ireland in hockey, including with her sister Moira, and in one season scored a mind boggling 90 goals. She emigrated to Canada in 1966 but will always be a Northern Ireland sporting idol.

PADDY HOPKIRK

RALLYING: MINI MARVEL WHO STEERED HIMSELF INTO HISTORY BOOKS

B: 14/04/1933

Paddy Hopkirk was so big in the 1960s that he was a hero to The Beatles with the Fab Four so taken by his spectacular Monte Carlo Rally success that they sent him a signed photograph saying "you're one of us now, Paddy". The Belfast man loved having the backing of John Lennon, Paul McCartney, George Harrison and Ringo Starr but this charismatic character enjoyed the support of the man and woman in the street just as much.

What Hopkirk did in 1964 is still considered one of motorsport's greatest triumphs encompassing a battle against the odds and proving that anything is possible when the right people are involved. Driving a little red Mini with a white roof, Hopkirk achieved the impossible beating the might and money of far bigger teams such as Ford and Mercedes to come first in the most famous race of its time. It was so huge over 20 million viewers in the UK tuned in to watch Hopkirk on the Sunday Night at the London Palladium television show after he had been flown back to Britain to take part. The boy from Windsor Avenue had wowed the public with his driving skills and that evening on the Bruce Forsyth hosted programme they fell for him even more as he exuded a natural charm and wit which he has carried with him all his life.

In his earlier years, though, not everyone saw eye to eye with Paddy who left Clongowes Wood College in county Kildare after falling out with the Principal and he was excommunicated by the Catholic Church for attending Trinity College, Dublin which at the time was regarded as a Protestant University. It wasn't until 1970 that a 100-year-old ban on Catholics going to Trinity without special dispensation was lifted. In 2019 Hopkirk told Laurence White in a Belfast Telegraph interview: "Because I didn't get permission from the Catholic Church to go to Trinity, I was automatically excommunicated." He added with a boyish smile: "That gave me the freedom to kiss girls without committing a mortal sin!"

Fascinated by cars from the age of nine when a local clergyman left him an invalid carriage in a will, Hopkirk, who has dyslexia, dropped out of University to work for Volkswagen in Dublin and it wasn't long before he was buying used Volkswagen Beetles to enter races. He earned his first rally victory in 1953 and that year entered the Circuit of Ireland - a race he would ultimately win on five occasions. With his reputation growing, Hopkirk landed his first factory drive in the 1956 RAC Rally and in the years that followed impressed with a series of excellent performances around the world including a class win at the Alpine Rally.

He finished third in the 1962 Monte Carlo Rally and sixth 12 months later driving a Mini. Then came 1964 alongside English co-driver Henry Liddon in a Mini Cooper S with the registration number 33 EJB. In those days big international rallying events were different to now with the Monte Carlo competitors starting out in nine locations across the continent, such as Minsk for Hopkirk, before joining up with other teams at Reims in northern France to race it out on treacherous roads in the Alps down to Monte Carlo.

The engine in Hopkirk's Mini Cooper S was about four times less powerful than Ford and Mercedes cars in the race but that didn't stop him being second behind Bo Ljungfeldt's Ford Falcon after stage one and using his incredible driving skills in the snow over the famous mountain road Col de Turini he took the lead. Ljungfelt may have posted the fastest time on the final stage but Hopkirk did enough to hang on to the overall lead though his victory was not confirmed until all the times had been added up manually. Eventually he was informed by journalists that he had pulled it off creating the biggest shock in rallying history and fuelling a tidal wave of pride and joy back home.

Princess Grace of Monaco presented the trophy to Paddy, who in an instant had become the most famous rally driver on the planet with the then Prime Minister Alec Douglas-Home, politicians from Northern Ireland and a host of celebrities, including the biggest band in the world, all passing on their best wishes with the victory not only changing Hopkirk's life but transforming the sales of Minis, which suddenly became the nation's most fashionable car.

Hopkirk would continue to race and win big with 1967 in particular impressive courtesy of a hat-trick of successes in the Circuit of Ireland Rally, Alpine Rally and Rally Acropolis. The next year during the gruelling London-Sydney Marathon, Hopkirk gave up a chance to win stopping to rescue rivals in the Bianchi-Ogier team whose car had caught fire after an accident. Forever young with a twinkle in his eye, in 1994, to mark the 30th anniversary of his Monte Carlo glory, he competed in the rally again in a Mini Cooper. Inducted into the Rally Hall of Fame in 2010 and six years later awarded the MBE, Hopkirk, based in Buckinghamshire, works hard for charity and is a wonderful ambassador for Mini, motorsport and Northern Ireland.

WENDY HOUVENAGHEL

CYCLING: THREE-TIME
CHAMPION OF THE WORLD
B: 27/11/1974

Wendy Houvenaghel was the late bloomer who went on to become a triple world champion, world record holder and Olympic medalist in track cycling. An honest performer in competition, she was the same away from the ruthless world of her sport telling me when she retired at 39 in 2014:

"Every athlete has a window of opportunity and I feel I made the most of every opportunity that I have been given. I didn't think when I started out that I would do as well as I did but I've always dedicated myself 100% to being a professional sportsperson and I am immensely proud of my consistently high achievements from the beginning and extremely grateful to all the people who have helped me along that journey."

Unlike many of Northern Ireland's sporting greats Houvenaghel's talent was not apparent from an early age because she wanted to study dentistry and did not start cycling until she was 27. From the Upperlands in county Londonderry, after graduating from the University of Dundee, she became a dentist in the Royal Air Force and was commissioned as a Flight Lieutenant in August 1998 before being promoted to Squadron Leader, completing her commission in 2004. By then Houvenaghel had taken up cycling as a way of keeping fit and discovered she could ride like the wind and while she worked part-time at a local dental surgery the more time she spent on a bike the more observers knew she was a quality performer.

Winning a hat-trick of National Time Trials from 2003 and the Individual Pursuit National Track title in 2005, the following year Houvenaghel was fast-tracked on to the Team GB Olympic Podium Programme for the 2008 Beijing Olympics and so started an incredible run of global success. Wendy became a multiple World Cup 3km Individual Pursuit Champion and European champion in the Team Pursuit in 2010 but best of all she enjoyed World Championship success in 2008, 2009 and 2011 in the Team Pursuit. What made the third of those World titles so remarkable was that at 36, Houvenaghel was twice as old as one of her GB team-mates Laura Trott, who was 18, with the third member of the squad, Dani King, just 20 as the Northern Ireland rider's experience and knowhow pulled the younger duo through to beat USA in a gripping final in Holland.

Houvenaghel also won four World Championship silver medals between 2009 and 2012, Commonwealth Games silver for Northern Ireland in the 3000m Individual Pursuit in 2010 and there was a second place in the 2008 Olympics in China in the same event with the woman from Upperlands missing out in the decider to team-mate Rebecca Romero after an impressive route to the final. It was at the next Games in London where Houvenaghel ought to have secured gold only to be denied in cruel and controversial circumstances.

Primed, ready and in what she felt was the form of her life, with sensational training times in the bank, the Cornwall based woman was surprisingly omitted for all three Team Pursuit races at the Velodrome by Team GB cycling officials who opted to only use Trott, King and Joanna Rowsell who surged to gold in world record breaking fashion on what became known as 'Super Saturday'. Indications leading up to the competition were that Houvenaghel would race in the semi-final or final but due to the rules because she did not ride at all she was ineligible for a medal and left the arena shocked and devastated. In a hard-hitting interview she blasted Team GB cycling officials and explained: "I warmed up and got ready for the final as I was told to do but then Shane Sutton (head coach of British cycling) came up to me and told me I wouldn't be riding. In that 10 second burst from him my Olympic dream was shattered."

Ironically months later with Houvenaghel performing well on the road she was selected to compete for Team GB again before retirement came in 2014 at the age of 39 when she talked about going back to dentistry. "It is a profession where, as a woman in my thirties, I'll be treated as an equal," she said in a parting shot over her treatment as the veteran of the cycling squad. While her London 2012 pain made front and back page headlines Houvenaghel deserves to be remembered for much more than that given she was a lady who bucked the trend, coming late to sport and leaving it as an Olympic silver medal winner and three time World Champion.

AARON HUGHES

FOOTBALL: NORTHERN IRELAND'S MR RELIABLE
B: 08/11/1979

It says much about the person Northern Ireland football great Aaron Hughes is that he was genuinely shocked and overwhelmed by the number of warm tributes that came his way when he retired from playing in June 2019 at the age of 39. That's Hughes, the modest man from Cookstown with humility tumbling out of him and one of the nicest guys in the game who managed to stay in the harsh and ruthless world of the Premier League for 17 years and made 112 international appearances, departing as Britain's most capped defender.

After announcing he was calling it a day, England hero and former Newcastle United team-mate Alan Shearer hailed Aaron's "brilliant career" and Northern Ireland captain Steven Davis labelled him an inspiration with Hughes admitting to me their praise and that from others left him feeling emotional. Hughes was never a flash player, he was never that footballer who would get you on the edge of your seat but what he did deliver was consistency, reliability and was always a team man.

At the Euro 2016 finals, in Northern Ireland's first major tournament for 30 years, Hughes was 36 and viewed more as a squad player than the starter he had been for most of the previous two decades yet there was no divine right attitude about him. He was overjoyed to be there, having suffered tough times for his country, and would have been content to carry the drinks if it helped the rest of the boys but with manager Michael O'Neill wanting experience, dependability and someone he could trust after a disappointing defeat in the opening game to Poland, he called on one of the oldest players in the competition to play and true to form Hughes produced an assured performance at full-back as Northern Ireland won 2-0 against Ukraine, keeping his place in the remaining games in France as the side made the knockout stages.

Hughes was the go to man for many a big name boss from Kenny Dalglish, who had faith in him at 18 to give him his debut in defence for Newcastle away to Barcelona in the Champions League, to former England managers Bobby Robson and Roy Hodgson, who was in charge of Fulham when Aaron was a rock steady centre-back driving the Craven Cottage club to the 2010 Europa League final. In total for Newcastle, Aston Villa and Fulham, the county Tyrone man was never sent off and played 455 times in the Premier League which at the time of writing is almost 150 appearances more than any other Northern Ireland international!

In the latter years of his career he featured for QPR, Brighton, Melbourne City in Australia, Kerala Blasters in India and Hearts and he didn't let any of them down, playing almost 700 matches overall. For Northern Ireland it started in 1998 as a teenager and ended 21 years later having played every position across the back line. In between he captained his country 48 times including in famous home wins over England and Spain and while there was a brief international retirement in 2011 he returned under O'Neill to be a crucial figure who set the tone for the success to come. Aaron only scored one goal for Northern Ireland but he kept scores of them out at the other end and is a legend with the supporters. Knowing him he would say others merit a place in this book more, but believe me he deserves his place.

DAVID HUMPHREYS

RUGBY: ULSTER'S EUROPEAN CUP INSPIRATION

B: 10/09/1971

David Humphreys would tell you off for even suggesting it but without the brilliant out-half Ulster would not have won the European Cup in 1999 and savoured the greatest rugby triumph in the province's history. He was the perfect 10 when Ulster needed one scoring and saving tries on the way to a magnificent occasion at Lansdowne Road when Dublin was invaded by almost 50,000 fans from the north, roaring their heroes on to a fabulous final victory over French side Colomiers. Captain marvel for Ulster, Humphreys was also superb for Ireland playing 72 times and scoring 560 points in an international career that lasted a decade.

The Ballymena Academy boy grew up idolising Liverpool star Kenny Dalglish and carried many of the same qualities of his hero such as a fierce will to succeed, a team before the individual mentality and an ability to make things happen. If his vision and intelligence kept him one step ahead playing rugby, he was also clued in away from sport studying law at Queen's University and Oxford where he is still remembered for scoring all of his team's points and producing a splendid display in the 1995 Varsity match against Cambridge in a 21-19 victory. With rugby moving towards professional status, Clive Woodward, who would later guide England to World Cup success, persuaded Humphreys to join London Irish where he revelled in learning his trade before returning home to play for Ulster in 1998 for what was the best season of his life. It certainly didn't start out that way with his close friend and then Ulster skipper Mark McCall informing Humphreys in a Belfast café that his playing career was over due to a neck injury. Reluctantly Humphreys took over the leading role but not for one second did he think he would be lifting a prestigious trophy within six months in a "thrown together side" of amateurs and professionals.

After riding their luck in the group stages, the fun really started in the December 1998 quarter-finals against French giants Toulouse when, urged on by a passionate Ravenhill crowd, Humphreys controlled the game with his tactical genius and knocked over two drop goals before saving his best to last with a miraculous try saving tackle in the closing stages, inspiring Ulster to a 15-13 victory. Nursing a dislocated shoulder after preventing the French from scoring and white as a sheet at the final whistle Humphreys said the win was "worth all the agony". There was ecstasy across Northern Ireland when Humphreys was declared fit for the semi-final against Stade de Francais, played just nine days into 1999 and with 20,000 at Ravenhill, courtesy of hastily erected stands to cope with demand, the noise was deafening as once again Humphreys stepped up to the plate. Amid a mad, frenetic, ear splitting afternoon against a superstar outfit it was Ulster's finest who delivered an out of this world moment to send Harry Williams' side to a thrilling 33-27 success. Collecting the ball inside his own half, Humphreys had the audacity to chip it forward for winger Sheldon Coulter who then passed to his skipper to race 50 yards and dive over the line. It was a classic try that had the whole country on its feet yet typical of Humphreys he stated that Coulter had done "all the hard work and I just had to run it in!"

With confidence soaring and a sea of red and white backing Ulster in the final there was no way they were going to lose to Colomiers with Humphreys dictating affairs and dropping a goal and the ever reliable Simon Mason kicking the other points in a resounding 21-6 result which allowed Humphreys to insist his pal McCall joined him to lift the European Cup. He said: "It was the highlight of my career. In terms of what it represented, what it meant to the players and the people of Northern Ireland it was the best."

A week later, illustrating the rollercoaster nature of sport, Humphreys missed a kick to earn Ireland a home victory over France, though he would put it right the following year slotting a late penalty to earn victory in Paris. First capped in 1996, the Ulsterman was a classy performer for the Irish with his creativity, positional kicking and frequent scoring, particularly evident in one world class display versus New Zealand in Dublin, though some never gave him the credit he deserved in a green shirt. In 1999 when Ireland were shocked by Argentina in a World Cup quarter-final play-off Humphreys scored all 24 points in a 28-24 loss though in his latter years with the team, the Dungannon player's rivalry with Ronan O'Gara for the number 10 jersey tended to dominate the narrative with the Ulsterman retiring from the international scene in 2006, having captained the side five times.

Regardless he was always Ulster's main man scoring a record 37 Heineken Cup points in a thumping win against Wasps in 2001 before two years later bagging 17 in a 27-21 victory over Edinburgh in the Celtic Cup final while in 2006 it was maestro Humphreys who floated over a timely long distance drop goal which hit both posts before going over in the dying moments to give Ulster, coached by McCall, a vital win over Ospreys and Celtic League glory – the last trophy the province won. Humphreys continued to deliver before he retired limping off the pitch with just eight minutes on the clock in his final game in 2008 against Cardiff Blues to applause from all quarters of Ravenhill. He became Ulster's Club Director of Operations building a team that would reach another European Cup final in 2012, in which his brother Ian played in the defeat to Leinster, before a shock switch to Gloucester as their Director of Rugby in 2014. As Humphreys departed, Rory Best summed up his priceless contribution saying: "David has not just been a part of Ulster rugby, he has been Ulster rugby."

EDDIE IRVINE

MOTOR RACING: FAB FORMULA
ONE REBEL WITHOUT A PAUSE

B: 10/11/1965

Playboy, wild thing, motormouth ... Eddie Irvine has been called them all and more over the years and is one of those sporting stars whose reputation tends to precede him but that should not detract from his superb driving ability in the unforgiving world of Formula One. Long after Irvine had retired and ahead of an interview with him at his Sports Complex in Bangor I was warned that he may prove testing but truth be told he was a joy, more charming than James Bond and as an interviewee pure gold dust shooting from the lip about F1, its drivers, himself and life in general.

When Irvine lost the 1999 World Championship with Ferrari by just two points, I was never sure he was given the credit he deserved but when asked about that his truthful answer was: "I didn't do it for anyone else. I did it for myself. I wasn't expecting lots of praise for doing things for myself, so that has never bothered me." Whether fast Eddie is bothered or not he deserves to be recognised having started out driving his father Edmund's single seaters, moving on and showing promise in Formula Ford, Formula 3 and Formula 3000 before a stint in Japanese F3000 with four wins in 1993 leading to Jordan team owner Eddie Jordan giving him a seat in F1 at the end of that year.

In trademark style there was no easing in for Irvine at Suzuka as he finished sixth in his first Grand Prix to earn a point only to outdo that in the headline stakes when the great Ayrton Senna punched him in the face after winning the race. The Brazilian was raging that Irvine had passed him to unlap himself with the Ulsterman believing the triple World Champion was driving too slowly! At the start of the 1994 season Irvine was banned for several races by the authorities who felt he was at fault for a collision in Brazil prior to establishing himself on the scene gaining a first podium spot at the Canadian Grand Prix in 1995, the year before he became number two to Michael Schumacher in the world famous Ferrari team.

The early years were frustrating but with the car improving and Irvine becoming more canny on the track 1999 would prove to be huge as he began the campaign with a first F1 triumph in Melbourne and when Schumacher broke his leg at Silverstone, it was the Conlig racer rather than the German who would go for World Championship glory with Ferrari. Successive wins in Austria and Germany took Irvine top of the standings in an exciting battle with McLaren's Mika Hakkinen who had regained the lead by the penultimate round in Malaysia, where Schumacher returned from his long lay-off to help his team-mate claim victory meaning that if Irvine finished ahead of Hakkinen in the final race he would be F1 champion. After the Malaysian Grand Prix there was controversy when both Ferraris were disqualified over the bargeboards on their cars and with Hakkinen moving from third to first in the race the ruling made him World Champion only for a successful Ferrari appeal to put his champagne on ice and set up a showdown in Japan. Unfortunately for Irvine third was the best he could do as the Finn won the race and retained his title by 76 points to 74 with the County Down driver leaving Ferrari in a pre-arranged move to a new Jaguar team, enjoying podium places in Monaco and Monza before quitting F1 in 2002, aged 36. Since then Irvine has been a successful property investor, with one of his buys an island in the Bahamas, and he remains as outspoken and compelling as ever.

MARTYN IRVINE

CYCLING: RIDER WHO SHOCKED THE WORLD
B: 06/06/1985

Martyn Irvine won a gold and silver medal in less than an hour at the 2013 World Track Cycling Championships in Belarus and to think he was once a self-confessed couch potato! The story of Newtownards man Irvine is as inspirational as it is remarkable and shows that when it comes to sport, it's best to never rule anything out. As a teenager Martyn used to hand sick notes to teachers at Movilla High School to avoid P.E. Growing up he had no interest in any physical activity, revealing to me in an eye opening interview: "I was a total couch potato until I was about 18. I even got sick notes for PE. I wouldn't have done anything at school."

Recalling how his successful cycling career started, Irvine added: "I was working in Bangor as a car mechanic and some of the lads there were really into their cycling and eventually it rubbed off on me. I'd been there since I was 16 but had no interest until I was 18 when they convinced me to get a bike. I went out riding after work and it snowballed from there. I started racing at 19 and I did my first Open race. By the time I was 21 I was racing in Belgium and I guess I had been bitten by the bug. I remember coming sixth in my first club race when to be honest I didn't really know what I was doing. I was just riding with my head down. I loved the racing side of things and saw training as a necessary evil. There was a lot of suffering in training but the racing made it fun."

By the time Irvine competed in the London 2012 Olympics for Ireland he was a seven time Irish National Track and Road champion and one year later at the age of 27 in Minsk came his finest hour. First he claimed silver at the World Track Championships in a highly competitive Individual Pursuit race and before 60 minutes had elapsed Irvine made history in the 15K Scratch race to become champion of the world. It was heroic stuff. The race was gruelling, exhausting and demanding for Irvine, who was hurting from his silver medal race, but he would not be denied. His motto that night was no guts, no glory and despite being almost out on his feet he broke from the bunch with 10 out of the 60 laps to go in the Scratch event and sprinted for home, somehow managing to hold off his rivals in a thrilling finale. Irvine's remarkable effort meant he became the first Irish male to win at the World Cycling Championships in 117 years!

Shortly after that triumph he suffered a fractured leg when competing in the Tour of Taiwan but would recover to finish third in the 2013 European Championships in the Omnium – cycling's version of the decathlon – and win World Cup gold in Manchester in the Points race (a 30 kilometre event). In 2014 he claimed another silver medal at the World Track Championships in the Scratch race in Colombia prior to retiring two years later. The Ards native couldn't resist a return to the saddle only to suffer a bad crash which cut short his comeback. With his riding days over Irvine is determined to help cyclists across the island and has worked as a track coach with Cycling Ireland. He has quite a tale to tell those willing to listen and learn about how a couch potato turned into a world champion.

PAT JENNINGS

FOOTBALL: LEGEND, WORLD CUP HERO AND GOALKEEPING IDOL

B: 12/06/1945

Pat Jennings is one of football's greatest ever goalkeepers who won 119 caps for Northern Ireland, played in over 1000 games, became a hero at both Tottenham and Arsenal and starred in two World Cup finals, bowing out at the age of 41. The respect and reverence in which Jennings is held in any company is something to behold and says as much about the modest nature, generosity and sincerity of the man as it does his magnificent ability between the sticks.

He staggered fans with the astonishing saves he used to make with the north London clubs and at international level but then Jennings was defying logic from an early age playing in an under-19 league in his hometown of Newry when he was just 11! Typical of the person, known throughout the football world as 'Big Pat', growing up and working hard as a forester in his teenage years he didn't feel a professional career in the game was on the horizon until he was selected to play for Northern Ireland in a youth tournament in England. Reflecting on his first trip away from his family, he once told me: "I literally came off the mountains where I was working in a timber gang up above Newry and 10 days later I was playing in the finals of this youth tournament at the world famous Wembley. In those days unless you played in the FA Cup final or for your country nobody got near Wembley so you can imagine what a thrill that was."

Jennings would return to work on the mountain but scouts in England had become aware of his talent and a month before his 18th birthday Watford signed him from Newry Town and from there he went from strength to strength. Jennings made such an impact in his first year at Watford that Tottenham and the legendary Bill Nicholson came calling in 1964, three years after they won the league and cup double. Jennings excelled at White Hart Lane and to this day is regarded as the club's best goalkeeper and rightly so given that in his 13 year spell there he was the solid base on which any success was built with FA Cup glory in 1967, League Cup victories in 1971 and 1973 and a memorable UEFA Cup triumph in 1972. As well as keeping countless goals out he actually scored one with a long kick against Manchester United in the 1967 Charity Shield and he claimed a host of individual awards including the Football Writers' Footballer of the season prize in 1973 and he was the first goalkeeper to be named PFA Player of the Year in 1976.

If that surprised no-one, what happened a year later stunned British football when the then Spurs boss Keith Burkinshaw felt Jennings, after 590 games for the White Hart Lane outfit and hardly a bad one among them, was surplus to requirements and he was sold to fierce rivals Arsenal. For just about anyone else such a move would have caused controversy and hate but not for likeable Pat who fitted in at Arsenal straightaway under manager Terry Neill and became a terrace hero playing over 300 times for the Gunners and being instrumental in them reaching three FA Cup finals in a row, winning the middle one in 1979, and the 1980 European Cup Winners' Cup decider which was lost to Valencia on penalties. In 1983 he was the first player in English football to reach 1000 senior appearances marking the occasion by keeping a clean sheet in a 0-0 draw with West Brom.

Jennings left Arsenal in 1985, lauded all over Highbury for his contribution, returning to Spurs and then joining Everton as cover and to keep himself sharp for a big finish to his stellar career in the 1986 World Cup finals in Mexico. If the one time GAA player delivered time after time for his clubs, he was even more important at international level in a record run of caps that spanned more than two decades kicking off as a Watford player alongside fellow debutant George Best in a 3-2 victory over Wales in 1964. The pair were room-mates and became close pals and while it is one of Pat's regrets that his genius friend never played in a major tournament, he is proud to have represented Northern Ireland at the World Cup finals twice having done more than most to get them there in 1982 and 1986. In virtually every international home or away team-mates of Jennings, the first Northern Ireland star to reach 100 caps, looked on in amazement at the miracle stops he would pull off with his big hands and feet all the while oozing a wonderful sense of calm, not least when Billy Bingham's side defeated hosts Spain in the 1982 World Cup finals or when he kept out England at Wembley in qualification for the 1986 tournament or when he halted West Germany in a famous 1-0 European Championships qualifying win in 1983. The list could go on and on for a man whose heroes growing up were Northern Ireland's Newry born star Peter McParland and the great Down GAA players. Pat played GAA himself as a youngster and felt the skills he learnt catching the ball then helped when he started playing professional football, leading to that glorious period at international level.

Jennings said: "We had been trying to qualify since I'd joined the team in 1964. We thought we were never going to make it. Then against the odds we qualified for the 1982 World Cup and to go out to Spain and beat the host nation in the finals was just incredible. Somehow we did it again four years later to qualify for the 1986 World Cup in Mexico. When you think about it now that was some achievement."

So too the fabulous football story of Pat, adored and known by all illustrated by the greeting Prince William offered the golf loving family man at an early 2020 visit to Windsor Park. "Now there's a man who needs no introduction," said the Duke of Cambridge as he approached Jennings, a giant in every sense and sporting royalty in Northern Ireland. Married to Eleanor, who he describes as "a great woman" and dad to their four children Mairead, Siobhan, Ciara and Patrick Junior, Jennings has had all sorts of notable honours lavished on him. His favourite? He says: "I never miss an opportunity to tell people wherever I go that there is a Pat Jennings park in my home town of Newry. That makes me very proud. It's where it all started. I've never forgotten that."

MARGARET JOHNSTON

BOWLS: INDOOR AND OUTDOOR WORLD CHAMPION IN A LEAGUE OF HER OWN

B: 02/05/1943

Margaret Johnston is the lady who started her sport in a Church Hall and became the best female bowler of all time being labelled rebellious, controversial and a maverick along the way. Full of witty one liners and never afraid to say her piece away from the rink, Johnston was so gifted on it with her smooth technique it seemed as though she could make her bowls dance winning SIX World Outdoor Championships, two World Indoor titles and Commonwealth Games gold twice.

It all began for the woman from the Upperlands in county Londonderry because there wasn't much to do when she was 20 in the little village of Tamlaght O'Crilly and she thought she would give bowls a go when the Church of Ireland minister formed a short mat bowling club. In her plain-spoken way, Johnston, who enjoyed hockey and netball at school, recalled in the Belfast Telegraph: "It was a night out, better than sitting in the house. There was little else in the village except the Mothers' Union and it was for old fogeys so it didn't appeal to me. I enjoyed the bowls from the start."

Having moved to Bellaghy she continued to play for fun in the local Masonic Hall but when it was damaged in a bomb during the Troubles the club moved and she ended up at the Ballymoney club where her talent blossomed. She reached the final of the Irish Singles in 1978 and by 1981, aged 38, was selected for the Irish team though as Johnston put it the decision to give her international honours did not go down well with "a lot of the old biddies who had been bowling for years and never got a chance".

As she gained experience playing at top level the big victories flowed. Her opening Irish National Championship arrived in 1983 with the first of four British Isles Bowls Championships coming in 1985 followed by a pairs gold medal alongside Freda Elliott for Northern Ireland in the 1986 Commonwealth Games and then Maggie, as she is called, took over the world. She was World Indoor Singles Champion in 1988 and 1989, World Outdoor Singles Champion in 1992, 2000 and 2004 and World Outdoor Pairs Champion with Phillis Nolan for Ireland three times running in 1988, 1992 and 1996 becoming the first person in 1992 to do the double in the same year. She was also Commonwealth Games singles Champion in 1994 and World Singles Champion of Champions a decade later claiming multiple podium places as well.

Despite all the success, bowls was never going to make Johnston rich. In fact with prize money limited there were occasions, with the cost of travel, that she was out of pocket. Working at different times as an auxiliary in a private nursing home and caretaker at a nearby primary school, the grandmother was keen for bowls to modernise and was not shy in clashing with officialdom about her desire to bring younger people into the sport. Perhaps her best known blast came after she refused to play in a home international series in Belfast because she did not like the use of sports psychologists and relaxation exercises as part of the build-up. Johnston, awarded the MBE in 1991, said: "I got to the top without all this nonsense. The relaxation classes amounted to lying on a cold, hard floor for an hour. I never won a game of bowls lying on my back!"

In 2008 after winning over 100 caps she retired from international competition but continued to bowl at an extremely high standard and returned to play for Ireland at the British Isles Fours Championship in 2018 having won the National Irish Championship Fours event a year before. You can't keep a great woman down.

JIMMY KIRKWOOD

HOCKEY: SEOUL MAN CLAIMED
GOLDEN MOMENT

B: 12/02/1962

Olympic gold medal winner Jimmy Kirkwood played hockey with a swagger and a style that left opponents bemused and bewildered and that's only part of the story because his cricketing ability led him to an achievement all too rare in modern sport - becoming a dual international. The Lisburn man enjoyed many sporting highlights though the brightest of all came in Seoul when, along with compatriot Stephen Martin, he helped the Great British hockey team triumph at the 1988 Olympics.

Kirkwood was renowned for his dazzling stick skills and forward runs and while he didn't start a match during the Games, the team management knew that in the Queen's University graduate they had a player capable of turning any encounter on its head. In South Korea, Kirkwood played twice in the group stages, in a 2-2 draw against the hosts and in an impressive 3-0 win over India that took the GB side into the semi-finals. On the gold medal being hung around his neck after a 3-1 final victory over West Germany, he would later remark: "You wondered did it really happen. You felt like a different person on the podium but it was hugely exciting and very special. Then we had tremendous receptions when we arrived home at the airport in London and again in Belfast."

Kirkland's sporting prowess with a stick or bat in hand was evident from his schooldays and that talent was rewarded when in 1981 at 18 years of age he won the first of 130 senior caps for Ireland which included appearances in multiple EuroHockey Nations Championships and in the 1990 World Cup when against Canada he was smashed in the face by an opponent's stick and ended up requiring 15 stitches.

The former pupil of Friends School was a popular and highly rated figure at international level, claiming 40 GB caps, and on the domestic hockey scene he was feared across the island as Lisnagarvey claimed numerous trophies, while in cricket this fine batsman and wicketkeeper will always be a hero at Lisburn Cricket Club for inspiring them to their first Challenge

Cup triumph in over two decades in 1985 and 13 years later coming out of retirement to help save the side from relegation. Kirkwood's ability with the bat led to him playing three matches for Ireland, a number that would have been considerably higher but for choosing hockey as his number one sport. It was the right call because only Jimmy, his good pal Stephen Martin and Lady Mary Peters have delivered gold to Northern Ireland from the summer Olympics.

JACK KYLE

RUGBY: GRAND SLAM MAESTRO FOR IRELAND

B: 10/02/1926 - D: 28/11/2014

There's a wonderful picture of Jack Kyle and Brian O'Driscoll shaking hands at the Millennium Stadium in Cardiff after Ireland completed the Grand Slam in 2009 with a dramatic victory over Wales. Captain O'Driscoll is in his green shirt, bathed in sweat, smiling broadly the way a winner does, while Kyle, dressed as smartly as ever in a sharp suit and overcoat, is generously offering his congratulations in a magical passing of the baton moment for Irish rugby. It had taken 61 years for the emerald isle to repeat the feat inspired by the brilliance of Kyle in 1948 when Ireland won their first rugby Grand Slam and no one was happier to see it than Jack, as genuine as he was great.

John Wilson Kyle, commonly known as Jack or Jackie, climbed Everest first and was Ireland's original superstar - the original and the best as voted by a gathering of rugby experts who in 2002 declared he was the finest player of all time to come from the island. No caps were awarded when Kyle made his first appearance for Ireland during World War II with official international recognition having to wait until 1947 when he played in a defeat to France in the Five Nations Championship. The following year a

13-6 victory in France kick started an extraordinary and historic campaign masterminded by the magnificence of out half Kyle who drove the Irish on with a try in an 11-10 success away to England prior to a 6-0 victory over Scotland at Lansdowne Road. The final match in the series was on Jack's home turf at Ravenhill in Belfast where Ireland defeated Wales 6-3 to claim Grand Slam glory and the Championship.

Who knew it would take over 60 years for Ireland to do it all over again? Certainly not Jack who told Ulster Rugby: "It was a wonderful thing to win all of our games and win the Grand Slam but we never imagined it would take 61 years before an Irish team would win another Grand Slam. Those of us who won the Grand Slam would have been dined and wined and feted because we were the old 1948 side and we began to think we were quite good! We never considered we were particularly good but every time there was a possibility of an Ireland team winning the Grand Slam the old photographs of the 1948 side would come out so it benefited us quite considerably."

After 1948 Kyle would keep inspiring as Ireland lifted more Five Nations titles in 1949 and 1951 and in between he gained new admirers in Australia and New Zealand with outstanding displays for the British and Irish Lions on their 1950 tour playing in all six Tests. They loved him over there and he continued to mesmerise for Ireland until 1958 with the then Irish Times rugby correspondent Paul MacWeeney capturing his abilities best in 1953 with a little help from The Scarlet Pimpernel after an amazing individual try versus France. The report read: "They seek him here, they seek him there, those Frenchies seek him everywhere, that paragon of pace and guile, that damned elusive Jackie Kyle."

By the time Kyle, labelled 'the Ghost' because he could be impossible to catch, finished with Ireland he had won 46 caps, a world record, and scored seven tries. Given all he achieved it seems funny to recount how he was first selected for Queen's University, where he was studying medicine, being handed a note in a chemistry practical informing him of details of a game in Dublin the following day.

Breathtaking and awe-inspiring as he was as a rugby player, the most uplifting part of Jack's life was away from sport when after retiring from club rugby in 1963 the Belfast Royal Academy student, with a fondness for travel, was contracted to work as a surgeon in Indonesia before moving to Zambia where he would work for over three decades as a consultant surgeon in Chingola, saving thousands of lives. Kyle would eventually return to Northern Ireland quietly helping others in any way he could including this writer when graciously accepting invitations to present awards at functions such as inducting fellow Ulster and Ireland rugby icon Mike Gibson into a sporting Hall of Fame.

Jack's modesty was as legendary as his ability to bamboozle opposition players and his daughter Justine, who wrote a fascinating book about her dad called 'Conversations with my Father', tells a tale of how as a young child she didn't have a clue that Jack was a rugby player, let alone one of the best ever, because he never mentioned it! Justine also explains that her father was born on February 10, 1926 rather than a month earlier, as some publications have suggested over the years, revealing that Jack once phoned one newspaper to clarify his date of birth only to be told he was incorrect which was the source of much amusement when the family celebrated his birthday on the proper date!

I was fortunate to chat with Jack a few months before he sadly passed away in November 2014 when he and Justine were kind enough to attend the launch of that year's Belfast Telegraph Sports awards and as always the maestro was pleasant, sincere and humble and far keener to talk about the accomplishments of others than himself. He was a gentleman and genius, loved and respected from Antrim to Auckland, and had that special quality of making people feel better about themselves after spending time with him, which was his greatest gift of all.

MAEVE KYLE

ATHLETICS/HOCKEY: DUAL STAR
WHO BROKE DOWN BARRIERS
B: 06/10/1928

If you want inspirational and influential look no further than the inimitable Maeve Kyle who was the first female athlete to compete for Ireland at the Olympics, won a European Championship medal at the age of 37, made her second appearance at the Commonwealth Games for Northern Ireland when she was 41 and before all that established herself as one of the best hockey players in the world.

Though Northern Ireland would become home later in life Kyle started her sporting journey in the town of her birth, Kilkenny, playing rugby and hockey with boys, swimming and running against them too, generally coming out on top. If athletics would help her create Olympic history it was hockey where she first excelled showing her skills at school and going on to play for Leinster, Munster and Ulster and 58 times for Ireland. Maeve's prowess was held in high regard within the game and she was included in the World All-Star team in both 1953 and 1959 so it was no surprise when she was in the first group of players inducted into the Irish Hockey Hall of Fame.

In Antrim in 1953 at a party after a hockey match Maeve met her future husband Sean Kyle who suggested she become a sprinter and that he would be her coach leading to her becoming the first woman chosen to race for Ireland at the Olympics in 1956. With Ireland a much more conservative place then and with many feeling a woman's place was in the home the public were fascinated by the story with some praising Maeve and others criticising her like one letter writer in the Irish Times who labelled Kyle's selection for the Games as "degrading to womenfolk" and questioning her for leaving her husband and young daughter behind.

Maeve, being Maeve, a woman who spoke her mind, was comfortable with her decision to go to Australia and felt entitled to do so thinking if men could compete for Ireland at the Olympics why couldn't women.

She would call herself an athletics suffragette and in time would be known as the lady who paved the way for hundreds of others though unlike modern stars Kyle had to foot a bill of £200 to pay her way to Melbourne with the trip from Dublin taking three weeks! Games rules stated women weren't allowed to run more than 200m so Kyle ran in the 100m and 200m in Melbourne and would return to the Olympics to do the same in Rome in 1960, meeting a charming young Muhammad Ali who was then known as Cassius Clay. Maeve did not get the chance to race in her best event - the 400m - and the 800m until 1964 in Tokyo, where she reached the semi-finals in both in what was her third Games, a record at that stage for an Irish competitor.

In 1966 at the inaugural European Indoor Athletics Championship she claimed a bronze medal in the 400m and there was still another major championship in Kyle when at 41 she made the final for Northern Ireland at the 1970 Commonwealth Games, 12 years on from first competing in the multi-sports event for the first time in 1958. Even after that Kyle kept running becoming a four time World Masters Champion in the 100m, 400m, high jump and long jump. Along with husband Sean, who passed away in 2015, Maeve co-founded Ballymena & Antrim Athletic Club in 1955 coaching a stream of athletes to success and in 2006 she was presented a Lifetime Achievement Award at the 2006 Coaching Awards in London. Revered for her coaching, as an athlete Kyle was a trailbrazer, a pioneer and the person who made it possible for hundreds of Irish females, north and south, to follow their Olympic dream.

DERMOTT LENNON

SHOWJUMPING: FIRST IRISH
WORLD CHAMPION
B: 12/06/1969

In 2002 Dermott Lennon did what some greats in his field couldn't and became Ireland's first World Showjumping champion just three years after making his debut in international competition. It was an astounding result for the man brought up in Ballynaskeagh on the outskirts of Loughbrickland in county Down and who began riding when he was six years old on a pony, minus a saddle or bridle, to round up cattle on the family farm. In time Lennon would learn to collect awards across Ireland but it was when he moved into the top level of the sport, mixing with the best on the planet, that he truly excelled.

It was in 1999 that he first rode internationally taking to it like a horse to hay jumping a double clear round in Athens to help Ireland to a Nations Cup success, a feat the team, with Lennon in assured form, kept repeating winning a record breaking 10 Nations Cup events that season. There was also a satisfying victory over the British squad at the Royal Windsor Horse Show in 2000 to win the Hallowe'en Cup and the next year the Ireland team clinched gold in the European Showjumping Championships for the first time in the nation's history with Lennon, fellow Northern Ireland rider Jessica Kurten, Kevin Babington and Peter Charles thrilled by a seminal moment.

Lennon was on board his beloved mare Liscalgot in that success and together he believed they could achieve World Championship glory in 2002 even though since the competition started in 1953 nobody from the island had cleared that final hurdle including Irish equestrian heroes Eddie Macken - twice a runner-up - and Gerry Mullins. In Jerez in Spain Dermott would conquer all before him in a field of 94 competitors from 21 nations to become the World Individual Showjumping Champion. Having reached the final after three days of intense competition, Lennon had to jump the course four times, once on his own horse and once on the horses of the other three finalists who all did the same. It was a demanding yet exciting test of horsemanship and using control and skill in equal measure Lennon passed with flying colours with just one fence down and a total of four faults in his four rides to seal an historic triumph beating 1990 French World Champion Eric Navet into second place. With Crossmaglen bred Liscalgot, which Lennon called 'Shirley' and described as a 'horse of a lifetime' when she died in 2016, injured Dermott missed out on the Olympics in 2004 and though he never matched his Jerez heroics he continued to ride on the circuit producing classy performances such as fifth place in the 2010 World Cup final. There were also victories including in the Olympia Grand Prix in 2011 and one just prior to the 2020 Covid-19 lockdown in the prestigious Big Tour speed class in Spain, almost two decades on from his greatest success.

MICKEY LINDEN

GAELIC FOOTBALL: DOWN'S
DOUBLE ALL-IRELAND HERO
B: 25/07/1963

In a team of stars it can be hard to stand out but that's what Mickey Linden did in the early 1990s winning two All-Ireland Championships with Down. What a player, up there with the GAA's finest who could kick points from the tightest of corners with either foot, create or score goals when his county needed them most and had that 'now we've got him, oh no we don't' speed to accelerate away from defenders making them look like they were pulling a horse and cart with Mickey driving a turbo charged red and black lamborghini.

Talk to a Down fan about Linden and they pause to enjoy memories and moments before waxing lyrical about all his qualities, tending to add with equal importance "and Mickey's always been a gentleman you know". Some think he was too nice at times but while he may not have been one for dirty tricks, it could still be a nasty experience chasing his shadow for 70 minutes.

Born into a GAA family with his mum Isabel a keen camogie player and his dad Eamon a canny footballer at club level for Mayobridge, Linden's ability was being lauded from his days as a pupil at St Mark's High School in Warrenpoint with his debut for the Down senior team arriving in 1981 as a teenager with immense promise. Two years later he would help the Mourne county to National League success and there were McKenna Cup triumphs in 1987 and 1989 but a bigger fish was about to be plucked from the lake with manager Pete McGrath building a top drawer team including Greg Blaney, Ross Carr, DJ Kane and James McCartan Jr that would win two All-Irelands in 1991 and 1994 with Linden at the heart of it.

In 1991 the corner forward was instrumental as Down won the Ulster Championship and he was man of the match in their superb All-Ireland semi-final victory over Kerry before unselfishly making a goal and scoring the most sublime of points in a 1-16 to 1-14 victory over Meath in the decider at Croke Park, bringing Sam Maguire north for the first time since Down were champions in 1968.

Down's win sparked a wave of Ulster glory with Donegal (1992) and Derry (1993) following suit before Linden and co came back for more in '94. The road to the Ulster Championship began with what BBC commentator Thomas Niblock described in 2020 as "perhaps the greatest game of all time" when Down overcame All-Ireland Champions Derry, having been beaten by them in the two previous summers, in a high intensity affair at Celtic Park with Linden breathtaking, chipping over point after point with the conviction of a man on top of his form. From there no one was going to halt the Down juggernaut, not even Dublin at Croke Park in a thrilling All-Ireland final when Footballer of the Year Linden was imperious and awarded the man of the match award after his side won 1-12 to 0-13.

Fit as a fiddle Down continued to get a tune out of Linden until he was 40 and he played for Mayobridge after that, making headlines again when he was 55, when exactly 27 years on from helping Down to the 1991 All-Ireland he produced a stunning score for his club in a reserve final against Burren. Now a driving instructor, at 50 Mickey competed in the 2014 Masters World Indoor Athletics Championships in Budapest, reaching the semi-finals in the 60m. Asked to name his all-time team, Down's legendary manager Pete McGrath told Irish News journalist Andy Watters: "When I look back at all the players I managed or played with, if you're looking for a corner forward then Mickey would be a no-brainer. The man's pace, his scoring ability, the fact that he taught himself how to kick better with his left foot than his right foot!" McGrath added that in the famous 1994 final Dublin couldn't cope with Linden and found him unstoppable, though they were not alone in that.

CIARA MAGEEAN

ATHLETICS: RECORD BREAKER
WELL ON TRACK
B: 12/03/1992

From the fishing town of Portaferry, Ciara Mageean grew up playing camogie to become a world class middle distance athlete winning medals at major championships and breaking records held by one of the most fabled sports stars across Ireland. Not only an exceptional runner, she is also renowned for her fun and honest post race interviews with enthusiasm, pure joy and her sparkling personality pouring out after every impressive performance on the track.

With camogie and hurling, in which her dad Chris excelled for Down, Ciara's favourite sports as a child, she didn't have a notion about being involved in athletics until she attended secondary school but after her PE teacher at Assumption Grammar in Ballynahinch suggested joining the cross country team her life started to go down a new path. By the age of 15 Mageean won her first Irish senior title at Belfast's Odyssey Arena in the 1500 metres and when she was 16 she broke the long standing 800 metres Irish junior record held by the great Sonia O'Sullivan in the Irish Schools Championships, where she also crossed the line first in the 1500m, the event in which she won a bronze at the 2008 Commonwealth Youth Games in India despite feeling unwell.

The progress continued in 2009 with silver at the World Youth Championships and gold in the European Youth Olympics while in 2010 she took 1500m silver in the World Junior Championships, competed at the Commonwealth Games for Northern Ireland in her first senior international competition making the final and was delighted to be named on the Ulster Schools' All Star camogie team as she continued to play her first love.

Not making it to the 2012 Olympics in London was a major blow as was an ankle problem that kept her out of action long term, the first of a number of disheartening injuries. There were some who feared for her track career but back she came to claim a bronze medal at the 1500m European Championships in 2016. That took heart, which Mageean has in spades, and in the same year she became an Olympian in Rio representing Ireland and breaking the Irish indoor records in the 1500m and mile prior to another significant medal in the 1500m, claiming bronze at the 2019 European Athletics Indoor Championships.

Entering 2020 Mageean was full of hope that she could kick on and despite the Tokyo Olympics being delayed by the coronavirus pandemic, the Portaferry woman enjoyed a stunning summer becoming the first Irish female to go under two minutes for the 800m and posting a time of 2 minutes 31.06 seconds to break former World Champion Sonia O'Sullivan's Irish 1000m record which had stood for 27 years. Mageean's blistering run in Monaco was the ninth fastest time ever at 1000m and she is sure she can go quicker in all the middle distance races promising a bright future to go with what she has already achieved.

STEPHEN MARTIN

HOCKEY: GOLD STAR
AT THE 1988 GAMES

B: 13/04/1959

Stephen Martin's place in Northern Ireland sporting history is assured. He is the nation's most successful Olympian with a gold medal and a bronze medal, captained both the Irish and Great Britain hockey teams and at one point had more international caps than anyone else. Yet at the age of 13 he was a heartbroken kid when he was told in a Bangor hospital that he wouldn't be able to play sport again after suffering a burst appendix. Martin refused to accept the prognosis, eased his way back into action by running and ended up becoming an Olympic champion. Northern Ireland is a place not blessed with many of those but the man known as 'Sam' stood tall on the top step of the podium, alongside countryman Jimmy Kirkwood, in the 1988 Games in Seoul having claimed a bronze four years earlier in Los Angeles.

As a young boy Martin was an extremely gifted golfer and often played alongside David Feherty, who went on to feature in the European Ryder Cup team, but it was discovering a love of hockey while playing with his brother Philip in the garden that would change Stephen's life as he went on to enjoy incredible success. An early highlight was winning a silver medal as a teenager for Ireland in the EuroHockey Junior Championships and with his blossoming talent he was picked for the full Irish squad before he was selected for Ulster. The former Bangor Grammar pupil and Ulster University of Jordanstown graduate would represent Ireland 135 times.

Great Britain, as they could back then, came calling in 1983 with Martin telling a lovely story about taking a picture of himself in the mirror in his GB kit ahead of his debut against the USA, thinking he may only ever play one game. He proved to be much more than a one hit wonder going to the 1984 Olympics in Los Angeles where he was an important figure in defence as the Great Britain squad upset the odds to earn a bronze medal, dramatically beating Australia 3-2, with the turning point a brilliant Martin clearance off the line.

Four years later from underdogs in LA the Great Britain team were amongst the favourites for Olympic glory in the 1988 Seoul Games. Martin did not play in the early matches but savoured a magical moment when he came on as a substitute in the famous 3-1 final victory over West Germany, on the date of his parents' wedding anniversary.

There was another Olympic experience in Barcelona 1992 and by the time Martin retired he had amassed a record breaking 229 caps in total for Ireland and GB, for whom he played 94 times and won bronze and silver in the 1984 and 1985 Champions Trophy tournaments. Awarded an MBE in 1993, he became a respected sports administrator for the British Olympic Association and Olympic Council of Ireland, though by then his medal winning exploits on the field of play had already earned Stephen an elevated status in Northern Ireland sport.

DAVE 'BOY' MCAULEY

BOXING: WORLD CHAMPION
ALWAYS VALUE FOR MONEY
B: 15/06/1961

Brave as a lion, Dave 'Boy' McAuley was a World Champion flyweight, had a record number of title defences and was involved in some of the most exciting fights ever to take place in Northern Ireland. Anyone who was at the King's Hall in Belfast to see the Larne man face Colombian Fidel Bassa in 1987 for the WBA crown will never forget it and if you haven't seen it do yourself a favour and view it on YouTube.

It was a stunning contest with McAuley down in the opening round before he summoned the strength to hit back and keep hitting back in an unforgettable toe-to-toe bout between two warriors who traded blows and knockdowns like there was no tomorrow. In various rounds McAuley, lifted by a raucous atmosphere, looked certain to triumph felling Bassa on numerous occasions with ferocious punching only to go down himself in the 13th from a searing assault and this time there was no getting up. It was voted Fight of the Year by the highly respected Ring magazine and 12 months on, they gave the Belfast rematch, another gripping war lost by McAuley on points, the same accolade.

Few other fighters would have had the stomach for more after those battles and McAuley did consider retiring but his iron will and desire to be the best in the business, combined with the canny man management and encouragement of Barney Eastwood, kept him dreaming and in 1989 the ambition of a lifetime was fulfilled when he shocked England's Duke McKenzie to bring home the belt. Facing McKenzie for the IBF World flyweight title at Wembley Arena few gave McAuley a prayer with the former viewed as the new ace in the British boxing pack and the latter supposed to be a busted flush. The Ulsterman had other ideas and in a highly accomplished performance and tactical masterclass, using his powerful left hook to great effect, he destroyed his opponent to emerge victorious on points. A joyous open top bus journey around his home town followed and with the confidence gained from the biggest win of his career, McAuley racked up the title defences, six in all, a then British and Irish record and was successful in five of them holding on to his belt until 1992.

It was a far cry from his early days in the sport having followed his brothers to the local boxing club. He won Ulster and All-Ireland flyweight titles but grew tired of the politics of the amateur game walking away in 1980 until three years later he decided to give the professional ranks a shot because he needed some money. Patiently he clocked up wins becoming British flyweight champion in 1986 prior to nine world title fights.

Even after reaching the pinnacle he never short-changed the fans with his famed never-say-die attitude still in evidence, particularly in the most memorable of his title defences when he rose from the canvas four times to defeat Colombian Rodolfo Blanco on points in another King's Hall thriller. You got your money's worth watching McAuley, who controversially lost to Blanco in a re-match in Spain when many felt he was a comfortable winner and feeling down after the defeat never fought again.

Tall for a flyweight, McAuley, who found it painfully tough making the weight for his division, jokily described himself as having a "cauliflower backside" because of the number of times he hit the deck but for a three year period he was on top of the world retiring to run the Halfway House hotel on the Antrim Coast and shoot from the lip in his role as a boxing pundit. He was offered big money opportunities to make a comeback with world titles at stake but the manner of the defeat to Blanco left a sour taste. Decades on the public still want to talk about his contests which enthralled a nation. "Every week people will approach me and say they remember my world title fights which is gratifying because it makes me feel that I have contributed something to the sporting history of Northern Ireland," said McAuley in CultureNI.org.

WILLIE JOHN MCBRIDE

RUGBY: THE ULTIMATE LEADER AND LION KING

B: 06/06/1940

As I write 835 players have the honour of being British and Irish Lions and the greatest of them all is Willie John McBride who could roar in red like nobody before or since and proved to be the King of the rugby jungle in an historic, epic and invincible tour of South Africa in 1974 that will never grow old. Mention Willie John McBride to rugby players from any era and there is reverence in their eyes and their words like loyal subjects talking about a leader they would go into battle for at the drop of a hat if the order came from him. To them he's their Gandhi, Mandela or Lincoln and still commands complete respect and awe when he walks into a room or opens his mouth.

A rugby icon and giant of a man it is strange to think that he started out in the field that he would dominate by making the numbers up in a house match at Ballymena Academy when he was 17. In a 2015 BBC NI documentary with Gavin Andrews he said: "They came to me and said, you're a big guy. If you play we'll have 15. I hadn't a clue about the game, but I was big and it wasn't a problem to me, I could shake people off."

Before that McBride was more interested in helping his mum and his siblings out on the family farm in Moneyglass close to Toomebridge in county Antrim after his dad had tragically died when Willie John was just four. He worked around the clock, early mornings, late nights but never on a Sunday and speaking to the Belfast Telegraph's Jonathan Bradley in a 2020 interview to mark his 80th birthday, McBride lavished the type of glowing praise on his mother that has come his way for decades.

At first a number eight, he became a second row with as much might as size playing briefly with Randalstown before moving to Ballymena and then came Ulster, Ireland and the Lions. For Ireland he made his debut in 1962, just four years on from playing his first ever game of rugby, and from early on those beside him knew he was a fearless competitor playing on for half an hour with a broken leg in his third cap versus France.

He would be influential in history making victories at home to South Africa and away to Australia, playing 63 times for Ireland up until 1975 when he scored his only try for the team in his final appearance at Lansdowne Road. Captain on 11 occasions, he received death threats for being an Ulsterman leading out Ireland but carried on.

That would have been some career all on its own but when you add his achievements with the Lions it takes Willie John into a different stratosphere. He toured FIVE times, his 70 appearances for the legendary four nation outfit is unlikely to ever be surpassed and his tally of 17 Test matches is more than anyone else too. His first tour was a four month long trek in 1962 to South Africa and as he recollected: "I went halfway across the world as a 21-year-old and as a little man from Moneyglass and came back more of a man. To have that experience, you can imagine how much you learn about yourself."

More tours followed, going to Australia and New Zealand in 1966 and back to South Africa in 1968 prior to a spectacular triumph in 1971 in the backyard of the All Blacks with McBride the pack leader. Up against New Zealand legend Colin Meads, the pair locked horns in a battle royale with neither giving a millimetre in a belter of a series. Canny coach Carwyn James wisely asked for McBride's tactical input during the tour and with a phenomenal all round unit the Lions won 2-1 with the final Test drawn, triumphing in New Zealand for the first time in history with Willie John declaring: "On previous tours we hoped we would win. This time we believed".

They took that same confidence to South Africa three years later in what is the most famous and celebrated Lions tour when with McBride appointed captain by fellow Northern Ireland man and coach Syd Millar, they embarked on the trip of their lives becoming invincible and immortal in the eyes of the sporting world. There was controversy that they went at all with South Africa under apartheid and excluded from competing in other sporting events such as the Olympic Games. Prime Minister Harold Wilson had asked them not to tour but the Lions went ahead and ended up with the support of the black population in Tests.

The undefeated Lions won the Test series 3-0 against the Springboks, won 21 out of 22 matches and drew the other one which was the final Test when most judges felt they were wrongly denied yet another victory. In the middle of it all McBride turned 34 and with his inspirational speeches as skipper and a burning desire to look after his team-mates, the respect the players already had for him exploded through the roof.

In previous Lions tours McBride had watched his buddies get roughed up on the pitch by 'bad boys', as he put it, and he was intent on making sure that would not happen in 1974 so he came up with the idea of the famous '99' call which was originally supposed to be '999' but the great man thought it would take too long to say with time being of the essence. Ahead of an encounter with Eastern Province, McBride heard that his players would be targeted so he outlined in a team meeting that they would be prepared. In a telling HSBC 2013 clip on YouTube McBride states: "I said to the guys if this happens we're all in it, all of us, we stand together, no handbag stuff, this will be for real and it will last seconds and we will teach them a lesson not to mess. If there's a call 99, we're all in." After 30 minutes it all kicked off with the pride of Lions charging at opponents and the message was out, McBride's men could not be intimidated which is exactly what he wanted.

The 99 call wasn't needed much after that though it did come back in the third Test when the Lions clinched the series with a 26-9 victory, having won 12-3 and 28-9 in the previous encounters. It should've been a 4-0 Test success but for some dubious refereeing during a 13-13 draw, though still McBride and his Lions returned home to Ireland, England, Scotland and Wales as heroes.

They played hard on the pitch and partied hard off it and tales of the latter are folklore such as one particular raucous night in Port Elizabeth when the Lions let their hair down and the story goes that amid the chaos and destruction the hotel manager raced into McBride's room screaming that his players were wrecking the hotel. Sitting on his bed in his underpants and smoking his pipe, Willie John said: "Are there many dead?" to which the manager retorted that he would call the police with McBride replying: "And tell me, these police of yours. Will there be many of them?" Lover of nature, McBride, living today in Ballyclare with darling wife Penny, would later coach Ireland, be a tour manager for the Lions, be amongst the first group inducted into the International Rugby Hall of Fame, be named 'Rugby Personality of the Century' by Rugby World in 2004, be presented with scores of other awards and be delighted to win the Pipe Smoker of the Year prize in 1998. A great grandfather, Willie John McBride will forever be the Godfather of the British and Irish Lions.

PHILLIP McCALLEN

MOTORCYCLING: ON HIS DAY
UNBEATABLE ON THE ROADS
B: 22/09/1963

Phillip McCallen was the boy who grew up on a farm to become one of road racing's most exciting and successful riders smashing records and entertaining crowds in equal measure. He famously competed on the edge in a daredevil style admitting that the drug of winning was addictive and at times he was unstoppable, such as at the North West 200 and Ulster Grand Prix, when on separate occasions he won FIVE times in one day, and at the Isle of Man TT stockpiling four victories in a week in a thrilling show of racing.

To some McCallen may have taken risks that even Evel Knievel would have winced at but he was also a highly accomplished rider who relished a duel when victory was on the line and worked his leathers off to grab it. He was a grafter from an early age and along with his brothers helped his mum Betty on their small family farm between Portadown and Tandragee after losing his dad Eric to Multiple Sclerosis when he was just nine. McCallen is rightly proud to this day that he did his bit delivering milk, bagging potatoes, plucking turkeys and other tasks to earn money, some of which he spent on a bicycle.

The racing bug bit and went into overdrive in his teens when he first jumped on a motorbike finding that with an engine life on the road was a whole lot faster, beating school pals Mark Farmer and Woolsey Coulter in impromptu races. While Farmer and Coulter decided on motorcycling careers, McCallen went to work nine to five in engineering and studied at night college to gain qualifications in the trade though all the while eating away at him was a desire to race against other riders and not just himself on the open road.

"My first race was at Aghadowey in 1983 and I got lost on the way there and missed practice, but still qualified for the final, my first time on a track," he recalled in the Belfast Telegraph. With support from the late Davy Wood, famed for being Joey Dunlop's manager, and his own investment in bikes by 1988 McCallen was challenging big names in the sport and winning Ulster and Irish titles. The following year a chance meeting with the legendary Dunlop led to Joey helping set Phillip up with the Honda team and from there McCallen turned into a winning machine.

In 1992 at the North West 200, he was on fire recording a record five wins in the 250cc race, both Superbike races, the Supersport 400cc and Supersport 600cc on a day of dominance that is still talked about decades on. The next year at the Ulster Grand Prix he bagged a treble in the 600cc, 250cc and Superbike races and went one better at the same meeting in 1994 before in 1996, four years after his North West five-timer, he left the fastest road circuit on the planet at Dundrod with a fistful of wins (two 250cc, two Superbikes and the 600cc) and a place in motorcycle folklore.

The victories kept coming including four in one week at the 1996 Isle of Man TT followed by three more on the iconic island circuit the next year on his way to 11 in total. There was also glory at the Macau Grand Prix but as well as daring victories there were serious injuries including two fractured skulls, numerous shoulder breaks, a broken pelvis, broken feet and a broken back. Time and time again the burning rubber and that competitive streak motivated him to return but he knew he could not go on forever. Injuries finally catching up with him and the death of a friend led to SuperMac seeing the end of the road. He said: "Simon Beck crashed in front of me in practice at the TT in 1999 and his death was the final link in a chain of events that told me it was time to retire."

McCallen was offered opportunities to ride again but steered clear becoming a straight talking media commentator on the sport he loves, building a successful business as a motorcycle dealer, with actor Daniel Day Lewis one of many satisfied customers, and spending time with his children and wife Manda who in her role as Miss North West 200 first met her husband to be the year he won five times at the prestigious race. It was meant to be, much like McCallen's compelling sporting journey.

SHIRLEY McCAY

HOCKEY: WORLD CUP FINALIST
WITH OVER 300 CAPS
B: 07/06/1988

From Drumquin in county Tyrone, Shirley McCay is Ireland's most capped hockey player, the most capped Irish woman in any sport ever and is one of the prime reasons why the Irish women's hockey team will finally take part in the Olympics next year. McCay is also a model of resilience and endeavour to go with her talent which has helped her play and stay at the highest level since 2007.

It would be fair to say that Drumquin, where McCay grew up on the family farm with parents Hazel and Robert and sister Lindsay, is not a hockey hotbed but encouraged by her Omagh Academy PE teacher Mary

Swann so started a career that would lead to Shirley amassing an astonishing 305 caps before the coronavirus pandemic lockdown put sport on hold.

McCay would prove to be instrumental in inspiring her school to a first ever all Ireland title as she swept through the underage ranks for Ulster and Ireland before becoming a senior international as a teenager making her debut against Canada. From there McCay, an outstanding player in defence or midfield, established herself in the side and was one of the first names on the team sheet with her drive matched by her consistency leading to a 100th Irish appearance in 2011 when she was overjoyed to be captain.

The same year illustrating her commitment, be it at club or international level, on the day she collected her journalism degree from Dublin Institute of Technology she drove through a busy city to join her team Old Alexandra mid-match to play against Pegasus in a league fixture. The caps continued to rack up but there was disappointment along the way as the Irish side missed out on Olympic qualification in 2008, 2012 and 2016, the last of which came in cruel fashion when Ireland lost to China on penalties for a place in Rio.

While dejected by that, McCay knew there was more to come from the Irish side, who had enjoyed success in the Women's FIH Hockey World League, and she was an influential figure as they stunned the sport to reach the final of the World Cup in 2018. In the London based tournament Shirley performed superbly in every game, scoring in a famous win over the USA, as underdogs Ireland claimed a silver medal losing the decider to the Netherlands. That remarkable run was followed in 2019 by Olympic qualification for the first time with McCay outstanding in the two legged play-off against Canada in Dublin when both ties ended scoreless before a dramatic penalties success saw Ireland progress with goalkeeper and McCay's fellow Northern Irish woman Ayeisha McFerran excelling in the shoot-out.

Working as a coach for the Ulster Hockey Union, McCay, who has won trophies at club level and played for Omagh Ladies, Randalstown, Ulster Elks, Old Alexandra, KHC Dragons in Belgium and Pegasus, has talked about retirement but she deserves her crack at the delayed Games in 2021 and a chance to increase her record number of appearances.

RHYS McCLENAGHAN

GYMNASTICS: GOLDEN BOY ON THE
POMMEL HORSE
B: 21/07/1999

He's the gifted young man from Newtownards who took the gymnastics world by storm beating the best in his burning desire to be the best and blazing a trail so hot that he has lit up a whole new level of possibilities for kids in Northern Ireland. Rhys McClenaghan, at 21, is the youngest of our 100 greatest sports stars but already is one of the most inspirational with what he has achieved and there is the promise of further deeds on the global stage. He wasn't out of his teens when he was breaking barriers and making history winning gold for his pommel horse routines in the 2018 European Championships and Commonwealth Games and in 2019 he became the first Irish gymnast to earn a medal at the World Championships.

In his early primary school years Rhys was a bundle of energy somersaulting in his house and climbing trees outside so mum Tracy took him to the Rathgael Gymnastics club in Bangor and it soon became apparent that the sport and her son were a natural fit. By the age of nine he was receiving support from the Mary Peters Trust with Lady Mary herself handing him a chocolate medal with his first monetary award.

As the years passed McClenaghan may have been teased by other children for his choice of sport but he was more bothered about improving his technique and his hard work bore fruit when, at 16, he produced an outstanding performance in the pommel horse to claim a bronze medal in the British Gymnastics Championships in Liverpool behind his heroes, World champion Max Whitlock and Olympic silver medalist Louis Smith. After a weekend to savour, McClenaghan was back in class at Regent House on the Monday morning but a month later he was making headlines again landing silver in the pommel horse at the Junior European Championships in a groundbreaking moment as the first Irish gymnast to win a European medal.

McClenaghan continued to raise his game and when he was victorious at the 2018 Commonwealth Games at the Gold Coast in Australia he had hit the big time, not just because of the gold medal but he overcame Olympic Champion, pommel horse god and his idol Whitlock in the process. The pair both scored 15.1 though with the Northern Ireland teenager's routine having a greater execution level he took the title and dedicated it to his proud mum and dad Danny for the sacrifices they had made for him when he was younger.

Rhys made a few of his own later in the year, training in his back garden after leaving Rathgael Gym when his trusted coach Luke Carson was made redundant by the club due to encountering what they called "significant financial challenges". It was a difficult and testing period for McClenaghan but he didn't show it in competition as he finished first at the artistic gymnastics World Cup and followed that up with a historic pommel horse performance at the 2018 European Championships in Glasgow, qualifying for the final which no Irish competitor had ever done before and then winning it with a then personal best score of 15.300 leaving Whitlock in his wake once more.

This was clearly a competitor not only with a stupendous talent but self belief to do extraordinary things and, by now training in Dublin, McClenaghan delivered another wonderful display to win bronze at the 2019 World Championships in Stuttgart. For all his impressive achievements to date there is a feeling that for the Newtownards gymnast the best may still be to come.

BILLY McCONNELL

HOCKEY: 1984 OLYMPIC MEDAL
WINNER
B: 19/04/1956

Billy McConnell, a native of Newry and intelligent and strong as a defender, won a bronze medal with the Great British hockey team in the

1984 Olympics in Los Angeles playing in every minute of every game. Lauded by his GB team-mates for his calming influence and commanding displays, he was also a big favourite when he played with Ireland.

He made his senior debut in green in 1979 and had what you would call a baptism of fire facing top nations Holland, Australia and New Zealand in early internationals. After showing he could cope in that company he became a key component in the Irish side and it wasn't long before the British selectors came calling, as was the norm then when a player from Northern Ireland showed class.

Along with the GB team he headed to America in 1984 with hopes of a medal, even though prior to the Games not many gave them hope of making an impression.

McConnell was central to Great Britain's success in the group games as they gained confidence with wins over Kenya, Canada, New Zealand and the Netherlands before a hard fought scoreless draw with Pakistan, who would go on to win the tournament. Following a narrow 1-0 semi-final loss to West Germany, GB claimed a nerve-wracking 3-2 victory over Australia to land a bronze with McConnell recalling that following a frantic finish there was sweet satisfaction at securing a medal. He said: "Australia entered the Games as the best team in the world but they were shattered after losing the semi-final to Pakistan. We played them two days later and after taking our chances had the lead in the closing stages. It was like the Alamo at the end with them all out attacking but we kept battling and got our reward. It was a dream to go to the Olympics in the first place and an unreal feeling to leave LA with a medal."

Billy was also a medalist at Champions Trophy tournaments for GB, for whom he was an ever present between 1982 and 1988 amassing 51 caps. Also a superb indoor player he made over 150 appearances for Ireland so it was no surprise when he was inducted into the Irish Hockey Association Hall of Fame in 2010. Reliable and consistent, McConnell could read the game brilliantly and from defence, and on occasion midfield, was an excellent distributor having a sixth sense for where to pass the ball. The Queen's graduate, who played for the University, Newry Olympic, Belfast YMCA and Holywood 87 at club level, moved into coaching where he has improved players and continually strived to enhance hockey across Ireland. Billy has not been shy in outlining his views on elements of the sport and when he says something it carries weight having been there, done it and brought home an Olympic medal.

OISIN McCONVILLE

GAELIC FOOTBALL: TOP ULSTER SCORER AND ARMAGH ALL-IRELAND HERO

B: 13/10/1975

Oisin McConville is the greatest scorer in Ulster GAA Championship history, hit the match defining goal in Armagh's only All-Ireland triumph and was instrumental in helping his hometown side Crossmaglen Rangers become an invincible outfit across the island. What makes McConville's achievements all the more remarkable is he scored many of those points and goals and inspired others around him when he was going through a crippling gambling addiction. Since first opening up about the issue and how it affected him so badly that he had suicidal thoughts, McConville, much like he was for club and county on the pitch, has become a standard bearer in Ireland in his bid to aid others, explaining the dangers of being addicted to gambling with his searingly honest testimony.

Speaking to Transworld Sport about the day Armagh beat Kerry at Croke Park to finally take Sam Maguire to the orchard county, McConville said: "In 2002 I got man of the match and for a lot of people that would have been their dreams coming true and for me it was in a sporting context. I was very pleased that a culmination of a lot of hard work had resulted in us winning the Holy Grail of an All-Ireland Championship but in the background of my life I was going through a gambling addiction which I had from 14 or 15 years of age. When we won that All-Ireland the first thing in my head was to get off the field to see if the horses that I'd backed the previous day had won. I lived for gaelic football but gambling had taken over my life at that stage. I was embarrassed and ashamed of what was going on but I couldn't arrest that problem until 2005 when I got help for it."

The goal that McConville scored in the 2002 decider for Joe Kernan's team against Kerry is the stuff of Armagh and Ulster GAA folklore not just because it turned the game in the favour of the team in orange but it also came after McConville had a first half penalty saved. The goal itself was a carefully orchestrated and clinically executed team effort which started with goalkeeper Benny Tierney and ended with McConville displaying immense composure, especially given what had gone before, to look up and pick his spot beating the Kerry goalkeeper Declan O'Keeffe, who had saved the earlier penalty. It was a classic finish by the ace marksman setting the county on their way to a 1-12 to 0-14 success and the Sam Maguire trophy for the first time.

From an early age McConville had an eye for goals and points and amassed an incredible record breaking 11-197 in the Ulster Championship winning seven Ulster titles in an extraordinary period for Armagh. McConville was prolific and in the first of those seven successes in 1999 against Down he put on a virtuoso performance scoring 2-7 in the final. The double All-Star winner was just as influential as Crossmaglen ruled Ireland in a way no Ulster club had done before with McConville part of 16 Armagh county title successes, including 13 in a row, 10 Ulster club titles and six All-Ireland club titles feeling the glory was not just important for the club but the community as a whole. Retiring in 2013, he did so as an Armagh legend and one of Ulster's best ever to play the game.

JENNA McCORKELL

FIGURE SKATING: RECORD
BREAKING CHAMPION ON THE ICE

B: 15/09/1986

Jenna McCorkell is Northern Ireland's greatest figure skater, with a record 11 British Championship successes to her name, two appearances at the Winter Olympics and international victories in a fiercely competitive sport. It all started at the Jet Centre in Coleraine when she was seven having been taken by a picture of a girl in a newspaper who had won an ice-skating competition, but when the venue in her home town closed down there was only one other ice-rink in Northern Ireland in east Belfast meaning early morning starts every day before school to keep her dreams on track.

That didn't stop her becoming the youngest skater picked for a Team GB squad when she was 10 and at 14 she competed at the World Junior Championships. As a teenager Jenna's alarm would ring at 4am and, along with her parents, she would make a 130 mile round trip going to practice at Dundonald Ice Bowl before returning to Coleraine for her lessons prior to taking the journey all over again after school to continue her training.

To further her career McCorkell left home at 15 to go to Coventry in England and by 2003 was competing in the World Senior Figure Skating Championships at the tender age of 16. Also that year she won the first of her British Championships, a competition she would dominate, triumphing every single time up until 2014, bar once when she had a broken leg. In UK figure skating terms the 11 victories is historic with only legendary British male skater Jack Page having the same number of titles.

A back injury ruled McCorkell out of the Winter Olympics in 2006 but she became the first woman from Northern Ireland to compete for Great Britain or Ireland at the Games in Vancouver in 2010 when selected for the GB team. While over the years many Northern Ireland athletes have gone to the summer Olympics, our winter Olympians have been few and far between with dedicated Jenna something of a pioneer going on to skate at the 2014 Games in Sochi in a sport where standards and demands, both physically and mentally, are sky high.

In the World Championships she finished 14th twice, was in the top 10 on two occasions in the European Championships and claimed seven international medals across the globe including gold at the Ondrej Nepela Memorial event and at the Ice Challenge in Graz. Having retired from the sport, McCorkell moved into business supplying the female skaters in television show Dancing on Ice with her own range of training clothing and she coaches around the world, though her heart lies at home with hopes that one day another Northern Ireland skater will compete at the Winter Olympics.

JIM McCOURT

BOXING: OLYMPIC MEDAL WINNER AND COMMONWEALTH CHAMP

B: 24/01/1944

It was at the 1964 Olympics in Tokyo that an American fighter who would later become known the world over as Smokin' Joe Frazier won heavyweight gold but at the time the people of Northern Ireland were more interested in Jim McCourt's journey. The west Belfast man captured bronze at lightweight for Ireland's only medal in Japan but it is impossible to escape the thought that the then 20-year-old ought to have been fighting for a different colour.

Boxing at the Immaculata club from an early age and inspired by previous Belfast Olympic medalists John McNally, John Caldwell and Freddie Gilroy plus Derry professional Billy 'Spider' Kelly, McCourt set off for the Far East determined to bring a special memento back for his boxing loving parents. The slick southpaw who loved to counter punch delivered convincing victories over Bun-am Suh from Korea, Pakistan's Ghulam Sarwar and Spaniard Domingo Barrera to reach the semi-finals and all this after hurting his left hand in his first fight.

With a medal secured the injury was so concerning that the Irish team wanted to pull him out of the competition but as McCourt told Sean McGoldrick in the compelling 'Punching Above their Weight: The Irish Olympic Boxing story' that close to tears he begged management to let him carry on. With his wish granted Jim put in another strong performance and was not alone in thinking he had beaten Velikton Barannikov only to be shocked when it was announced that the judges had scored the fight 3-2 in favour of the Soviet Union fighter.

The majority of those watching were thrown by the decision which remains one of the most controversial in Olympic boxing history and let's face it there have been a few since! Initially McCourt felt he had let people down back home by not reaching the final though nothing could be further from the truth as he discovered arriving in Belfast where a brass band was playing for him at the train station and he was carried shoulder high with fans across the city congratulating him on his bravery and outstanding boxing ability.

The following year in Dublin at the National Stadium the crowd were in raptures when McCourt proved a point defeating Poland's Olympic champion Jozef Grudzien who had beaten Barannikov in the Games final in Tokyo. There would be another bronze at the 1965 European Amateur Championships following a semi-final loss to that man Barannikov in Berlin but in 1966 gold was struck by McCourt at the Commonwealth Games in Jamaica for Northern Ireland at Light Welterweight. Rated as one of the finest amateur boxers of his generation, McCourt won seven Irish titles at three different weights and was Ireland's flag bearer at the 1968 Mexico Olympics going out early after falling ill in the stifling heat. When the legendary former undisputed world heavyweight champion Frazier came to Belfast in 2003 he met McCourt with the 1964 Olympics a topic of conversation.

SIR TONY McCOY

HORSE RACING: GALLOPED TO
GREATNESS AND TITLES GALORE
B: 04/05/1974

When Tony McCoy rode his first winner as a 17-year-old the flame was lit and with an obsessive desire and hunger for more he kept on winning and winning and winning moving him to a different level than the rest on his gallop to become the best jump jockey of all time. The man from Moneyglass was Champion jockey a staggering 20 years in a row until he retired in 2015, claiming more National Hunt winning rides than anyone else, passing the post first in every big race and driving himself on at every meeting whether it was a low key affair at Wetherby or the Cheltenham Festival.

Racing to his 4000th triumph in November 2013 aboard Mountain Tunes at Towcester to set yet another landmark, McCoy was almost 1500 victories ahead of Richard Johnson, who was second on the all-time winners list, while Richard Dunwoody, another brilliant Ulster jockey, had 1,874 successes in Britain and Ireland before he retired and Peter Scudamore, yet another great, ended his career with 1,692. McCoy's numbers are outrageous and all the more so because when he was breaking all these records he was also breaking virtually every bone in his body.

Asked about his injuries over the years he would rhyme them off so matter of factly it was like he was putting together a grocery list for the supermarket. "I broke my ankle, my leg, my arm, my wrist, my lower back, middle back, shoulder blades, collarbones, sternum, all my ribs, cheekbones," he would calmly say seeing it as part of the job, leaving those listening open-mouthed in amazement. He also punctured his lung and knocked his teeth out in the line of duty but no matter the pain or severity of a fall, McCoy was not for one hospital beds as he continually found the strength, mentally and physically, to get back on the horse sooner than seemed medically possible. No wonder Irish great Ruby Walsh used to declare "he is made of concrete" when his friend and rival would show superhero powers of recovery to make a lightning quick comeback to action after his latest break.

It was when passionate Arsenal supporter McCoy was nine that he fancied the idea of being a jockey and by the age of 12 he was certain what the future held for him, recalling: "I knew that was all I wanted to do. I was riding horses from I was very young and when I was 12 I used to go down to a friend of my dad's, the late Billy Rock, who was a trainer in Cullybackey. I'd go there every weekend during my summer holidays and I was with him from then until I left school. It was him that suggested I go to Jim Bolger's yard in Kilkenny. It was tough but for any young person who wants to be successful you should go and work for people that are high achievers and Jim Bolger was very much a high achiever."

It was with Flat trainer Bolger that McCoy rode his first winner at the age of 17, in 1992. He says: "I remember it well. It was in Thurles and on a horse called Legal Steps. After that I just wanted to get another and then another." That he did switching to National Hunt racing and moving to England where he claimed the conditional jockey championship with a record 74 winners in the 1994/1995 season before being crowned champion jockey for the first time the following campaign leading to Anthony Peter McCoy, or AP as he is known, dominating in unprecedented fashion.

The consistency of the county Antrim native was compelling as he won races day in day out, year in year out sometimes travelling hundreds of miles to land one more success even if the champion jockey title was in the bag. There was a notable double at the 1997 Cheltenham Festival when he won the Champion Hurdle on Make a Stand and the Gold Cup riding Mr Mulligan, with his 1000th victory coming a couple of years later prior to the 2001/2002 season when he achieved his greatest feat overtaking the record number of wins in a season by Sir Gordon Richards (269) with an astonishing 289.

Win number 2000 arrived in 2004 with number 3,000 in 2009 one year before a much celebrated and memorable Grand National success at his 15th attempt, riding Don't Push It, which in turn led to him being the first jockey to be voted BBC Sports Personality of the Year in 2010, and two years later he savoured his second Gold Cup victory on Synchronised. There were also more Champion Hurdle successes with Brave Inca in 2006 and Binocular in 2010 and a cracking victory on Best Mate in the 2002 King George VI Chase. It was in 2013 with beaming wife Chanelle watching in the stands with daughter Eve by her side and baby son Archie in her arms that McCoy brought up the 4000th win steering Mountain Tunes to race clear with a force of will that had served him so well for so long.

Taller than most jockeys, McCoy, as disciplined as a Kung Fu Master, created all this history on the back of a punishing schedule and a gruelling regime to keep his weight down. He tended to race around a stone and a half lighter than his natural weight hence the saunas and strictest of diets, which on occasion included licking the flavour from a crisp before throwing it away. In February 2015, after riding his 200th winner of the season at Newbury on Mr Mole, he shocked the sporting world when he announced that he was quitting a couple of months later but while the sport was going to miss its biggest name and biggest draw that early warning gave National Hunt Racing fans the opportunity to pay homage to its greatest star for the rest of the season. Ultimately he would finish with 4,358 winners - 10 of which were on the flat and 4,348 over jumps in Britain and Ireland - and while he wasn't victorious in his last race on Box Office at Sandown the reception he received afterwards was fit for a King. Knighted in 2016, the peerless, record breaking, history making Sir Anthony McCoy will always be King in the sport of Kings.

RAY McCULLOUGH

MOTORCYCLING: RACING'S QUIET MAN WITH A WINNING TOUCH
B: 03/07/1941

Mention the name Ray McCullough to bike fans of a certain vintage and their faces light up and they go weak at the knees thinking back to how he used to thrill them on Northern Ireland's roads. Joey Dunlop became the greatest road racer of them all but the original 'SuperMac' was the man before the man, adored by the racing public in the 1960s and 1970s, and the rider every other competitor wanted to beat. Such an unassuming, quiet guy you would never imagine he was the same person with the leathers and helmet on roaring into the distance at the speed of a bullet and not slowing down for anything or anyone.

When the Ulster Grand Prix hosted a round of the World Championship Grand Prix for the last time in 1971, the wet conditions were horrendous and during the 250cc race English rider Phil Read, who was in the running to win the World Championship, gestured towards McCullough to slow down but while Read retired from the race, Ray kept going and pulled off a stunning victory ahead of Jarno Saarinen and Dieter Braun.

There were plenty of other highlights for McCullough, not least when he was taking on Joey Dunlop in one of Northern Ireland's most compelling sporting rivalries. While Dunlop was part of the Armoy Armada, McCullough was the leader of the Dromara Destroyers with the racing fraternity fascinated by these two world class performers going wheel to wheel in what to many was the golden era of the sport. They would go at it hammer and tongs, trying to outdo each other on every corner and straight, watched on from every vantage point by thousands and while the fans and media revelled in the battles, behind the scenes after races, no matter who came out on top, the pair would have a chat about the drama that had gone before. To underline the respect when McCullough ended up in hospital after a crash, Dunlop, still wearing his leathers from that day's racing, was one of the first visitors he had.

Although not one for leaving Ireland to compete, when the big boys like Italian legend Giacomo Agostini came to town McCullough relished the challenge winning over 100 races on the road, succeeding with the smoothest of styles that made him the envy of other riders. Between 1971 and 1982 he was victorious seven times at the Ulster Grand Prix with three in the 250cc class and four in the 350cc, breaking lap records in both in 1976, and he also enjoyed multiple victories at the North West 200, including the only ever dead heat race at the event in 1977 when it was ruled that he and Tony Rutter crossed the line together.

A winner at the Southern 100 and one time King of Kirkistown, McCullough attracted onlookers enthralled by his speed from he was a teenager, like when he used to ride a Norton Dominator to work to Portadown so fast that people came out to see him take the big bends close to Gilford. After breaking down in his first two races at Tandragee and Cookstown in 1960, he won his third at the Temple and from there racing became his passion, even helping Queen's University Professor Gordon Blair with the development and design of two stroke engines for bikes. In his day McCullough was an artist on a bike and while he would never say that himself, the way he is greeted and treated like a superstar at parade laps and motorcycling functions around the country tells you how highly he is regarded.

WAYNE McCULLOUGH

BOXING: WORLD CHAMPION AND OLYMPIC HERO
B: 07/07/1970

Known as the 'Pocket Rocket', Shankill Road man Wayne McCullough was never afraid to take on the best, had a chin and heart that even the fiercest punchers couldn't break and he delivered one of the most masterly displays ever by a British or Irish boxer on foreign soil to win a world title.

In 1995 McCullough flew to Japan to fight WBC World bantamweight champion Yasuei Yakushiji in his Nagoya playground where the holder of the belt was king and considered unbeatable as he made a fifth defence. McCullough, though, and his legendary American coach Eddie Futch, who had trained Joe Frazier and Larry Holmes among others, had other ideas putting together a game plan that would see the Belfast man fulfil a dream he had been waiting for since he was 15.

It was the WBC World title McCullough craved more than any other and during an intense battle he did what Yakushiji felt was impossible as he outfought and out thought the home favourite over 12 gripping rounds with a barrage of well conceived jabs combined with uppercuts that forced the champion back for the majority of the contest. The Belfast man was sure he had done enough to win when the final bell sounded but thousands of miles from home with little support nothing is guaranteed and so when it went to a split decision there were fears justice had not been done. Thankfully and deservedly McCullough was given the nod and would hold on to the belt for another couple of years before embarking on a journey that took him to world title shots at super-bantamweight and featherweight against fighters that others in the sport would dare not tangle with.

As a kid McCullough would take anyone on, excelling in an impressive amateur career winning over 300 fights and being selected as a teenager to represent Ireland at the 1988 Olympics. If the Seoul Games are most remembered for Canadian sprinter Ben Johnson's cheating, McCullough, at 18 the youngest member of the team, was praised for his integrity in carrying the Irish flag at the opening ceremony. He would only win once but four years later at the Barcelona Olympics a more experienced and canny McCullough was victorious in his first four contests fighting through the pain barrier after suffering a broken cheekbone in his semi-final points success over Gwang-Sik Li from Korea.

Somehow in the bantamweight final McCullough, still hurt from his previous contest and with blood dripping from his eye, turned it into a classic just losing out on points to Cuban great Joel Casamayor. In between his Olympic appearances, in 1990 McCullough won flyweight gold for Northern Ireland at the Commonwealth Games in Auckland and bronze in the same division at the World Cup in Mumbai.

A year after his Olympic silver, the Pocket Rocket turned professional but rather than stay in the UK, he decided to base himself in Las Vegas having signed up with American manager Mat Tinley and with his career going in the right direction, thanks to multiple wins in double quick time, he was handed a savage test in Atlantic City in June 1994 facing tough Mexican and former World Champion Victor Rabanales. It was pure theatre in an all-action affair which McCullough won to set up his dream 13 months later, emerging as the first fighter from the UK or Ireland to win a belt in Japan.

What McCullough achieved in the Far East wasn't just monumental for boxing in Northern Ireland, inspiring a whole host of young pretenders like Carl Frampton, it was one of the greatest on the road wins in the sporting history of the country. There would be successful defences in Belfast and Dublin as McCullough's popularity grew with politicians, actors and performers, such as U2's Bono, singing his praises and in his home town he was never afraid to break down religious barriers visiting gyms and encouraging youngsters in Protestant and Catholic areas.

In later years McCullough would open up about how on the outside all appeared rosy in his life around that time but in reality he was suffering from severe depression and having suicidal thoughts. It was the bravest admission of all from a fighter renowned for showing guts and never being knocked down when he had the gloves on.

Moving up to super bantamweight he controversially lost a close call in 1997 to World Champion Daniel Zaragoza in a cracker and then went to World title war with heavy hitting knockout specialists Naseem Hameed at featherweight and Erik Morales at super bantamweight, being defeated on points on each occasion though he disputes the Hameed verdict. There was a comprehensive loss to Scott Harrison in 2003 for the World flyweight title and while many thought that would be that McCullough was determined not to wind down his career coming back to lose twice in 2005 in World super bantamweight clashes with Mexican Oscar Larios. Three years later he finally called it a day after 27 pro wins, seven losses and an eventful and distinguished career packing as much in as he could. Settled in the States with wife Cheryl and daughter Winona, McCullough is now a WBC peace and goodwill ambassador and a thoughtful coach passing on tips and advice he learnt becoming a true Northern Ireland boxing hero.

GRAEME McDOWELL

GOLF: US OPEN WINNER WITH WONDERFUL RYDER CUP PEDIGREE

B: 30/07/1979

It was in June 2010 on the 18th green at the iconic Pebble Beach Golf Club that Kenny McDowell uttered the words "You're some kid" as he hugged his son Graeme who moments before had become US Open Champion. It was a stunning victory built on patience, graft, craft and touches of class from a Portrush man who as a boy had told his mum Marion that he would be a professional golfer. Even mystic Graeme McDowell though would have struggled to predict what would happen at the 2010 US Open as he became only the second Northern Ireland player to win a major championship 63 years after Fred Daly had broken the duck and the first British player to triumph at the US Open since Tony Jacklin 40 years previously.

What McDowell also did was set off a remarkable chain of events inspiring countrymen Rory McIlroy and Darren Clarke to follow in his footsteps and claim major championships of their own.

McDowell had travelled to California in good spirits after playing beautifully to win the Welsh Open a couple of weeks before but he was still viewed as an outsider and that didn't change much after an opening level par 71. By the end of his second round, however, there was a buzz surrounding G-Mac whose 68 had given him a share of the lead only for him to fall three behind American Dustin Johnson after another 71 ahead of the final day with Tiger Woods, Ernie Els and Phil Mickelson also in the mix.

In the fourth round with conditions extremely difficult when the going got tough McDowell got going and as big names fell off the tightrope the Portrush native stayed on showing an inner calm amid the storm, refusing to let his dream be blown away.

Using his golf brain, honed as a kid when he and his brothers played at the Rathmore club until it was dark, the Ulsterman produced gutsy iron shots and clutch putts at key moments giving himself a one shot lead going to the last with Frenchman Gregory Havret now his nearest challenger. With the heat well and truly on "the Irishman wearing a cardigan", as one American commentator remarked, stayed cool and smart making a par for a 74 and an overall level par score which was good enough for the US Open Championship trophy and a warm embrace from his proud father as he joined Jack Nicklaus, Tom Watson, Tom Kite and Tiger Woods as winners of the tournament at Pebble Beach.

In the days that followed McDowell would appear on a late night American talk show and visit the set of his favourite TV programme Entourage before flying to Northern Ireland for a memorable homecoming at Rathmore Golf Club.

Life could have been so different for McDowell had he not opted to leave Queen's University, where he was studying engineering, to transfer to the University of Alabama at Birmingham and shine on the college golf scene. "I was at Queen's, took my engineering exams and passed everything and then took temporary withdrawal from the course. I felt America calling me. College golf was something I really, really fancied and I wanted a shot at it," he recalled.

In 2002 having smashed records set by Tiger Woods, McDowell won the Haskins Award, presented to the outstanding collegiate golfer in the United States, and in the same year he turned professional triumphing in that season's Volvo Scandinavian Masters on only his fourth start on the European Tour. Highs, including more tournament successes, and lows followed with the ever honest McDowell never afraid to tell reporters about where his game was at, leading to 2010 when it all came together in spectacular fashion.

Four months after the US Open, McDowell was the hero for the European Ryder Cup team when in the final singles match it all came down to him and American Hunter Mahan at Celtic Manor. The atmosphere was as tense as it was electric and while he may not be a big hitter, like so many of today's golfing stars, if you wanted a man to play for your life McDowell would be on the shortlist as he proved in nerve jangling circumstances sinking the ball from 15 foot on the 16th hole with what he described as "the best putt of my life" to take control of the match which he duly won on the next sparking crazy celebrations on the 17th green.

Later in the year with self-belief oozing out of him McDowell claimed the Andalucía Valderrama Masters and beat Tiger Woods in a thrilling play-off in the Chevron World Challenge. There have been tournament victories around the world, outstanding performances in the Ryder Cup and much reflection since such as in 2015 when he admitted that he had lost the "desire and urge to practice" after marrying his wife Kristin and having a daughter but he has continued to compete - and win - doing it his way and becoming a successful business owner in Florida in the process.

Fun to be around he is able to join in with jokes about his transatlantic accent in the knowledge he is Northern Irish born and bred and a hero all over the island, helping sick and under privileged children thanks to his G-Mac Foundation. He may reside in America but his roots remain important for McDowell who after being named the Belfast Telegraph Sports Star of the year in 2010 told me the inspiration behind his success. He said: "Growing up in Portrush it was inevitable that I would play golf, but without what my parents did for me I wouldn't have gone on to do so well. It's made me very proud to be able to help them and give them the things they deserve in life. We come from a very humble background, a very working class background and my mum and dad worked very hard to give me everything that I wanted as a kid. They have been unbelievably supportive throughout my career."

BARRY McGUIGAN

BOXING: WORLD CHAMPION
FIGHTER WHO UNITED THE
COUNTRY
B: 28/02/1961

The saying used to go "leave the fighting to McGuigan" and that's exactly what happened on June 8, 1985 when Northern Ireland stopped to watch

Barry box for the WBA featherweight championship at Loftus Road, home of Queen's Park Rangers, against Panamanian superstar Eusebio Pedroza. Around 27,000, most of them Irish, were inside the football stadium shouting themselves hoarse for McGuigan and 20 million television viewers were willing the Clones Cyclone to storm past the crafty champion, who had successfully defended his title an astonishing 19 times.

Before the gripping contest there wasn't a dry eye in the house when McGuigan's father Pat belted out Danny Boy after it took the challenger 12 minutes to find his way to the ring with expectant fans swarming round their hero like bees round honey. Once the first bell sounded the then 24-year-old went to work surging forward at Road Runner pace firing out combinations, determined not to give his taller and much more experienced opponent a second to think and with every punch that McGuigan landed the roars in the west London night air were so thunderous they drowned out the chimes of Big Ben. The volume levels shot through the sky when McGuigan knocked down Pedroza with a piercing right to the chin in the seventh and the din was constant as a blistering fight progressed with the great Panamanian putting up a brave display in the face of destiny.

McGuigan had never been beyond 10 rounds but had to battle on for 15 to become world champion with the crowd chanting "here we go" in the final seconds knowing their man was about to claim a dominant, unanimous and famous points victory. It was a magical night, with 75,000 turning out in Belfast and 200,000 in Dublin in welcome back parades for the new champ, and backed up by McGuigan three months later when he returned to the scene of so many memorable victories defending his belt in style at the King's Hall against unbeaten American Bernard Taylor. In 1985 there was no more popular sportsperson across Britain and Ireland than McGuigan, proved by him being voted BBC Sports Personality of the Year beating cricket legend Ian Botham into second place.

McGuigan grew up in the Republic of Ireland in Clones close to the Irish border but in the 1978 Commonwealth Games, aged just 17, fought and won bantamweight gold in Edmonton for Northern Ireland. In 1980 he competed for Ireland in the Moscow Olympics before turning professional with a decision to make in the middle of the Troubles as he outlined in an interview with RingTV.com stating: "The support of my hinterland was all in Northern Ireland. So I thought, when I go pro, I could do one of two things: I could go to Dublin and box out of the Boxing Union of Ireland, which wasn't an organization of any great notoriety. There wasn't great support for professional boxing. In the north, for some reason, there was great support for professional boxing. So I thought, well, I can move half-a-mile up the road and be in the north, live with my family, train in Belfast, be promoted in Belfast but I had to take out citizenship and that was a whole different ball game because we were right in the middle of the worst period of politics, or what is euphemistically called, 'The Troubles.' There was a lot of tension, murders. There were certain sections you couldn't go and I was an Irish guy, taking out British citizenship."

In 1981 McGuigan had his first professional fight, the same year as he wed childhood sweetheart Sandra in a union between Catholic and Protestant and as the years and fights went by it was commonplace that the two communities would come together to cheer on Barry in the ring, hence the phrase "leave the fighting to McGuigan" during a period when carnage and sorrow on both sides was all around Northern Ireland.

Managed by Barney Eastwood, he built up his reputation with victories in the Ulster Hall and also fought in the Lakeland Forum in Enniskillen, which is still talked about in county Fermanagh, before going to the King's Hall in Belfast where better opponents were despatched including Puerto Rico's Juan La Porte, setting him on his way to the night of his boxing life in London. Speaking to the Independent's Alan Hubbard in 2011 McGuigan, who was seen as the light amidst dark days, said: "I had broken all the rules, a Catholic who married a Protestant, an Irishman who fought for the British title. There were people dying of bullets and bombs and so much depression. It was very important for me that I didn't wear colours or play any anthems. I wore the UN flag of peace on my shorts and always felt a responsibility to help create a harmonious situation."

After beating Taylor there would be another winning defence against Danilo Cabrera in 1986 prior to later that year suffering from dehydration in the blazing heat of Las Vegas as he lost his title on points to American Steve Cruz in an outdoor fight. There would follow a split with Eastwood and a costly legal battle. McGuigan returned to the ring in 1988 winning three contests before losing his 35th and what turned out to be his final professional fight against Jim McDonnell in Manchester in 1989.

Articulate McGuigan, who has been inducted into boxing's Hall of Fame, would go on to be a respected pundit in the sport, a regular on television, work with Academy Award winner Daniel Day Lewis in the making of movie 'The Boxer' and manage fighters including Belfast hero and world champion Carl Frampton, before their parting in 2017. In McGuigan's life he has faced family tragedy with his brother Dermot committing suicide and his beloved 33-year-old daughter Danika dying of cancer in 2019 while in 1982 in one of his early pro fights he had a knock out win against a Nigerian called Young Ali, who collapsed in a coma and later died. That was a shattering experience for a young McGuigan who dedicated his World title success to Ali on the 1985 night at Loftus Road he brought the UK and all of Ireland to a standstill.

JIMMY McILROY

FOOTBALL: GRACEFUL WORLD CUP SUPERSTAR FOR NORTHERN IRELAND

B: 25/10/1931 - D: 20/08/2018

Jimmy McIlroy was a gem of a footballer, with the creative mind of Michelangelo and as selfless as your mum. It is no wonder that greats of the game like Danny Blanchflower and Stanley Matthews used to adore playing alongside him. Considered one of the finest players in Northern Ireland's history and a star turn in the iconic 1958 World Cup team, Burnley declared he was their greatest ever, when he sadly passed away in 2018, and with good reason given his majestic performances for the Turf Moor outfit over a 13 year period which included their last top flight league title win and their last FA Cup final appearance.

Called "Ulster's gift to Burnley" by former Blackpool and England hero Jimmy Armfield, McIlroy grew up in Lambeg in county Antrim honing his football skills on the street with a tennis ball, signing for Glentoran and playing in the same team as a young Billy Bingham. A year later in 1950, Burnley bought the inside forward for the best £7,000 they ever spent beginning a love affair between the two which would eventually lead to a stand in the stadium being named after Jimmy and him given the freedom of the town in 2008. McIlroy had it all; balance, intelligence, touch, passing ability, was stronger than defenders first thought, deceptively quick and scored goals...131 for Burnley in 497 appearances though it would have been more but for consistently setting up team-mates when he could have easily netted himself.

For Northern Ireland he started out in 1951 winning his 55th and final cap in 1965 with the nation's first World Cup finals in between when his elegance on the ball and effort off it, featuring in all five games in Sweden, helped the team earn a surprise quarter-final berth. Influential in the finals he was instrumental in getting there hitting the target in a famous 2-1 success over Italy in a glorious Windsor Park occasion when Northern Ireland qualified for their first major tournament. In total, McIlroy scored 10 times at international level, including three against England, one of which was in an historic 3-2 win at Wembley in 1957, and his understanding with captain Blanchflower was telepathic with the pair of them combining the same year for the first passing penalty on record in a 3-0 victory over Portugal with Danny passing from the spot rather than shooting for goal and Jimmy slotting in. The confused referee disallowed it with McIlroy successfully scoring the re-taken the kick. In later years Johan Cruyff and Jesper Olsen, Lionel Messi and Luis Suarez and Thierry Henry and Robert Pires would copy the McIlroy/Blanchflower move.

A hero at home, there was even more adulation for McIlroy at Burnley as he inspired the side to the 1960 First Division Championship (or Premier League as it is known now) with vital goals and vision and invention that carved open defences for team-mates. Like McIlroy, the Burnley team were a joy to watch lifting the club's second title, and first since 1921, by one point from Wolves and making it to the quarter-finals of the European Cup the year after when the maximum wage for footballers was abolished with McIlroy one of the first players to be paid £100 a week. Burnley finished second in the title race in 1962 and reached the FA Cup final, losing 3-1 to Blanchflower's Tottenham and while at different points Jimmy had chances to join Manchester United, whose manager Sir Matt Busby was a huge admirer, and Italian team Sampdoria he opted to stay loyal to Burnley, before in 1963 the football world was shocked when the Turf Moor club sold him to Stoke City for just £25,000, a decision and fee that left Burnley supporters raging and threatening protests.

For McIlroy it afforded him the opportunity to play with England's fabled winger Matthews and they led defenders a merry dance as Stoke won promotion to the First Division. While with Stoke, the Northern Ireland man rejected an offer from Argentine giants River Plate and in 1966 he became player-manager at Oldham leaving two and half years later before in 1970 taking charge of Bolton, after Nat Lofthouse left the role, exiting just two games in following a dispute over selling players. He went back to Burnley, became a journalist for the Blackburn Evening Telegraph and Burnley Express, played golf, painted and enjoyed spending cherished family time. As the years went by Jimmy didn't watch too much football though he once revealed he liked to see Eric Cantona in action with his grand-daughter telling him, much to his amusement, that back in the day he was as good as Manchester United's French star. No harm to Eric and his sardines and trawlers, but gentleman Jimmy, who was 86 when he died, oozed more class.

RORY McILROY

GOLF: MULTIPLE MAJOR WINNER
AND ALL-TIME GREAT
B: 04/05/1989

From the moment nine-year-old Rory McIlroy chipped a ball into a washing machine on Gerry Kelly's UTV chat show, the people of Northern Ireland have been talking about him and today they are not alone as the whole world discusses, debates and dissects the career of the Holywood star who is rated amongst the finest golfers of all time.

Watching McIlroy at his absolute best is akin to gazing at an eagle soaring through the sky; smooth, unstoppable and a thing of wonder. In Northern Ireland's pantheon of sporting greats, he's up there with George Best for God-given natural talent and when he's on top form there is no one better to watch with a golf club in hand. McIlroy also has achievement, with big time victories, to match his ability and you know he's not finished yet, not by a long iron.

At the time of writing, McIlroy has four major titles, winning them so early in his career that he joined icons Jack Nicklaus and Tiger Woods as the only players to have won that number by the time they were 25. It's some company to keep but from the day he picked up a plastic golf club as a toddler there has been a sense of fate in the story of McIlroy who, having already finished top of the leaderboard at The Open, US Open and US PGA tournaments, is destined to win the Masters one day and complete the majors set, joining an elite list of Grand Slam Champions Gene Sarazen, Ben Hogan, Gary Player, Nicklaus and Woods.

Mentored by long time coach Michael Bannon, even as a primary school pupil McIlroy's swing stood out with his mum Rosie and dad Gerry, a fine player himself, making sacrifices to give the Holywood Golf Club member as much opportunity as possible. Rosie worked night shifts in a factory and Gerry put in long hours as a cleaner and barman to fund the passion of their son, who has always appreciated the efforts, support and love of his parents.

Aged nine McIlroy, with a jaunty stride that would become a sign of his mood on the course, was victorious in the Under-10 World Championships in Florida and later he would be a winner at the Ulster Boys Championship. In 2005 at 16 he played in the British Masters in his first professional tournament, shot an 11 under par course record 61 at Royal Portrush in the North of the Ireland Championship and was the youngest player to win the West of Ireland Championship and the Irish Close Championship, both of which he successfully defended the next year. McIlroy's professional career has been so thrilling, outside of golf what he did as an amateur tends to be forgotten but it really was something else, claiming the European Amateur title in 2006 and in 2007 winning the silver medal as the top amateur at The Open in Carnoustie, where Dubliner Pádraig Harrington lifted the Claret Jug.

Seven years later McIlroy would be doing the same, dedicating the coveted prize to his mum and landing his dad £50,000 from a bet Gerry placed in 2004 that his son would win The Open within a decade, though there were many more memorable moments in between.

Turning professional at 18, Rory would be the youngest member to secure his European Tour card and after a few near misses clinched his first pro title at the Dubai Desert Classic in 2009 when his flowing, fluid swing had peers drooling about what the young man could do. Anything he wanted as it turned out, producing a blistering final round course record of 62 (-10) at Quail Hollow in 2010 to capture his first PGA tour title in America and be the youngest winner on that Tour since Woods.

Majestic McIlroy, it seemed, was primed for his first major title, and it looked sure to come at the 2011 Masters at Augusta where he played scintillating golf to be four shots clear at the end of the third round. Still in control with nine holes left, McIlroy's hopes started to crumble when he made a triple bogey on the 10th after a wildly wayward tee shot and following a bogey on 11 and double bogey on 12, when he four putted, his dream was shot to pieces as he finished with an eight over par 80 and in 15th place. It may have become known as the 'McIlroy meltdown' but several years later he would tell BBC NI sports presenter Stephen Watson "it was the most important day of my career" and that it was "a huge learning curve".

At the time what impressed most was how philosophical the then 21-year-old was, graciously congratulating winner Charl Schwartzel and saying he would have many more chances to win a major. The next one would be just two months later when he took an early lead at the US Open, stayed out in front and by the finish was so far ahead none of the other golfers could see him. McIlroy won by eight shots at Congressional for his first major triumph breaking records galore including at 22 being the youngest US Open champion since Bobby Jones in 1923 and the youngest major winner since Woods in 1997. Best of all it was on Father's Day and his dad was there to see it and hug his boy on the 18th green with more major celebrations coming in 2012 when McIlroy raced away with the PGA Championship at Kiawah Island to claim another staggering eight shot major victory, regaining the world number one spot he had held, and bettering the previous biggest winning margin in the tournament set by Nicklaus.

Wins across the globe continued and in 2014 there were two more major successes to savour with an immaculate Open victory for the big Manchester United supporter at Hoylake in Liverpool beating pals Sergio Garcia and Rickie Fowler in a thrilling last round.

There was also a phenomenal PGA Championship triumph in fading light at Valhalla with some final round shots from golfing heaven to finish one shot clear of Phil Mickelson and cap the year of his sporting life as he became the third youngest player to win four majors.

McIlroy wasn't just the best golfer around, he was one of the most admired men on the planet as millions hung on his every stroke and word with his interviews and press conferences sometimes as compelling as his drives. Over the years McIlroy has been candid in his thoughts about everything and anything from the Ryder Cup, which he once called an exhibition before falling in love with the event and emerging as a mighty force in Europe's successes, to President Trump, with whom he has played, and his own form once admitting he felt 'brain dead' on the course after a poor Open round.

He may be a multi-millionaire but to pals he has had since his days at Sullivan Upper school he remains a normal bloke and likes to do normal things, one of which cost him a chance to defend his Open title in 2015 when he suffered an injury playing football with his friends. Since his fourth major victory, McIlroy has triumphed in numerous tournaments including the World Golf Championship, Arnold Palmer Championship, Players Championship, the Irish Open, which he has been proud to host raising a shedload of money for good causes, and the FedEx Cup as well as lifting countless awards.

Now living in America with his wife Erica and their daughter Poppy Kennedy McIlroy, born on August 31, 2020, Rory was reminded how much he is revered at home at the 2019 Open at Royal Portrush when after a disappointing opening round of 79 he was roared all the way round the north coast course as he shot a stirring 65, missing the cut by one stroke. Devastated and emotional at not making the weekend, it was still a rewarding experience for the player given the meaningful connection with those who have felt part of his life since seeing him on the Kelly show and watched him grow into a swashbuckling superstar who constantly puts Northern Ireland on the world sporting map. Not just a favourite son in his own land, McIlroy is a global hero and should soar like an eagle for many years to come.

MICHAEL McKILLOP

ATHLETICS: PARALYMPIAN MIDDLE
DISTANCE MULTI-GOLD MEDALIST
B: 27/01/1990

In the Paralympics, Michael McKillop is the master of middle distance events with gold medals from Beijing, London and Rio to go with all his world records, world titles and an inspirational back story. Before he was three years of age McKillop was diagnosed with cerebral palsy, a condition which affects the right side of his body, he was then bullied at school, discovered at 15 that he had epilepsy and in more recent times has bravely opened up about his battle with mental health issues and through it all he has found the strength of character to become one of Northern Ireland's most decorated athletes.

Running talent was in the genes courtesy of dad Paddy and mum Catherine and it became evident when Michael won the Ulster Primary School Cross Country Championships that their boy could go far. Coached by his father it wasn't long before he did, winning the 800m, with what became a trademark sprint to the finish, at the age of 16 in the T37 category at the 2006 World Paralympic Championships, a year after representing Ireland at the European Championships. There was better ahead when in 2008 and still a teenager he raced home in the T37 800m in front of 90,000 spectators in the famous 'Bird's Nest' stadium in Beijing to land gold in the Paralympics, smashing the world record in the process. McKillop was invincible and incredibly wouldn't be beaten in 13 years of Paralympic competition up until 2019 as he dominated his 800m and 1500m events with further success at the 2011 World Championships before doing the double in electrifying style at the 2012 Olympics.

The Glengormley native knew the Games in England's capital would be special when in a pre-Olympics test event he was the first male athlete to set a new world record in the London stadium though they turned out to be even more memorable than he imagined. It was no surprise as he claimed two golds in his specialist distances but McKillop was left stunned when his mother presented him with his 1500m medal in an historic and emotional family moment. Arranged by Paralympics partner Procter & Gamble, for whom Catherine was an ambassador, it was the first time a mum had presented her son with a gold medal with the rest of the McKillop clan watching proudly from the stands. To complete a perfect Paralympics, McKillop was also given the prestigious Whang Youn Dai Achievement Award, chosen by the International Paralympic Committee (IPC) and presented to the athletes who exemplify the best spirit of the Games.

There would be more World Championship glory for passionate Arsenal fan McKillop in 2015 and 2017 and in between another gold in the 1500m at the Rio Paralympics in 2016, a year in which he sought professional help for mental health issues he had spoken about with sincerity and honesty. A brilliant motivational speaker, capable of inspiring with his words as well as deeds, McKillop has also competed in able bodied competition, becoming the first Paralympic athlete to represent Ireland at an IAAF cross country championships, and despite injuries in recent years this high class athlete is determined to have more Paralympic success before he calls it a day.

JIMMY McLARNIN

BOXING: WORE WORLD WELTERWEIGHT CROWN WITH DISTINCTION
B: 19/12/1907 - D: 28/10/2004

Jimmy McLarnin has often been referred to as Ireland's greatest fighter and across the Atlantic Ocean he is viewed as one of the finest welterweights in the history of the sport. All this and he was smart enough to get out of the game feeling healthy and satisfied with what he had achieved at a time when too many of his peers couldn't leave it alone.

McLarnin, who in 2004 died at the grand old age of 96 after a happy life with his wife Lillian and their four children, only lived in Northern Ireland for his first three years but the legendary Hillsborough-born boxer was always true to his Irish roots. One of 12 children, Jimmy emigrated with his family to Vancouver in Canada and as a 10 year-old boy he found he could use his fists when other kids attempted to take over the street corner where he sold newspapers.

After turning professional at 16, under the wing of coach and mentor Charles 'Pop' Foster, he started making waves in Canada but he wasn't making enough money so opted to try his hand in the USA and while he lost his first title fight, aged 20, to world lightweight champion Sammy Mandell in New York in 1928, the decision was vindicated as he became one of the most respected boxers in the country, avenging the defeat to Mandell twice in non-title fights and beating a host of other highly rated stars to get another shot at a world championship belt in 1933. This time McLarnin would be victorious knocking out Young Corbett III in two minutes 37 seconds to become welterweight champion of the world leading to a thrilling trilogy in front of massive crowds against Barney Ross who controversially won two of the fights with McLarnin successful in the middle contest.

The Hillsborough native, nicknamed 'the Belfast Spider' and 'Babyface', loved mixing it with the best around battling with world champions from various weight classes and was a fearsome puncher prior to hand injuries seeing him transform to a more tactical operator, but having made his money and been clever with business investments he retired at 29 in 1936, though not before overcoming revered duo Tony Canzoneri and Lou Ambers in his final two fights.

He departed, according to the International Boxing Hall of Fame to which he was inducted in 1991, with a record of 62 wins, 11 defeats, three draws and one no decision. The two-time welterweight world champion rejected several offers to return preferring to focus on family, acting and business interests. Always one for a quip to leave people smiling, McLarnin once said: "Boxing's a very hazardous business and I'd always felt that anybody who goes into it for fun has to be out of their entire cotton pickin' mind but then I started to make money and when I was 19 I had $100,000 in the bank, so all of a sudden I realised boxing was for me!"

JOHN MCNALLY

BOXING: FIRST OLYMPIC MEDAL WINNER IN THE RING ON THE ISLAND

B: 03/11/1932

John McNally will forever be known as the first Irish boxer to bring home an Olympic medal, claiming a silver at bantamweight at the 1952 Games with many neutral observers believing it ought to have been gold. What McNally achieved in Helsinki set Ireland on a magnificent medal winning trail in the ring and taking Northern Ireland fighters alone into account at least one has made it on to the Olympic rostrum in virtually every decade since the Belfast man showed the way.

Just 19, McNally returned a hero from the Games and while he never played on it, it was a phenomenal achievement for a teenager who in his early days trained in the Immaculata club before moving on to St Mary's and winning an Ulster juvenile title. Pushing on to secure Irish honours back then was complicated by schoolwork as McNally recalled in Barry Flynn's fascinating Legends of Irish Boxing book. "I was at the time a pupil at the Christian Brothers' School in Hardinge Street but, due to my examinations, I was not permitted by the Brothers to go to Dublin to compete for the Irish title. That really upset me inside but I did learn the lesson in hindsight that there was more to life than boxing," he said.

McNally would enjoy success in the Irish juniors at flyweight prior to earning the Irish bantamweight senior prize and a place in the Olympics. In Helsinki McNally was imposing and inspired defeating Alejandro Ortuoste from the Philippines, European champion Vincenzo Dall'Osso from Italy and South Korea's Kang Joon-Ho to reach the final, where he controversially lost on a split decision to Finland's home town favourite Pentti Hamalainen.

Newspaper journalists reporting on the fight were left perplexed feeling the Northern Irishman had been robbed by the decision, one that I asked McNally about in 2012 to which he replied: "People have been asking me that for 60 years. I'd rather not say," telling you exactly why he is known as Gentleman John.

In 1953 McNally followed up his Olympic silver with bronze in the European Championships and in the same year won the Golden Gloves Championships while representing his continent, turning professional in 1954 though the ruthless nature of the pro game wasn't for him and he opted out after 25 fights. Without gloves John used his hands to entertain in another way playing the banjo in popular folk group 'The Freemen', doing it with style.

TERENCE 'SAMBO' MCNAUGHTON

HURLING: HALL OF FAME
SAFFRON STAR
B: 18/09/1964

There's a cracking Christmas story from years ago about Antrim and Ulster hurling legend Sambo McNaughton turning up to hand out selection boxes to children at the St Paul's GAA club in Belfast with excitement levels high as he entered the room. As Sambo dished the presents out Santa style to the kids, rather than rip open the cardboard to get their hands and lips around the various chocolate bars, there was a mad clamour for pens and pencils so that the little ones could request their guest to sign his autograph on their boxes. That's hero status, which over the years has been well earned for all that he has done for his sport in the province. Had it been the mobile phone era, the big man would have ended up being included in more selfies than Justin Bieber!

McNaughton grew up on a housing estate close to Cushendall and started playing at under-12 level and in a typically open interview with GAA.ie he talks about how hurling, one of the toughest sports in the world to master, helped him as a boy, declaring: "I was born with a very bad speech impediment and found it hard to communicate but the one thing I was good at and didn't have to speak in was hurling."

By the age of 16 McNaughton was playing senior hurling for his club Ruairí Óg Cushendall going on to win numerous Antrim and Ulster titles with them and emerging as a marvellous all round player who could be as influential in defence or attack. He had a passion for the game that was infectious but also obsessional to a point where he would later admit he put hurling before his family at times. With Antrim he won two All-Ireland B titles in 1981 and 1982 becoming as big and as dominant as a skyscraper for his home county. Aggressive as he was skilful, Terence was one of the major reasons why the Saffrons reached the 1989 All-Ireland final, creating a mighty shock in a semi-final success over Offaly under the capable management of Jim Nelson. Putting that achievement into context, the only other time a team from the north made it to an All-Ireland hurling decider was in 1943 when Antrim were hammered by Cork.

Unfortunately by the end of his career, McNaughton would be labelled one of the greatest players never to win the Liam MacCarthy Cup with his county losing to Tipperary at Croke Park in the 1989 final as they let all the pre-game hype and attention get to them. Straight talking McNaughton told Anthony Daly on the Irish Examiner GAA podcast: "We forgot about the match, we were carried away."

In 1991, the year McNaughton won an All-Star, Antrim lost in a titanic contest against Kilkenny in the semi-final with Sambo feeling had they reached the final then things would have been different, though he is proud that for the guts of a decade Antrim competed at top level in the league with the best in Ireland. Selected at left wing-back on a special hurling Stars of the 1980s team, McNaughton was inducted into the GAA Museum's Hall of Fame in 2019 long after an inter-county senior career that spanned 1980 to 1997 when fans would turn up just to watch this all-action hero, easily recognisable due to his lack of hair. He went into coaching, including a spell in charge of Antrim, and remains as passionate about hurling as ever and is loved in his county just as much.

PETER McPARLAND

FOOTBALL: NORTHERN IRELAND'S
FINEST WORLD CUP GOAL GETTER
AND FA CUP HERO
B: 25/04/1934

Northern Ireland reaching the quarter-finals of the World Cup may seem like some fanciful notion but go back to 1958 and the sensational scoring ability of Peter McParland made the unthinkable happen. Aston Villa fans will tell you the Newry native did that consistently for them and the history books confirm it with his goals in FA Cup and League Cup finals securing indelible triumphs for the midlands club during a phenomenal career that hit its peak in the World Cup in Sweden where in the early stages of the tournament he was being lauded as much as a 17-year-old Brazilian boy called Pele.

Starting out in the League of Ireland with Dundalk, McParland scored twice on his debut at 16 in 1950 and soon had a trial at Leeds United but after just a day at Elland Road homesickness hit him hard and he returned to continue playing for Dundalk where club secretary Sam Prole landed him a job as an apprentice coppersmith and put him on a diet of steaks to bulk him up. It worked a treat as McParland enjoyed the food and became a force to be reckoned with leading to Aston Villa snapping up the tall winger in 1952.

It didn't take long for McParland to become a firm favourite in England due to his ability to race past big name defenders and score with his feet and head. Come 1957 he was the most talked about man in football when he played the defining role in the FA Cup final against Matt Busby's Manchester United who had won the title that season and were odds on to do the double.

In one of the most controversial incidents in FA Cup history just six minutes into the Wembley decider McParland had a header saved by goalkeeper Ray Wood but with his momentum taking him forward he ended up shoulder charging the United number one. While that type of challenge was deemed fair in those days it left Wood with a broken cheekbone and he had to be carried off. McParland's Northern Ireland team-mate Jackie Blanchflower went in goal for the league champions who were down to 10 men and effectively stayed that way even though Wood would later come on and play outfield at different times during the match! As for McParland he was hurt too but determined to play on because his parents had travelled over to see the game and later would say his challenge on Wood was a case of self-preservation. Booed every time he touched the ball by infuriated United supporters, McParland, who had inspired Villa to the final with his goals, scored one of the greatest diving headers ever witnessed at the stadium and followed that up with a blistering volley to earn his side a stunning 2-1 success. When McParland, paid £71 in bonus money for winning the Cup, was next back at Villa's training ground he had scores of nasty letters waiting for him including one where a stranger was threatening to kill him.

The following year McParland only received letters of praise after his exhilarating performances for Northern Ireland, who excelled in the country's first experience of a major tournament. Making an unforgettable entrance to the international scene 19-year-old McParland netted on his debut against Wales in 1954 after just 30 seconds and added another in the same game yet incredibly did not score again at that level until the World Cup in 1958 when he hit the target in a 3-1 defeat to Argentina and grabbed a priceless double in a 2-2 draw with World Cup holders West Germany which took Peter Doherty's side into a group play-off against Czechoslovakia.

McParland was immense in the knockout encounter inspiring Northern Ireland to come from behind with an equaliser before the break and then snatching a winner in extra-time. The team may have lost to France in the last eight but McParland, who played every minute in Sweden, and his pals returned home as superstars.

When the Northern Ireland squad for the Euro 2016 finals was named, Peter was a special guest of the Irish FA and his legendary sense of humour was to the fore when recalling 1958, declaring: "Pele became the golden boy of football in that tournament. He scored six goals. I mustn't have done too badly because I got five!" McParland is Northern Ireland's highest scorer in the World Cup finals and in total netted 10 goals in 34 games for Northern Ireland with his captain Danny Blanchflower insisting: "Peter's inspirational play helped to put us on the world map. He used his brains to save his legs. He had a wonderful flair of turning defence into attack with one simple pass. Peter was the finest ever inside forward of British football."

Three years after Sweden came another epic experience when he scored the winner for Villa in their two legged League Cup triumph over Rotherham in 1961. In an interview with the Sunday Life he said: "Someone asked me about the game when I was at the Tower of London ahead of the 2020 League Cup Final that Villa were in. There is no known film of the game, so I told them that for my goal I beat three men, nutmegged the centre-half, ran round the goalkeeper and knocked it into the net. Then I came clean and told them it was a porkie pie and was, in fact, a tap-in from about two feet. I was the first player to score in an FA Cup Final and a League Cup Final which was really nice."

Leaving Villa as a club legend in 1962, McParland would play for Wolves, Plymouth, Worcester City, Toronto Inter-Roma in Canada, Peterborough, Atlanta Chiefs in America, where he won the title, and Glentoran, who he also managed to championship success. He would also have colourful spells as national coach in Cyprus, Kuwait, Hong Kong and Libya where his time ended because of a decision made by one of the world's most infamous dictators. McParland told the Daily Mail: "I went to Libya, Colonel Gaddafi's country. Gaddafi wasn't liked but the players said they had a good life as long as they didn't say or think anything. Gaddafi visited once. A whole gang of people cheered him and one of the players said: 'They're being paid to cheer him!' It ended one year at Christmas. The secretary rang me up and said 'Gaddafi's only gone and banned football!'"

Few others could stop McParland, who after finishing with the game settled in Bournemouth, worked in property, enjoyed travelling around the globe, played a lot of golf and to this day can tell stories like few others.

JACKIE McWILLIAMS

HOCKEY: OLYMPIC GAMES MEDAL
WINNING STAR
B: 18/02/1964

Jackie McWilliams is the only female hockey player from Northern Ireland to have won an Olympic medal which was the highlight of a long and distinguished playing career at club and international level. Games glory for McWilliams came in Barcelona in 1992 as part of the Great Britain team having previously played for Ireland in the days when it was possible to switch.

To put the influence of McWilliams into context, in every game that she started in the Olympics in Spain, the GB team were victorious and in those matches she didn't start they lost. Jackie was a late substitute as the British were defeated by the Netherlands in their opening tie but she was the one change to the line-up in the next group encounter against South Korea, coming in to strengthen the defence in a vital 3-1 victory. In the final group game McWilliams showed her resilience and ability as GB overcame New Zealand 3-2 in the "hottest weather conditions" she had ever played in but she didn't figure in the semi-final loss to Germany leading to a win or bust match versus South Korea with the bronze at stake.

The Great British women's hockey team had never won a medal at the Olympics so the 1992 play-off was huge in their history as the Randalstown player returned to the team, playing brilliantly in a thrilling contest which GB won 4-3 after extra time sparking jubilant scenes. Jackie told me: "At the time making history didn't register, initially it was pure relief and then the joy was unbelievable that we had accomplished something special together. It was such a good feeling inside and out. I had only joined the GB system in 1989 and being a Northern Ireland girl I had to try to get used to different methods and they had to get used to me and my sense of humour but we gelled so well and I always loved being part of a team in sport and in life generally and standing on the podium it felt like my heart was jumping out of my chest."

In men's hockey Stephen Martin, Jimmy Kirkwood and Billy McConnell brought Olympic medals home to Northern Ireland in the 1980s but for McWilliams to be the first lady to do it filled her with enormous pride and although she never saw it this way, the Games success placed her on a different plane earning her legendary status in her homeland.

In all Jackie played 64 times for Ireland and made 34 appearances for Great Britain in an era when internationals were nowhere near as frequent as they are now while at club level she was the inspiration behind many a trophy for Randalstown, starting out at 13 years of age and enjoying "fantastic years" before joining Ballymena where she continued to play and influence those around her until she retired at 47. Hockey ran in the family because the Ballymena Primary School teacher and Ulster great, who went on to become a respected coach, was delighted when her nephews Paul and Mark Gleghorne represented Ireland and Great Britain respectively at hockey in the Olympics, though unlike their awesome aunt they didn't win a medal.

JEREMY McWILLIAMS

MOTORCYCLING: MOTO GP VICTOR
AND VETERAN NORTH WEST
WINNER

B: 04/04/1964

Jeremy McWilliams is the last man from Northern Ireland to win a race in the Moto GP Championship, which is the Champions League of motorcycling, and in 2019, at the ripe old age of 55, he became the oldest rider to come home first at the North West 200. Six years earlier, at 49, he topped the podium for the first time on the famous coast roads showing the keen racing brain that was always a hallmark of his riding on Grand Prix circuits around the globe.

McWilliams didn't enter the sport until relatively late with his wife Jill recalling in an interview that he started at 23 and had to borrow a set of leathers for his first race. McWilliams had a good job in electronics with Chubb doing security work but soon what began as a hobby became more serious when the Glengormley man found he could win on short circuits in Northern Ireland. From being a local star, McWilliams was taking on the best in the world when he was racing in the 500c races in the Moto GP Championship from 1993 and doing it on a machine that simply wasn't as powerful or quick as others.

Even so he would consistently be in the points and his tallies improved when he switched to 250cc landing podium places before going back to the 500cc class and producing a classy ride from 15th on the grid to finish third at the 2000 British Grand Prix at Donington Park with legendary Italian Valentino Rossi victorious. Leading on his Aprilia at one stage it was an emotional race for Jeremy who dedicated his place on the rostrum to the great Joey Dunlop, whose funeral had taken place a couple of days before.

The first Grand Prix win of Jeremy's career would come the next year on the renowned Assen circuit in Holland where he dominated the 250cc race after taking an early lead. It was a highly professional job from the Northern Ireland man as he used his experience to make the best of a drying track to romp home becoming the first British rider to win a GP since the 1980s. While 2001 brought the stand out moment in his time in Moto GP, McWilliams believes it wasn't his best race with a contender for that the day he finished second behind Japan's Tetsuya Harado after beating Rossi and fellow Italian World Champion Loris Capirossi in a titanic battle in Germany in 1998.

McWilliams was a man who could mix it with the best and while he continued to compete in Moto GP he also raced in the British Superbikes Championship, won the 2010 British Harley-Davidson XR1200 Trophy and entered the North West for the first time in 2012 winning his first race there in 2013 in the Supertwin event. For some that might have scratched the itch but not veteran McWilliams who still has the enthusiasm of a kid and the riding intelligence of a seasoned campaigner, captured by his fabulous 2019 North West victory riding for a team led by another exceptional racer Ryan Farquhar.

There have been broken bones along the way and half a finger amputated, but the remarkable McWilliams is still going strong and in the middle of his busy schedule he found time to act in a movie with Scarlett Johansson called Under the Skin. Maybe Hollywood should think of making a film about Jeremy's wonderful life.

KRIS MEEKE

RALLYING: WORLD STAR WITH GLOBAL WINS TO HIS NAME

B: 02/07/1979

When Dungannon's Kris Meeke was victorious in Rally Argentina in 2015 he became the first British driver to win in the World Rally Championship for 13 years and what made his triumph even more special was he emulated his mentor, the late Colin McRae, who was first in 2002. Meeke produced a drive of authority to finish ahead of his Citroen team-mate Mads Ostberg by 18.1 seconds and then dedicated his success to the legendary McRae, who before being killed in a helicopter crash in 2007 had supported the county Tyrone native at the beginning of his career.

Meeke would win four more rounds in the World Rally Championship (WRC) over the course of 2016 and 2017 with an attacking driving style that thrilled spectators and was admired by peers. Rallying is well known for being an unpredictable white knuckle ride but the daring Meeke was something else in entertainment terms at the highest level of the sport which is why so many fans were disappointed in early 2020 when he said it was unlikely he would be competing again full-time in the WRC.

After winning Rally de Portugal, along with Irish co-driver Paul Nagle in an early round of the 2016 series, a couple of months later Meeke produced a record breaking drive for victory in Rally Finland when he set a pace that was the quickest in the history of a World Rally Championship round. Rally Finland is akin to the Masters in golf or Wimbledon in tennis or Monaco in Formula One, it's the race everyone wants to win and even McRae and Richard Burns, Britain's two World Rally Champions, never managed it but Meeke's average speed record of 126.60kph saw him not only succeed on the famous 'Grand Prix of Gravel' but become the first British driver to take the race and only the sixth non-Nordic winner in its 65-year history.

That night in his hotel room he happily gazed at one of the most coveted trophies in sport and further WRC victories would come in 2017 at the Mexico Rally and Rally Catalunya in Spain where he was hugged at the finish by wife Danielle and young daughters Isabella and Alexandra.

What makes Meeke's success somewhat different to many of his contemporaries is that initially he had designs on design where cars were concerned. After gaining a degree in Mechanical Engineering from Queen's University in Belfast, Kris worked at the Ford World Rally Team, M-Sport, as a Computer Aided Designer. He had known rallying all his life with dad Sydney revered in the industry for his preparation of cars for top names, including multiple Irish Tarmac champion Bertie Fisher, but wanted to go down his own path before in 2000 he entered a competition in Motorsport News, in conjunction with Peugeot UK, to find a young rally star and won it hands down.

Opportunities came Meeke's way in rallies across the UK and he took them leading to McRae supporting his development in 2002 and Kris winning the British Junior title. In 2005 he finished third overall in the Junior World Rally Championship winning the Monte Carlo Rally in the process and while ups and downs followed, Meeke's class was evident as he claimed the prestigious Intercontinental Rally Challenge title with Peugeot in 2009. There were more impressive performances for a factory backed Mini team in their first season in WRC in 2011 with Citroen coming calling in 2014 to offer him a full WRC season with that first historic victory in Argentina and other big wins not far away. Should he never race in the WRC again, thrill seeker Kris, who enjoys snowboarding and skiing and has ridden his bike on some of the Tour de France mountain stages, can recall his five global victories with relish and know long after the great Paddy Hopkirk he put Northern Ireland rallying on the world map again.

SYD MILLAR

RUGBY: WORLD CLASS PROP AND
LIONS STAR
B: 23/05/1934

When John Sydney Millar was throwing a rugby ball about in Ballymena as a boy he never dreamed about being awarded the Légion d'Honneur from the French government, becoming one of the shrewdest coaches in rugby or one of the sport's finest administrators. It's to his eternal credit that he achieved all of the above and so much more after he made his childhood dreams come true starring for Ballymena, Ulster, Ireland and the British and Irish Lions.

There will be many who will look up to 'Syd' for the sterling and defining work he did after he stopped playing but this is a man who should also be on a pedestal for his outstanding efforts on the pitch. There was a period when Millar, equally adept on either side of the scrum, was rated as the best prop on the planet and in 2016 Rugby World listed him in their top 10 loose head props of all time which would have brought a smile to Syd's face knowing he started playing as an out-half. During a fantastic career that saw him win 37 Ireland caps and go on three Lions tours he maintained a ball carrying ability he learnt as a schoolboy number 10 and in the front row, relishing the set piece, was ranked amongst the most technically astute props to ever squeeze into a shirt.

The oldest of six children and educated at Ballymena Academy he first played for Ballymena Rugby Club in 1950 helping them become a senior team and then proving to be a major asset in the pack he earned Ulster honours in 1957 and a first Ireland cap in 1958. Strong, physically and mentally, there was a spell when Millar was out of the Irish team but he fought to regain his place and ended up playing in green until 1970, finishing with victory over a Welsh side chasing a Grand Slam.

Millar toured with the Lions as a player on three occasions, starting in 1959 in Australia and New Zealand prior to the 1962 trip to South Africa. Left out in 1964, he roared back to Lions duty at the age of 34 in 1968 for another journey to face the Springboks, proudly captaining the team on two occasions. Syd returned to South Africa in 1974 as coach of the greatest Lions side, making fellow Ballymena man Willie John McBride the captain and going through the entire tour unbeaten, winning a remarkable 21 of their 22 matches.

Millar also coached Ireland between 1973 and 1975 guiding the team to Five Nations glory in 1974 and in 1980 he was team manager for the Lions in South Africa. That same year, having never lost his love of playing, at 45 years of age he won the McCambley Cup with Ballymena Sixths!

President of Ulster Rugby and the IRFU and chairman of the International Rugby Board, Millar has held the loftiest of positions and amongst the vast number of personal awards bestowed on him he has been inducted into the IRB Hall of Fame and awarded the Légion d'Honneur, France's highest honour, choosing to have the ceremony at Ballymena Rugby Club. Without question Millar's has been a life well lived in rugby contributing more to the sport than most and being a high class player to boot.

RINTY MONAGHAN

BOXING: CHAMPION OF THE WORLD BELFAST HERO

B: 21/08/1918 - D: 03/03/1984

John Joseph Monaghan was his name but everyone knew him as Rinty, the undisputed flyweight boxing champion of the world who could sing just as well as he could fight. Rinty Monaghan was Belfast's first boxing world champion inspiring many born in the city to follow in his illustrious footsteps.

The boy from the docks, always with a twinkle in his eye, had an extraordinary life and while he is an iconic figure in Northern Ireland sport, the Wartime NI website tells how he was also an entertainer of note touring western Europe alongside the likes of Gracie Fields, Vera Lynn and

George Formby to lift the spirits of the troops when the second World War was raging. By then he had already built up a reputation in the ring having started boxing on the streets as a boy with fish suppers the prize for winning rather than world title belts. As for that nickname, the caring child in him used to bring home stray dogs and he adored Rin Tin Tin, a much loved dog in the movies, leading to his grandmother calling him Rinty, which stuck for the rest of his days.

From his first 'professional' fight as a 14-year-old, the public lapped up Monaghan who after boxing matches used to belt out numbers such as his trademark tune 'When Irish Eyes are Smiling' to the packed houses earning him extra money from the spectators who would throw coins into the ring. In those early days Rinty dutifully took the cash home to his parents.

With his busy, fiery, all action style Monaghan looked set for titles galore until a young hard-hitting Glaswegian Jackie Paterson knocked him out at the Oval, home of Glentoran Football Club, in 1938. That kicked off a fierce rivalry though it was interrupted due to the War with Rinty serving in the Royal Navy before being recruited to the Entertainments National Service Association performing song and dance routines for soldiers, including in Normandy shortly after D-Day. He formed a band after the War, did comic turns and even some acting as his popularity grew around the country but he was not finished with the fight game – in fact he was only really starting as he claimed the Ulster Flyweight title in 1945 and the following year gained revenge against champion Paterson, stopping him in the seventh round in a non-title fight in Belfast.

In October 1947, after impressive wins over England's Terry Allen and French pin-up Emile Famechon, Monaghan took on and overcame Salvador Dado Marino from Hawaii on points in Harringay stadium for the vacant world flyweight title though unfortunately for Rinty the bout was not recognised by the British Board after Paterson, forced out of a battle with Marino a few months before due to weight problems, won a High Court injunction preventing them from recognising the fight's status.

You can imagine the hysteria that greeted Monaghan and Paterson five months later in March 1948 when they both made their way to the King's Hall ring for one of the most anticipated world title fights ever in Northern Ireland. Rinty had trained harder than ever running up Cave Hill to enhance his fitness, chopping down trees for more strength and eating raw eggs and goat's milk and it worked as he defeated Paterson in the seventh round sparking wild celebrations in the arena as jubilant supporters tried to storm the ring with bonfires lit across the city in recognition of him becoming the undisputed flyweight World, British and Empire champion.

There would be successful title defences and a European crown prior to him calling it quits in 1950 with a record of 51 wins, six draws and nine losses. The St Patrick's Christian Brothers' pupil did himself, his wife Frances, their four children, his family and Belfast proud leaving the stage as a British, European, Commonwealth and World title winner.

He continued to sing after his boxing days were over and worked in a variety of jobs from a taxi driver to a petrol pump attendant and one day laughed his socks off in the 1970s phoning up a local radio station who had wrongly announced his passing telling them "I'm not floored yet".

He died in 1984 but his place in sporting folklore is assured and marked by a plaque in his honour at the King's Hall and a 10 foot high bronze statue at Cathedral Gardens in Belfast. In his heyday everyone knew this boxing great illustrated perfectly by the story of a letter sent to him by an English film crew wanting to do an interview. The address on the letter read: 'Mr Rinty Monaghan, Champion of the World, Ireland' and quickly reached the man himself who once said: "Life really has been a load of laughs for me. I was only serious when I stepped into the ring."

DERMOTT MONTEITH

CRICKET: SPIN BOWLING GREAT
FOR IRELAND
B: 02/06/1943 - D: 06/12/2009

Dermott Monteith is widely considered the finest bowler in the history of Irish cricket claiming a fantastic 326 wickets for Ireland between 1965 and 1984. The Lisburn cricketer could bat as well but it was his sublime spin bowling that took the biscuit and batsmen by surprise leading to dismissals of the great and the good. Monteith played 76 times for Ireland and with self-belief dripping out of him felt he was up there with the best left arm spin bowlers in the world and few disagreed. He starred in the days when Ireland weren't involved in a flurry of internationals, taking on England and the like or featuring in World Cups yet minus all that he made a huge impact on the sport that has stood the test of time.

With Dermott there was always a swagger and the one time Queen's University student was never afraid to shake things up scoring a half century on his international debut against the MCC at Lord's before making his name at that level as a top class bowler taking his wickets at an average of just 17.37 runs. He claimed a five wicket haul 27 times and on seven occasions snaffled 10 wickets in a match, including 13 once in a victory over the MCC which was some effort for someone who started out as a fast bowler at Royal Belfast Academical Institute prior to being converted to spin.

A cavalier cricketer, who was fun to watch, he captained Ireland in 37 games and while some questioned the appointment his knowledge of the game came to the fore finding ways to win matches when a draw or defeat loomed. Irish players being given a shot at county cricket was rare in Monteith's era but at the age of 38 he was snapped up by Middlesex playing for them in the early 80s, earning praise for his performances from captain Mike Brearley and helping them win the County Championship.

Monteith, a successful club cricketer for Lisburn, was always up for a challenge and the bigger the name the better in a battle at the crease with legendary figures Hanif Mohammed, Viv Richards, Gordon Greenidge and Rodney Marsh amongst his victims. As a batsman Monteith tended to play lower down the order than perhaps he should have done, totalling 1712 runs and scoring an international high of 95 versus Scotland in what turned out to be his final Ireland match in 1984 with his career cut short after he was left for dead following a hit and run accident in Bangor. Thankfully Dermott survived and later became president of the Irish Cricket Union and acted as a national selector for the Ireland cricket team he had served so well, sadly passing away at the age of 66 in 2009. Paying tribute after his former team-mate died, Ireland team manager Roy Torrens said: "Dermott was a magnificent cricketer and a trail-blazer in every way, being one of the first Irishmen in the modern era to make a mark in county cricket and he was great to play alongside."

BILLY MURRAY

KICKBOXING: FROM BULLIED BOY
TO MULTIPLE
WORLD CHAMPION
B: 05/06/1958

It was John Lennon who said "before Elvis there was nothing" in reference to the influence and impact Elvis Presley had on music and while it is true to say the effect has not been on the same cosmic scale it's a quote that could easily apply to Billy Murray and what he has done for Kickboxing in Northern Ireland. "Before Billy there was nothing" yet now the country has multiple World and European Kickboxing Champions and thousands of people of all ages besotted with the sport for worthy reasons, be it to keep fit, increase their self-esteem, have fun or with ambitions of competing at elite level.

What Belfast man Murray has done over the years is to form a movement and his extraordinary, feelgood story is one that cannot be told enough. He was the shy kid who was bullied and found it within himself to use the experience to become champion of the world four times over. Coming home from school one day Billy was attacked and so traumatised by the episode it was almost a couple of months before he would leave his home or return to school in case he encountered the bullies again. He thought about learning self-defence with his mum buying him a book called 'Beginners Guide to Kung-Fu' and his dad taking him to a boxing gym in east Belfast. Soon he was learning Karate and Ju Jitsu before trying his hands and feet at Kickboxing discovering a new found self confidence and that he was actually pretty good at it, winning a first amateur Ulster title in 1982 and an amateur world title in 1987 before turning professional.

Training hard and studying the finer details and techniques of the sport, good would become great as this self coached sportsman became European Champion in 1988 and won his first pro world title at welterweight in September 12, 1989 defeating American Richard Hill. Murray had lost to Hill in their previous contest but with the atmosphere and noise bouncing off the walls in the Ulster Hall, the result would be different this time with Billy adamant that was the night that set him on his way.

He told me: "It was a surreal moment. I can remember sitting backstage on my own before that world title fight. When I became a coach I made sure that I never left any of my fighters on their own because backstage can be such a lonely place and it can destroy a fighter. So many thoughts were racing through my head as I heard all the cheers inside the Ulster Hall. It was such a nervous time and there was so much expectation on my shoulders to win the first Kickboxing world title in the country. I always enjoyed fighting away from home because there was far less pressure. At home I was promoting the event, financing the event and training myself. The roar when I came out to fight was incredible. There was always something special about the Ulster Hall with the acoustics in it and people so close to you and that night it was so packed they were hanging over the balcony. It was some fight and thankfully I became World Champion."

Murray would go on to achieve stunning success, becoming a four weight world champion, the first Irishman to do so, claiming titles at Super Welterweight, Light middleweight and Middleweight and he was rated as one of the best exponents of his art as he travelled around the globe to take on all comers. After coming out of retirement at the age of 42, Murray won title number four, the coveted WKN Muay Thai world title, at a heaving Waterfront Hall in his home city beating Thailand great Chartsing though even then he wasn't finished with his final bout in 2006 when he was 47!

Behind all the personal glory and sacrifices that led him to it, Murray had started up the ProKick Gym on Wilgar Street in east Belfast during the Troubles bringing Catholics and Protestants together by using the power of sport and while a select band of club members have gone on to be champions of Europe and the World, for most it offers enjoyment and makes them feel good about themselves. Trainer and promoter Billy is a co-founder of The Peace Fighters initiative and ex-Crusaders and Linfield footballer Ian Young, who became a kickboxing World Champion under Murray's guidance, says: "What Billy did becoming a four weight world champion in kickboxing was astonishing. He is a pioneer of the sport and respected across the world and all his success in the ring helped him do other important things like building bridges between our communities. He's a great man as well as being one of the best kickboxers of all time."

CAROLINE O'HANLON

NETBALL/LADIES GAELIC FOOTBALL: WORLD CLASS STAR ON THE BALL AT THE DOUBLE
B: 08/08/1984

Caroline O'Hanlon isn't just a remarkable sportsperson, she is a remarkable woman combining her job as a doctor with being a world class netball star and an all-time great in ladies Gaelic football. At club, county or international level O'Hanlon has shone in not one but two sports dictating play from midfield in GAA or performing brilliantly at centre in netball winning a host of individual prizes and lifting her teams to memorable successes.

Over a stellar career dating back to her schooldays this is a woman who from the beginning of the 21st century has been equally at home in the orange of the Armagh ladies Gaelic football team and the green of the Northern Ireland netball side making more appearances for both than any other player in history and bringing her ball handling skills, agility and speed to the two codes. What O'Hanlon also possesses is an ability to try something unexpected and inventive to create opportunities out of nothing for grateful team-mates.

The Queen's University graduate has been courted to play other sports such as rugby and Aussie Rules but Dr O'Hanlon has stayed loyal to Gaelic football and netball.

From Bessbrook, O'Hanlon followed in her farmer dad Charlie's footsteps into the GAA inspiring her club Carrickcruppen to multiple county titles and Armagh to Ulster Senior Championship glory as well as helping the Orchard county to an All-Ireland final and being key to All-Ireland Intermediate and NFL Divisional success. She was named All-Ireland Senior Player of the year in 2014, has won three All Stars having been nominated an Ulster record 11 times, been included in the NFL Team of the season more than anyone else on the island and represented Ireland in an International Rules series.

You would think that might be enough to be going on with in terms of sporting achievement, but then there's her netball accomplishments and to put in context how well respected O'Hanlon is on the world stage she was shortlisted in 2020 by go to Australian website Netball Scoop as one of the best centres in the sport over the past 30 years.

Caroline, who started playing netball at primary school, was in the starting line-up, aged just 17, when Northern Ireland played in the 2003 World Cup, an event she has now played in three times, the latest of which was in 2019 defining her longevity at the highest level. In that time she has been the star player for her country inspiring them as captain to an all-time high ranking of eighth, played twice in the Commonwealth Games, carrying the Northern Ireland flag at the 2018 opening ceremony, won silver medals at the 2012 and 2017 European Netball Championships and was named player of that tournament.

There's also been two Nations Cup wins with Team NI and O'Hanlon has led her Lisburn based club Larkfield to numerous trophies while in 2019 she played a thrilling role in Manchester Thunder's Netball SuperLeague title glory becoming the first Irish woman to play in a SuperLeague final craftily orchestrating a comeback victory over Wasps, cementing herself as Northern Ireland's best ever netball player.

MARTIN O'NEILL

FOOTBALL: INSPIRATIONAL WORLD
CUP SKIPPER AND TWO TIME
EUROPEAN CUP WINNER

B: 01/03/1952

Martin O'Neill is rightly regarded as a successful manager but before jumping into the hotseat and winning a plethora of trophies in England and Scotland, he was a fabulous footballer who, as captain, led Northern Ireland to their most iconic victory, predicting the outcome beforehand, and he holds the distinction of being the last European Cup winner from the country.

O'Neill also happens to be great company with his stories and wit but try it on with him and you will be sorry such as when he put French and Italian World Cup winners Patrick Vieira and Fabio Cannavaro in their place when the trio were ITV pundits for the 2014 World Cup. Making a point to host Adrian Chiles, who had cheekily observed that the bespectacled Martin may not have been brave in a defensive wall leading to grins from Vieira and Cannavaro, O'Neill reminded them all he played the game to a high standard, stating: "They are two World Cup winners but actually when it comes to the Champions League, which used to be called the European Cup, I've won two of them!" Knowing the answer was zero and gazing towards the sheepish pundits, he added: "I'd just like to know how many of them you have won." Classic Martin.

Those European Cups that O'Neill referred to relate to the astounding back to back triumphs for Nottingham Forest in 1979 and 1980 when the genius of Brian Clough rubbed off on the man from Kilrea and his teammates. Given O'Neill's rich history with Forest it is telling that before they dominated Europe he didn't see eye to eye with Clough's predecessor Allan Brown and thought about leaving England and returning to Queen's University where he had been passionately studying law prior to signing for the Nottingham club in 1971.

Clough and midfielder O'Neill had their moments but the pair were like kindred spirits as the Derry native became a significant figure at the City

Ground with Forest winning promotion to English football's top flight and then remarkably claiming the club's only league title the following year in 1978 with a League Cup success thrown in to boot. O'Neill was superb, scoring vital goals and delighting his team-mates with his energy and effervescence which continued into the next season when he was one of the best performers at home and abroad as Forest won another League Cup and reached the European Cup final.

O'Neill scored in the quarter-finals and shone in the semi, but was gutted to be left on the bench for the 1-0 final win over Malmo with Clough worrying about a hamstring issue for the midfielder who felt he was fit to play. O'Neill's replacement Trevor Francis netted the winner and while the Ulsterman had a cherished European Cup medal his determination to feature in the biggest club game of all helped drive Forest back to the final in 1980 where Clough's side beat Hamburg by a single John Roberston goal.

That season there was also European Super Cup success against Barcelona which brought back happy memories for Martin, who in 1971 had scored a cracking goal for Irish League side Distillery in a 3-1 European Cup Winners' Cup defeat to the Catalan giants, having netted twice at 19 years of age for the Whites a few months before in a 3-0 Irish Cup victory over Derry City to earn a place in continental competition. With scouts watching the teenage sensation, a move to professional football was certain and while O'Neill left Forest in 1981 he would go on to play for Norwich, Manchester City and Chesterfield before injury forced him to retire in 1985.

As a kid Sunderland fan O'Neill loved GAA and savoured the day when he and his mother travelled to Croke Park to watch the 1958 All-Ireland football final with his brother Leo in the Derry panel that was defeated by Dublin. Martin was a super player and after his family moved to Belfast, he was instrumental in his school St Malachy's winning the MacRory Cup in 1970. That same year he was mightily disappointed when his school lost in the Hogan Cup final at Croke Park. In 1971 St Malachy's reached the semi-finals of the MacRory Cup but the Antrim County Board refused to permit the use of Casement Park because Martin had been playing soccer which was viewed as 'a foreign sport' and in breach of GAA rules. In the end the game was played in Omagh with St Malachy's losing to St Mary's CBS from Belfast. The rule was later removed. In 2008 O'Neill admitted in a speech about Irish identity that he had been perturbed by the experience.

Forever a man with the courage of his convictions, proud Irishman O'Neill took some abuse from home fans in the 1970s when he first turned out for Northern Ireland but gradually became one of the nation's favourite players with his personality and pursuit of success crucial as Billy Bingham's team qualified for the 1982 World Cup finals. In O'Neill, Bingham saw a strong character and clever tactician who could be his manager on the pitch which is why he made him captain.

Gerry Armstrong tells the story that before Northern Ireland's never to be forgotten 1-0 victory over hosts Spain in the World Cup, O'Neill informed all the players that the underdogs would triumph and also how they would do it. Some of Martin's team-mates thought the skipper had been out in the Spanish sun too long but not for the first time he was proved right hugging a jubilant Bingham after the final whistle in a memory to hold dear.

O'Neill played 64 times for Northern Ireland between 1971 and 1984 scoring eight goals and winning the Home Nations tournament yet despite overtures from the Irish FA never managed the national team. After working in insurance following his playing career, Martin had success in management bringing silverware and promotion to Wycombe, two League Cups and European football to Leicester City and every domestic trophy, including the treble, and a UEFA Cup final appearance to Celtic.

Dedicated to his family, O'Neill left Celtic in 2005 to care for his wife Geraldine who was diagnosed with cancer. He returned to management in 2006 to make Aston Villa punch above their weight before a topsy turvy spell at Sunderland and a rollercoaster ride with the Republic of Ireland taking them to the Euro 2016 finals ahead of a sour end followed by a brief stint in charge of Forest. Fascinated by criminology and keen to attend murder trials, intelligent and articulate O'Neill was never the prototype 1970s/80s footballer, but he was a hugely successful one for club and country and in case anyone forgets he has TWO European Cup triumphs to his name, the only man from Northern Ireland who can say that.

SEAN O'NEILL

GAELIC FOOTBALL: DOWN GREAT WITH HAT-TRICK OF ALL-IRELAND WINS

Down GAA legend Sean O'Neill was an exceptional player with ball in hand or at his feet and was revered across the length and breadth of Ireland for his ability which was a significant factor in his county bringing home three All-Ireland titles in the 1960s. GAA fans of a certain vintage rave about the qualities of O'Neill and how he could catch the ball on the run at speed, cause havoc for defenders with his creative mind, score for fun and do it all with a style that spectators adored. In the years that followed he would be named in the GAA's Team of the Century and Team of the Millennium.

A Sigerson Cup winner with Queen's in 1958, O'Neill was in the Down senior side a year later when they claimed their first Ulster title. He swung into the sixties by helping the Mourne county win the All-Ireland in 1960 beating Kerry in the final to bring the Sam Maguire trophy north for the first time – the only Ulster side to win it previously had been Cavan.

O'Neill was still a young man but was already a key figure in the side and when they retained 'Sam' in 1961 he was considered one of the most impressive players in the land. In front of a record Croke Park crowd of 90,556, old highlights of the match show O'Neill scoring a point from a free and a sparkling goal as Down defeated Offaly 3-6 to 2-8 in a dramatic decider. The hat-trick of triumphs came in 1968 with a 2-12 to 1-13 victory over Kerry with the Irish Times report on the final explaining how the tone was set by the superb O'Neill, playing at full-forward, scoring a point early on and finding the net shortly after in a typically influential performance.

Sean's credits don't end there with three National League titles, eight Ulster senior Championship medals, eight Railway Cup successes and multiple All Stars on a glittering CV. One of Ulster's most decorated heroes, he was selected at right-half forward in the GAA's Centenary Football team in 1984 and their Millennium team in 2000 though the John Mitchel club man, who was Footballer of the Year in 1968 and named as the Ulster

Footballer of the Millennium in 2000, was comfortable in any position in the forward line.

As a coach he guided the Down Minor team to 1977 All-Ireland glory and Queen's to Sigerson success in 1982 and has championed the GAA since his days at Abbey CBS Grammar School in Newry. It seemed right that Sean was honoured in 2013 at Queen's with the inaugural and prestigious Paddy O'Hara Medal of Honour, named after the man who guided the University to their first Sigerson Cup success in 1958.

O'Neill was one of the most accomplished GAA players of his or any other generation and when he received an Honorary Degree from Queen's in 2019, the University's Pro-Vice Chancellor Professor David Jones said: "Sean has proven over decades to be a man of outstanding talent, integrity and solidity. He stands in our midst as one of the greatest Gaelic footballers in the history of the game - a true legend of Irish sport."

BERTIE PEACOCK

FOOTBALL: PARKHEAD, WINDSOR PARK AND WORLD CUP HERO
B: 29/09/1928 - D: 22/07/2004

Northern Ireland legend, Celtic legend, Coleraine legend and according to Sir Alex Ferguson, Bertie Peacock deserves to be remembered as one of the true greats of football. In Belfast's Europa Hotel in 2008, four years after Bertie's death, the Milk Cup committee held a gala dinner honouring Peacock with Manchester United icon Ferguson making the trip to speak in glowing terms about his good friend and one of his favourite footballers.

Peacock was admired by all with his mild manner, generosity and ability to put people at ease as endearing as the qualities he showed during a wonderful playing career resulting in him being the first international footballer from Northern Ireland to have a statue erected of him in his home town in 2007.

A plumber by trade after brief spells with Coleraine and Glentoran he moved to Parkhead with the Celtic FC website detailing that the Bhoys were alerted to his talents after he played in a RUC Fives tournament in the summer of 1949. He would become a super captain of Celtic and a huge favourite with the fans in the 1950s with his industry, ability to keep possession and knowledge of the game constant features of every 90 minutes.

Jock Stein, the man who inspired Celtic to European Cup glory in 1967, loved playing alongside Bertie in a famed half-back line, which also included Bobby Evans, and labelled Peacock 'a human dynamo'. It was the perfect description of a player who covered ground so quickly he left opposition players wondering if there were two or three Bertie Peacocks on the pitch. He was also known as 'the Little Ant', in a nod to his size and neverending work-rate.

At Celtic, where he initially formed an effective partnership with countryman 'cheeky' Charlie Tully, Peacock won a host of trophies including the league and cup double in 1954, another Scottish Cup in 1951, the club's first League Cup in 1956 and perhaps most famously lifting the team as skipper to a stunning 7-1 victory over Old Firm rivals Rangers in the 1957 League Cup decider in a derby etched in the history of the Parkhead outfit.

When it was time to leave Glasgow behind in 1961 after 12 years, 453 appearances and 50 goals Peacock had offers across England and Scotland but chose to become manager of Coleraine, who he guided to their first and only league title in 1974, and he also took charge of Northern Ireland giving George Best and Pat Jennings their debuts.

While forever a Celtic idol Bertie's place in the pantheon of Northern Ireland playing greats is also assured having been a star performer in the legendary 1958 World Cup team that reached the last eight of the competition. He first played for his country in 1951 and would win 31 caps in 10 years with the highlight being the trip to Sweden when he shimmered against the best on the planet. In conversations with anyone involved with the 1958 side, they would tell you about how Peacock, without fuss or fanfare, could influence big games which shows why he was picked in a star-studded Great Britain side to face the Rest of Europe in 1955.

In later life, along with Jim Weir and Victor Leonard, Peacock was a co-founder of the prestigious and world renowned Milk Cup tournament and was assistant in the 1982 World Cup finals to manager Billy Bingham, who played with Bertie in 1958 and knew he was a man he could trust.

MADELINE PERRY

SQUASH: BIG TIME WINNER ON THE COURT

B: 11/02/1977

Madeline Perry is not one of Northern Ireland's most well known sports performers but she should be, given her heroic triumph over adversity story and everything that she achieved on the squash court. Banbridge woman Perry was a professional in her sport for 17 years, won numerous big tournaments around the globe, became the oldest woman in squash history to make it into the top 10 in the world and with her consistency, fitness and talent was at one point the number three ranked player on the planet.

She hit that mark in 2011 four years after being the victim of a vicious mugging outside a restaurant in Milan, where she was preparing for a tournament, leaving her with a broken temporal bone in her skull and bleeding and bruising to the brain. Speaking to me some years after the incident she recalled: "I think there was a danger of dying but luckily I had a very small bleed so it didn't put any pressure on the brain. I was in hospital in Italy and when I got out I wasn't allowed to fly because I had some sort of bubble of air close to the brain so my mum, who had come over from Northern Ireland, and I got the train and boat back to Belfast. It was a long journey home."

Perry admitted to feeling angry that her career had been stalled revealing it took a year for her to feel right again on court, but when she got there she made it count performing even better than she had done previously. Madeline reached the World Open semi-final in 2008 and defeated world number one Nicol David on her way to the 2009 British Open final before recording a stunning Australian Open triumph in 2010, beating England's Alison Waters in a gripping final 11-5, 12-10, 6-11, 4-11, 13-11 to clinch her biggest victory. It was a success not only greeted with joy by Perry's family and friends but the squash fraternity, inspired by how Madeline had fought back from such a horrifying experience to win the Women's Squash Association (WSA) World Series competition, one of the most prestigious events around.

In total Perry, renowned for her attacking nature and movement, was victorious in 12 WSA events which was some going given when she turned pro in 1998, after completing a geography degree at Queen's University, "it was only supposed to be for 12 months". Another impressive feat during her career was when aged 37 in 2014 she became the oldest top 10 competitor ever on the female circuit.

Madeline won well over 100 caps for Ireland, played in eight World Team Championships, competed in the Commonwealth Games for Northern Ireland on five occasions, was a record 15 time victor of the Irish National title, won six Irish Open crowns, the last of which was her final individual competition, and helped the Irish to a bronze at the European Team Championships just before retirement in 2015. Her next adventure as a project manager for the charity Raleigh International was a touch more extreme as she slept in the jungles of Borneo for three months, helping with various construction and infrastructure projects, before moving into coaching.

LADY MARY PETERS

ATHLETICS: OLYMPIC GOLD MEDAL
WINNING ICON
B: 06/07/1939

Lady Mary Peters is Northern Ireland's Golden Girl, admired and loved all over the world and standing alone as her country's only Olympic champion in an individual sport having won the pentathlon in world record breaking style at the 1972 Munich Games. Today Mary is recognised for a colossal contribution to sport in Northern Ireland providing not just inspiration but financial assistance to hundreds of young stars courtesy of the charitable Trust established in her name. Featured in this book are some of those to benefit from the first lady of Northern Ireland sport who at 33 years of age in Germany earned Britain's only athletics gold medal of the Games excelling on the track and field.

You won't meet anyone prouder of Northern Ireland than Mary, but originally from Halewood near Liverpool she didn't live in what became her home country until she was 11 when her family re-located to Ballymena due to her dad's work. Later the family would move to Portadown but tragically her mum died of cancer when Mary was just 16.

It was at Portadown College where she was head girl and hockey captain that she developed an interest in athletics and encouraged by her father it quickly became evident that she had a rare talent. Motivated by the memory of her mother, Peters threw herself into the sport and even when her dad remarried and left Northern Ireland she decided to stay and concentrate on her athletics. By 1956 Mary had competed in her first pentathlon which was a multi-event with five disciplines, the 100m Hurdles, Shot Put, High Jump, Long Jump and 200m and two years later, while still a teenager, she gained valuable experience at the British Empire and Commonwealth Games.

Giving up a teaching job to focus on her athletics career she was first selected for Great Britain in 1961 in the shot, finished fifth in the pentathlon at the European Championships in 1962 and fourth in the same event in 1964 on her Olympic debut before grabbing a silver medal in the shot at the 1966 Commonwealth Games and hampered by injury she was ninth in the pentathlon at the Mexico Olympics in 1968.

After 10 years of international competition and training hard every day others may have called it a day but as she hit 30 Peters was determined that the best was still to come and she was proved right winning gold for Northern Ireland in the pentathlon and shot at the 1970 Commonwealth Games in Edinburgh. With the Troubles raging in Belfast and bombs exploding around the city on a regular basis, Mary flew to Germany for the 1972 Olympics with the Great British team dreaming of bringing some much needed good news to Northern Ireland.

The pentathlon proved to be one of the most exciting events in the Games with Peters going head to head with home favourite Heidi Rosendahl who had already won gold for West Germany in the long jump. You would have thought that the fans in the Munich stadium would have been against Peters, who was the main threat to Rosendahl, but with her bubbly personality, smiles, energy and never-ending effort there was much warmth for Peters in the arena as she led after day one by 301 points thanks to a strong 100m hurdles and shot followed by a personal best 1.82m in the high jump.

She needed the advantage with high class sprinter Rosendahl starting day two by almost breaking her own long jump world record and closing the gap considerably with only the 200m to come. Millions of television viewers in Britain were gripped as late, great commentator Ron Pickering roared 'Come on Mary' as she raced down the home straight chasing Rosendahl who finished in 22.96 seconds with Peters 10 metres behind in 24.08 seconds. Unlike these days there was no instant confirmation of total points scored and Peters had an agonising wait to find out if she had won the gold she craved before Rosendahl, having heard the result, graciously approached, hugged and congratulated her rival on her wonderful success. In the end Peters won by just 10 points with a score of 4801, breaking the world pentathlon record and becoming a national treasure overnight giving Northern Ireland the good news she had desired.

In a telephone call to a Bavarian mountain restaurant hours after her triumph, the then Sports Editor of the Belfast Telegraph, Malcolm Brodie, asked what Peters would like from the people of Northern Ireland to mark her glittering achievement with Mary replying an athletics track so there would be proper facilities for people in Belfast and after a mighty fundraising effort the Mary Peters Track was built offering athletes an ideal place to train to this day. There is also a statue of the great lady at the track celebrating her glory in Munich though in 1972 not everyone was happy with Mary's success because she received a death threat from the IRA following her Olympic heroics but it didn't stop her from appearing at a special homecoming party in Belfast where thousands turned up to salute the athlete who set 25 British records in her career and became the first Northern Ireland star to be voted BBC Sports Personality of the Year.

There would be one more gold in the pentathlon at her fifth Commonwealth Games in Christchurch 1974 with Mary driven on to succeed for her long time coach Buster McShane, who had died in a car accident nine months earlier. In retirement Mary didn't take it easy and has been busier than ever from opening a health club, setting up her Trust, being a successful British women's team athletics manager at the Olympics and going to numerous ceremonies where she has been honoured to be awarded title after title including Lord Lieutenant of the City of Belfast and Lady Companion of the Order of the Garter. In 2018 Mary came through open heart surgery to replace an aortic valve and is adored everywhere she goes having always been at ease in any company be it royalty, the Rolling Stones, who she met and shared champagne with at a 1964 gig at The Ulster Hall, huge sporting stars inspired by her past feats, young athletes with dreams of making it big or members of the public. To each and every one she will forever be our Golden Girl.

JONATHAN REA

MOTORCYCLING: MULTIPLE WORLD
CHAMPION SUPERMAN
B: 02/02/1987

Jonathan Rea is a modern day Northern Ireland sporting phenomenon who in 2015 won his first World Superbike title and then kept on winning it, smashing records and setting new standards in the sport as he was crowned champion in 2016, 2017, 2018, 2019 and 2020. It is quite something to become the best at what you do but to stay there year in year out in the ruthless profession of motorcycling requires remarkable levels of consistency and resilience plus an insatiable desire to succeed and serious racing prowess.

Six-time World Champion Rea has those qualities in abundance and has become one of the biggest heroes his homeland has ever known. He has also raced twice at MotoGP earning points on both occasions but it is in World Superbikes that he has earned legendary status with more fastest laps, podium spots, wins, points and titles than any other rider.

With his grandad John one of the first sponsors for the late, great Joey Dunlop and his dad Johnny a fine racer himself, winning a Junior race at the Isle of Man TT in 1989, Jonathan was comfortable in the environment in which he has made his name from an early age with his father recalling that his son was riding a motorbike before he was riding a push bike!

Much as Rea savoured racing growing up, with his first love motocross, his parents told him that he had to study hard and secure good marks at school in order for him to ride bikes and it worked a treat as Jonathan became an A star student at Larne Grammar. For all his academic aptitude Rea only saw one career ahead and it entailed going as fast as he could on two wheels and beating anyone racing against him. With his background in bikes, some may feel that success was written in the stars for Rea but his tale, which merits huge admiration, is as much about putting in the hard yards, having the character to overcome injury setbacks such as a shattered femur at 17 when he was told he'd never race again and not giving up in pursuit of his dream.

Talk to people who knew Jonathan as he was making his way and they tell you about his humble nature that has never changed despite all his success, helping make him one of Northern Ireland's most popular sporting stars. With his talent there is every chance that Rea could have become a world champion in motocross, but the decision to move into circuit racing in 2003 was a shrewd one as he illustrated his quality with strong performances and race wins in the British Superbikes before being offered the chance to move into the World Supersport Championship in 2008, finishing second in his first year.

By 2009 he had a full-time ride in World Superbikes with the Ten Kate Honda team where in a rollercoaster five year spell he had the highs of 15 race victories and numerous podium finishes and crushing injury lows, some of which kept him out for months on end. In 2015 he moved to Kawasaki and from their first race together at Phillip Island in Australia it was a winning partnership that continued to pop open the champagne with 14 victories that season, as Rea cruised to the World Superbike Championship.

If title number one was clinched early, Rea had to wait until the final round in Qatar to retain his crown in 2016 before making history by claiming a third successive championship with 16 victories in 26 races and the highest points tally ever (556) in World Superbikes. There were more records when Rea made it four in a row in 2018 going past the mark of 59 World Superbike triumphs set by Carl Fogarty and in the same year there was much mirth when it was revealed that while Jonathan was the king of the tarmac he didn't hold a licence to ride motorbikes on public roads!

Regardless the winning machine, who spent most of his childhood in the county Antrim village of Kilwaughter, continued to do what he did best and landed his greatest title in 2019 after all seemed lost early in the season when Ducati rider Alvaro Bautista took a commanding lead in the Championship. Rea roared back to become the first rider to have five World Superbike titles on his CV and with that victory, as with every success there was an acknowledgement of his fans in Northern Ireland and the huge part his family have played most notably Australian born wife Tatia and young sons Jake and Tyler. Title number six arrived in October 2020. Not even a worldwide pandemic could halt Jonathan's charge to glory.

BRIAN REID

MOTORCYCLING: WORLD CHAMPION

BIKER WITH THE RIGHT FORMULA

B: 03/09/1956

In motorcycling terms Brian Reid is one of Northern Ireland's fab four listed alongside Ralph Bryans, Joey Dunlop and Jonathan Rea as the sport's only world champions from the place he calls home. What a select band to be in for Reid who is immensely proud of the company he keeps having raced himself into history in 1985 by winning the Formula Two World Championship and then proving his class by retaining the title the next year.

Racing was in Reid's blood with his uncle Ian McGregor, one of the original Dromara Destroyers, taking him to meetings as a young boy and buying him his first bike, a Triumph Tiger Cub, for a tenner when Brian was nine years old. He couldn't get enough of it and before his teenage years were up he was revelling in his first race at Fermanagh's St Angelo airfield in 1976 and then a road race at Dundrod in the Killinchy 150 on a 250 Yamaha.

While enjoying competing on the open roads and becoming a Dromara Destroyer himself like McGregor, Ray McCullough and Trevor Steele, it wasn't until after Reid's first victory at Carrowdore on a 125 Morbidelli that his career accelerated thanks to support and a Yamaha 350 from the late Mick Mooney of Irish Racing Motorcycles. In 1982 Reid carved out a piece of history when he was the first rider to triumph in three Irish road racing championships in the same year winning the 250, 350 and 500cc titles and after moving into Formula TT world championship racing in 1984 he finished third before becoming World Champion the following year, clinching the crown in the final round at the Dundrod Ulster Grand Prix after race victories in Portugal and Spain.

Reid dazzled in 1985 and to underline his ability he won the Formula Two World Championship again in 1986 cementing his legend in leathers status. With Dunlop taking home a fifth World Formula One title that year it wasn't until 2015 that Northern Ireland would have another world motorcycling champion and Rea marked the occasion by wearing old helmets of his predecessors 29 years on. 'Speedy Reidy' would have further glory in the Regal 600cc Championship in 1989 and 1990 and victories at the Ulster Grand Prix, Isle of Man TT and North West 200 and there was family delight when cousin and jockey John Reid won the Epsom Derby in 1992. Two years later Brian's career ended at the Temple 100 after suffering serious injuries when his bike hit the wreckage from a crash that took the life of rider Ian King. In 2017 Reid, whose son Simon is a talented young rider, told the Belfast Telegraph's Jim Gracey: "I broke a femur, elbow, both wrists and a shoulder. I was in a wheelchair for three months and couldn't even clean my teeth by myself. I wanted to race again, I could have raced again, but I couldn't have fallen off again. I'd a good career so at least I had a wealth of memories to ease me into retirement."

JOHN REID

HORSE RACING: FANTASTIC FLAT
JOCKEY WHO WON BIG
B: 06/08/1955

Banbridge man John Reid is a flat racing great who won the Epsom Derby, Prix de l'Arc de Triomphe and just about every other big race going and competed at the top level of his sport for almost three decades. Retiring as a jockey in 2001 after over 2,500 victories worldwide and a remarkable 48 global Group 1 successes, he continues to be hugely respected within the horse racing industry. Renowned for his racing brain and attention to detail, Reid started out as a teenage apprentice in Ireland before making the move to England with his first big win coming in 1978 on board Ile de Bourbon in the King George VI and Queen Elizabeth Stakes, a race he would triumph in again almost 20 years later in 1997 when he produced one of the rides of his career to see Swain beat Pilsudski by a length in a thrilling contest.

In between came a glorious triumph in the 1988 Prix de l'Arc de Triomphe in Longchamp when in a perfectly timed run to the finish Reid brought Italian trained horse Tony Bin home in front. Legendary Irish trainer Vincent O'Brien had wanted John to ride another horse in the race but the county Down jockey was so confident that Tony Bin could deliver in France's most prestigious race that he asked O'Brien to be excused and was proved right surging ahead in the final furlong. Another classic victory came in the 1992 Derby when Reid produced an accomplished performance in the most famous flat race of all using his racing savvy and skills to take 8/1 shot Dr Devious into the lead in the closing stages and stay clear leaving greats like Lester Piggott, Willie Carson, Pat Eddery and Steve Cauthen plus a young Frankie Dettori and their mounts trailing behind.

There were other fabulous moments in a brilliant 28 year career such as a stunning win with Dr Devious again in the Irish Champion Stakes at Leopardstown, two victories in the 1000 Guineas (1982 and 1994) and a super St Leger conquest on Nedawi in 1998. A multiple classic winner in Ireland he enjoyed Irish Derby glory in 1987 and abroad he was triumphant in numerous countries including Italy, France and Germany taking the honours in the 2001 German Derby before finally deciding to retire. He had thought about quitting two years earlier after sustaining a serious injury but a love of the sport and a desire to be in the winners circle again kept him going until he was 46 when he called it a day. Cousin of motorcycling World Champion Brian Reid, John was an expert jockey that owners in Ireland, the UK, where he rode 1,937 winners, Europe and beyond could rely on. He has proved equally popular since in the racing game doing fine work in roles such as the Jockeys' Association President.

HUGH RUSSELL

BOXING: PICTURE PERFECT
OLYMPIC MEDALIST
B: 15/12/1959

Since the Olympics began in 1896 boxing has proved to be Northern Ireland's most successful sport in the greatest show on Earth though after the 1964 Games and before 1992, only one man brought back a medal and that was the brilliant Hugh Russell. The Belfast native is now one of most respected newspaper photographers in the UK and Ireland, producing illuminating and historic pictures for the Irish News but in his former life, as he describes it, Russell was one heck of a fighter. Following in his elder brother Sean's footsteps, he first entered a boxing gym when he was nine years old learning his trade in the Holy Family Club under the guidance of legendary trainer Gerry Storey, who instinctively knew Russell had the qualities to make a mark.

As a young amateur he was Irish Champion, represented Ireland and in 1978 travelled to Edmonton as a teenager with the Northern Ireland team for the Commonwealth Games, claiming a bronze medal in the flyweight division. Next, at 20, he set his sights on the 1980 Olympics in Moscow. Russell would later recall in the Irish Examiner that as he was getting to work in the ring, in what was the old USSR, such was the interest on the New Lodge Road, where he was brought up, rioting during the Troubles would stop so everyone could watch the local hero fight on television. He cruised to victories early on in the competition before defeating Yo Ryon-Sik from North Korea in a tight and tough contest and although he lost to Bulgarian Peter Lessov in the semi-finals Hugh would go home with a bronze taking Ireland's first boxing medal in 16 years.

He told Culture NI: "I'm fortunate to have an Olympic medal and am in a very exclusive club. As good as it is to be an Olympian, to be an Olympic medalist is very special and I don't think it is something that is ever forgotten about. On the world stage an Olympic medal is recognised massively and no matter what country you are in around the world or from what sport when you mention you have an Olympic medal people raise their eyebrows and smile."

Russell didn't just pick up a prize to treasure in Moscow, it was also the place where he first bought a camera which he would learn to use in award winning style. Before becoming a photographer, Russell moved into the professional ranks of boxing with the principle aim to win the Lonsdale Belt, an ambition he achieved in 1985, following in the footsteps of the great Freddie Gilroy. With his ginger curly locks, Hugh, who was known as Little Red, clinched the British bantamweight title in 1983 and a year later became the British flyweight champion and the first boxer to win the respective titles in that order. Russell is also remembered for two riveting, bruising and atmospheric bantamweight battles against fellow Belfast man Davy Larmour in the Ulster Hall, with the pair winning one apiece.

In 1985, at just 25, he retired having won the Lonsdale belt outright though Hugh continues to give something back to the sport having represented Northern Ireland on the British Boxing Board of Control and overseeing weigh-ins and fights in his home city, where he is so admired.

ELISHA SCOTT

FOOTBALL: KING OF THE KOP AND IRISH GREAT

B: 24/08/1893 – D: 16/05/1959

Over the years three Northern Ireland goalkeepers have, at different times, been rightly considered the best in the world ... Pat Jennings, Harry Gregg and Elisha Scott who joined Liverpool in 1912 and left in 1934 and is still the club's longest serving player. If you ever want to know how Belfast's Scott is viewed at Liverpool take a walk around Anfield and close to the Main Stand you will see seven granite benches placed in a landscaped walkway as part of the redevelopment of the ground. They are dedicated to 'the men who built Anfield' with Scott honoured alongside Bill Shankly, Billy Liddell, Bob Paisley, Kenny Dalglish, John Barnes and Steven Gerrard in what amounts to a most magnificent seven.

When asked in his later years who was the greatest goalkeeper of them all, Everton legend Dixie Dean said no one came close to Scott, who was both a friend to drink Guinness with and the deadliest of rivals on Merseyside derby day. Ironically Scott could have been a Blue rather than a Red after starting out in Boys Brigade football, joining Linfield as a 14-year-old and then signing for Broadway United before his older brother Billy, the Everton and Irish goalkeeper, recommended him to the Goodison Park side who thought five foot nine inches 'Lish' was too young and too small.

When Billy told the Liverpool chairman John McKenna about his brother, the Anfield club snapped him up in 1912 and at 19 on New Year's Day in 1913 Scott made his debut keeping a clean sheet against Newcastle, who were so impressed by the kid in the opposition goal that they offered £1,000 for him. It was massive money then but promptly rejected by the Reds who could see the Irishman's potential, though just as he was establishing himself in the team the First World War intervened and Scott returned home where he played for the newly formed Belfast United and Linfield ahead of joining Belfast Celtic as an amateur winning the Irish League title and Irish Cup and then going back to Liverpool after the War.

From 1920 he was a regular and an idol with the fans emerging as the first King of the Kop due to his agility and ability to make staggering saves while for opponents he was an intimidating presence between the sticks despite his stature. In the middle of games Elisha was not shy in dishing out some colourful language which annoyed some of his team-mates but he made up for it with his performances propelling Liverpool to their third league title in 1922 and another one the following year.

A talismanic figure at Anfield he would continue to be the main man at the club for over a decade making a record number of appearances (468) not surpassed until 1957 by legend Liddell. Everton, hoping to make up for their original mistake, had tried and failed to sign Scott during his time on Merseyside but looked like landing him in 1934, however, as Liverpool's official club website explains the controversial move was shelved after the Liverpool Echo was overwhelmed by letters of protest from angry

Liverpool fans. He did leave that year though not before in an extremely rare event he was allowed to address the fans with an emotional speech at his final Anfield match leaving the toughest of Kopites misty-eyed.

In 1939 Scott was voted as Liverpool's greatest ever player by the fans and today there is a weighty argument to say he merits being in the club's all-time XI. Scott took over as player/manager of Belfast Celtic overseeing a magical period in the club's history winning 10 league titles, six Irish Cups and countless other competitions continuing to take charge of the team until they withdrew from football in 1949 six months after a mob attacked Belfast Celtic player Jimmy Jones in a game with Linfield at Windsor Park.

On the international front Scott made his debut in 1920 playing until 1936 when he was 42, appearing a record 31 times and with the Ireland team (long before it was called Northern Ireland) not the strongest he was often the busiest player on the pitch producing miraculous saves in virtually every match. There weren't too many victories for the Irish in those days but one that stands out is a home success over England in 1927 in which Scott played a vital role. Elisha died in 1959 and 50 years later the Belfast Celtic Society organised a moving ceremony at his grave in the city cemetery unveiling a headstone adorned with the crests of Belfast Celtic and Liverpool in a fitting tribute to a football icon.

JASON SMYTH

ATHLETICS: QUICKEST
PARALYMPIAN EVER AND MULTI-
GOLD MEDALIST
B: 04/07/1987

When Jason Smyth was eight years old he was diagnosed with a genetic disorder called Stargardt's disease which had a serious impact on his eyesight but while it may have stopped him from fulfilling his dream of being a footballer for Liverpool, it didn't prevent him from becoming the fastest Paralympian of all time. Visually impaired Smyth, from Eglinton, is known as the Usain Bolt of the Paralympics and no wonder given he has won eight outdoor world titles and five Paralympic gold medals.

He is an inspiring, driven character who tells it straight in interviews, be it admitting he wasn't a big athletics fan growing up or that successful Paralympians don't tend to get the publicity or money that they deserve.

Smyth came to terms with his condition early on telling me in one of our earliest conversations in a matter of fact manner: "My grandad had it, then it skipped a generation and I picked it up when I was eight. The best way to explain it is if, say, you were looking at something and saw it clearly from 10 metres I would have to look at it from one metre. I have under 10 percent of perfect eyesight and things around me are very blurry but I have coped with it and learnt to adapt." He jokes about the need for two television sets in his house as when he is watching from two inches no one else can see the screen!

As a kid Smyth knew he was much faster than his friends but didn't take his talent seriously until a teacher at Limavady Grammar School suggested he should go to the City of Derry Athletics club. Aged 18 and still doing his A-Levels Smyth was victorious at the World Indoor Paralympic Athletics Championships in the 60m and at 19 he became a double world champion outdoors winning the 100m and 200m in the T13 Vision Impaired category. When he was 21 he repeated the trick to stand on top of the podium twice at the 2008 Paralympics in Beijing, breaking his own world records in the process. It was the start of an era of complete and total domination for Smyth who, competing for Ireland, proved to be invincible in international competition racing to four more World T13 titles at 100m and two more at 200m and a host of European crowns. The meeting he enjoyed most was the London Paralympics in 2012 when family and friends, along with 80,000 admiring spectators, cheered him on to another sparkling double as he scorched to world records – 10.46 seconds in the T13 100m and 21.05 seconds in the T13 200m.

It was a special year for Smyth who months after sprinting to glory in England's capital city married his American sweetheart Elise in the world famous Salt Lake Temple in Utah, which is the headquarters of the Church of Jesus Christ of the Latter-day Saints better known as the Mormons.

Clean living Smyth is proud of his faith which has been passed down the generations in his family since his paternal grandparents were amongst the first converts to join The Church of Jesus Christ of the Latter-day Saints in Derry.

Smyth won his fifth Paralympic gold in 2016 in Rio and was primed to add to that tally in Tokyo 2020 until the Games were postponed for a year due to the coronavirus pandemic but determined to continue re-writing the record books and cement his legacy, he will be confident there is more success to come.

Without question one of the finest Paralympian sports stars ever, it is worth pointing out that Smyth made history as the first Paralympic athlete to race in the mainstream European Championships in 2010 and just missed out on a place in the 100m final, won a bronze medal with the Irish 4 x 100m relay team in the First League European Team Championships in 2011 and was only 0.04 seconds away from qualifying for the 2012 Olympics.

Always keen to improve he has attended numerous training camps in Florida over the years with the top American sprinters, never feeling intimidated thanks to his easy going and laid-back nature. He says: "I have tried to change perceptions in my career. Just because you can't see it doesn't mean you can't run fast. I have won gold medals and broken world records and would never have had those experiences if I had full sight and feel with the challenges I have faced I have become a stronger person."

PAUL STIRLING

CRICKET: TOP IRISH RUN SCORER
AND OUTSTANDING OPENER

B: 03/09/1990

It was England's World Cup cricket winning captain - and Irishman - Eoin Morgan who in August 2020 described Paul Stirling as one of the most destructive opening batsmen on the planet. Morgan had just watched Stirling, from Newtownabbey, dismantle his bowling attack to score a match winning 142 runs off 128 balls to inspire Ireland to a marvellous One Day International (ODI) victory over England in Southampton. That the victory came with one ball to spare in a thrilling encounter only further heightened the value of Stirling's knock which contained nine fours and six sixes with Morgan saying: "He's as dangerous an opening batsman as there is around the world. I know guys do not like bowling at him, he hits good balls for four or six and, on his day, he can take a game away from you."

Former Belfast High School pupil Stirling has had that ability since starting out at Cliftonville Cricket Club and moving on to Carrickfergus before Middlesex snapped him up. Also capable of taking wickets with his underrated spin bowling and a reliable catcher, he has become an Ireland hero since winning his first cap, aged only 17, against UAE in Abu Dhabi in 2008. Two years later he smashed a ferocious 177 against Canada, which was the highest individual score for Ireland in an ODI and in 2011 he cracked the then fourth fastest century in World Cup history versus Netherlands in a blistering opening stand with captain William Porterfield. That was the same year in which he bagged his first ton against a visiting Test nation, with Pakistan feeling the heat and his power.

From a young protege he has matured into a standard bearer for modern day Irish cricket and one of the nation's finest batsmen of all time scoring more runs for the team than anyone else in the ODI and Twenty20 forms of the game. There is no sign of him letting up having opted in 2020 to leave Middlesex, where he spent 10 years, played almost 200 games, scored more than 6,000 runs and won the county championship, in order to continue playing at international level when tasked with making a choice between county and country after Ireland had gained Full Member status.

The first player to pass 4000 Irish runs in ODI cricket, he played in Ireland's Test debut in 2018 and in 2019 scored more T20 runs (748 at an average of 41.55) than anyone on the international stage. At the start of 2020 he smacked 95 runs off just 47 balls in a T20 victory over West Indies with astonishingly 67 of those coming in 25 balls during a six over Powerplay which was a T20 international best, and several months later he was starring again with his superb century to beat England. Stirling's brother Richard and father Brian, an international rugby referee, have also been fine cricketers in Northern Ireland but they know Paul, who signed for North Down after leaving Middlesex, is the pick of the bunch. What we all know is this class player is going to score many more runs for Ireland and break many more records.

DENNIS TAYLOR

SNOOKER: CROWNED WORLD CHAMPION
AFTER GREATEST FINISH EVER
B: 19/01/1949

Dennis Taylor was responsible for keeping 18.5 million people up past midnight so they could watch him beat the great Steve Davis in a black ball fight and claim the World Snooker Championship at the Crucible Theatre. In the 1985 final Coalisland native Taylor was a massive underdog taking on the best player on the planet who was going for his third world title in a row and fourth in five years and all looked to be going to plan for the Londoner when he opened up an 8-0 lead only for Taylor to mount a magnificent comeback to trail only 9-7 overnight. If the first day was fun, the second was so filled with tension it gripped you to your seat watching on television as the frame score moved to 17 apiece with 18 needed to lift the trophy. The final frame would last 68 minutes and deliver a record TV audience after midnight and give BBC 2 its largest viewing figures ever but more importantly it would end with Taylor being crowned world champion after the most dramatic final of all time.

With four balls left on the table, Taylor needed them all and after showing admirable nerve to sink the brown, blue and pink then came that nerve-wracking battle on the black with both missing chances amid a fraught atmosphere before Taylor finally made one count after Davis had blown a golden opportunity. As the black entered the corner pocket, the Tyrone man lifted his cue above his head in exaltation and relief at a dream come true as a pale Davis looked on in disbelief. It was the final to end all finals and won by our Dennis.

Several months before Taylor's life – and attitude to it - changed when he was told that his dear mother Annie had passed away suddenly with a massive heart attack. "I was doing well in a tournament in Newcastle playing some of the best snooker of my career and that's when I got the devastating news about my mum who was only 62. Everything stopped then and I didn't want to pick up a cue after that. It was the most horrible time of my life," Dennis told me in 2017.

Taylor had no interest in snooker as he mourned his mother's loss, but after the family persuaded him to play in the Grand Prix in Reading, inspired by the memory of Annie, he performed superbly to reach the final and defeat Canadian Cliff Thorburn 10-2. It was his first major title. "I wasn't even going to play in that tournament. It was my family who persuaded me to do it for my mum. That's exactly what I did. It was a very, very emotional time but at least I won it for my mum," he said.

That victory gave Dennis the confidence to shine at the Crucible in Sheffield. Six years on after losing his first World Championship decider to Terry Griffiths, he savoured a miraculous 18-17 success. "At the Crucible I was chatting away to my mum in my head so that kept me in a good frame of mind. Even when I was way behind I never gave up," he added.

Over three decades on from his world title win, Taylor is a more recognisable face than most of the modern day players thanks in part to his 'upside down' glasses, which helped his vision at the table, a razor sharp wit, ready smile and the most talked about world title win of all. Taylor's relationship with Northern Ireland's other snooker legend Alex Higgins had its difficult moments but the Coalisland man was extremely sad when the Hurricane passed away in 2010. Dennis defeated Alex 9-8 in a brilliant Masters final in 1987 and together the pair of them, along with Eugene Hughes, won the World Cup team event in 1985, 1986 and 1987 for Ireland. A hugely popular character in sport, Taylor became a respected snooker commentator when his playing days finished and has taken part in a host of prime time TV shows including Strictly Come Dancing.

ANTHONY TOHILL

GAELIC FOOTBALL: MIDFIELD GIANT IN DERRY'S ALL-IRELAND TRIUMPH
B: 02/08/1971

Anthony Tohill was a colossus for the successful Derry GAA team in the 1990s with a towering presence that put the fear of God into opponents and told those in the trenches beside him that everything was going to work out just fine. In 1993 he sampled the thirst quenching taste of All-Ireland glory and in a highly decorated career also won two Ulster Championships, four Allianz League titles, four All Stars and was outstanding for Ireland against Australia in the International Rules Series.

A man mountain of a midfielder he had the strength of Sansom, more skill than some gave him credit for and a character never to give up which was first fashioned when he played against his older brothers on the family farm just outside the village of Swatragh. He learnt life lessons in the fields with his siblings and under the tutelage of intelligent coach Adrian McGuckian at his school St Patrick's Maghera his marks on the pitch soared.

It was in 1989 that Tohill made a major breakthrough, not just in terms of honours but in how he was looked upon by GAA fans across Ireland as, after a startling comeback victory over St Colman's, Newry in the MacRory Cup final, he helped St Pat's lift the Hogan Cup for the first time in their history and then played a significant role as the Derry Minors claimed the All-Ireland Minor trophy.

A long and illustrious GAA career beckoned for Tohill though not before he was one of the first Irishmen to be snapped up by an Australian Football League (AFL) team at 18 years of age to play Aussie Rules with Melbourne Demons, who were impressed by his attitude and attributes. Tohill left home in January 1990 and was back 18 months later after what he told GAA.ie was "a wonderful experience" ended by clubs having to cut costs and squad sizes across the AFL with Tohill not helped after previously suffering a broken leg playing in a GAA game Down Under.

The loss for the Demons was an almighty gain for Derry and while he was offered opportunities to return to play in Australia, Anthony stayed put and was the centre of attention as the Oak Leaf county savoured the best period in their history. Under perceptive manager Eamonn Coleman they won the National League final in 1992, beating Tyrone with talisman Tohill turning the game on its head late on with a right footed goal and a left footed point. The big one, the one Derry had never won, would be captured the next year when a team of style and substance overcame Cork 1-14 to 2-8 at Croke Park with Tohill contributing points and a big performance, as he had done on route to the final, in the county's greatest day of all.

The same year he won the Sigerson Cup with Queen's and in 1995 and 1996 there would be back to back National League triumphs for Derry and an Ulster Championship in 1998 before he captained the side to another League success in 2000 when he collected the last of his four All Stars. He was also skipper of the 2001 Ireland International Rules team which famously won both Tests in Australia, leading by example with words and deeds in one of four tours he experienced. In the middle of all this Tohill, who retired from playing in 2003, had a trial with Manchester United and played for Derry City, though it was in GAA that this giant of the game made a monumental impression.

COLIN TURKINGTON

MOTOR RACING: MULTIPLE
TOURING CAR CHAMPION DRIVER

B: 21/03/1982

The highly charged and achingly hard fought British Touring Car Championship (BTCC) has been going since 1958 and in that time, despite the exceptional motorsport talent in the country, Colin Turkington is the only Northern Ireland man to have won it. Even more impressive is the fact that no one in the history of the prestigious event has won it more times than the masterly Turkington, who is widely recognised as one of the best Touring Car performers in the world. Writing this now the Portadown driver has four BTCC titles, starting off his glory run in 2009, doubling up in 2014, making it a hat-trick in 2018 and racing to a record equalling success in 2019 and with the prospect of more triumphs to come Turkington could rev out on his own in the BTCC all-time list and ahead of another Touring Car great, 1970s and 1980s hero Andy Rouse.

Like many a successful driver, Turkington, at the age of 10, started out in karting and although initially it was a hobby, his prowess behind the wheel meant he progressed quickly, winning the Ford Fiesta Championship in 2001 while still a teenager. The next year he was brought on board as a driver for a glamorous new set-up who were sponsoring a team in the BTCC. It was Team Atomic Kitten and with the hit girl band involved in an enticing mix of music and motorsport Colin, then 19, was thrust into the spotlight. The pop stars exited stage left after one year but Turkington did well enough to earn himself a spot on a manufacturer backed team and stayed in the BTCC. At the same time he was studying for a business degree at Stirling University in Scotland, later admitting that with his dedication to racing he missed out on partying and some classes but finished the degree.

That dedication has played an important role in his success, as he is known for attention to detail and collecting as much information as possible on different circuits to give him an edge. What he is also renowned for in his sport is his style of driving, preferring to be smooth and slick rather than becoming involved in the rough and tumble of Touring Cars. In an interview marking being named Motorsport Hero in the 2020 Autocar Awards, he said: "I've always tried to go about my racing in a fair manner, to race hard but fair. If I'm going to win something, I want to win it in the right way. It's more rewarding to pull off a great overtake than nudge somebody off the road."

In 2009 came his first British Touring Car Championship victory courtesy of six race wins in a BMW 320si E90 with the West Surrey Racing team prior to delivering podium places and wins in the World Touring Car Championship and Scandinavian Touring Car Championship before making a return to BTCC, clinching the title again in dominant fashion in 2014. His third title in 2018 meant the world after his mum Mavis had passed away, with Turkington telling Sammy Hamill in the Belfast Telegraph: "It was always my dream to win the BTCC championship and I had won it twice before but this time mum wasn't there with my dad Trevor so this one was for her. That's what makes this one special. It's in her memory." He retained the crown in 2019 in thrilling and dramatic fashion by just two points becoming champion in the final race after a breathtaking drive in his BMW 330i M Sport to cement his place amongst the Touring Car greats, paying warm tributes, as is his way, to those who helped him including his team and wife Louise and their children Lewis and Adam.

JOHN WATSON

MOTOR RACING: FORMULA ONE HERO
WITH MIRACLE GRAND PRIX WINS

B: 04/05/1946

John Watson was the first Northern Ireland driver to win a race in Formula One, was close to winning the 1982 World Championship and rates as one of the finest over takers ever in the sport, famously and historically coming from the back of the grid to take the chequered flag in a US Grand Prix in Long Beach. Unlike many of his contemporaries who included James Hunt, Niki Lauda, Mario Andretti and Alain Prost, Watson could be understated with F1 legend Jackie Stewart once labelling him "too nice" when comparing the Belfast man to other drivers, but make no mistake 'Wattie' is one of his country's all-time motorsport greats and arguably the best of the bunch.

Born into a motorsport loving family and with dad Marshall a keen racer himself it wasn't long before John developed a passion for four wheels which was heightened at the age of nine when he saw icons Juan Manuel Fangio and Stirling Moss racing at Dundrod. From that moment Watson wanted to be a racing driver and when he was old enough to compete across Ireland he showed his class with notable wins at Phoenix Park and an exceptional performance in 1969 in the European Championships at Thruxton going from 20th to fifth in a second hand Lotus 48 Formula 2 car before crashing. The following year he raced in F2 in a Brabham BT 30 after being backed by his father and though John broke his arm and leg and fractured his ankle in 1970, lost friends to the sport and found the financial costs a struggle being a privateer, determination to race at the top level drove him on.

In 1973 he finally made it to what he viewed the pinnacle, a Grand Prix drive in Formula One, winning for the first time in 1976 in Austria with American team Penske, shaving off his beard after promising to do so when he was victorious. That same year Watson helped save Niki Lauda's life after the Austrian's Ferrari was engulfed in a fireball during the German Grand Prix. Penske dropped out of F1 but with some assistance from Bernie Eccelstone, Watson joined Brabham, establishing himself as a top line competitor before racing politics and Lauda arriving as the team's kingpin saw him move to McLaren in 1979 leading to an exhilarating and emotional home victory in the British Grand Prix at Silverstone two years later.

That was followed by an even more impressive success on the Detroit street circuit in 1982 roaring through for victory from way down on the grid, Belgium Grand Prix glory and a shot at the F1 title that season which ended with the battle going down to the last race and Keke Rosborg pipping Watson to the crown by five points. In 1983, in what is still regarded as one of the greatest racing displays in F1, Watson miraculously surged past the field at Long Beach for his fifth and final GP victory, having started 22nd with no one ever having won from that far back. Watson, who raced 154 times in F1, would go on to finish runner-up in the 1987 World Sportscar Championship with Jaguar ahead of moving into broadcasting where he remains as respected as he was on the track.

NORMAN WHITESIDE

FOOTBALL: WORLD CUP HISTORY MAKER AND WEMBLEY WONDER

B: 07/05/1965

Norman Whiteside made his Manchester United debut at 16, broke a record set by Pele when he played in the World Cup finals for Northern Ireland at 17, scored his first goal at Wembley at the same age, netted his first FA Cup final strike at 18, won the British Championships with his country at 19, produced a stunning effort to win the FA Cup at 20 and was 21 when he was on the scoresheet in the World Cup finals. The Shankill Road man achieved more in the first five years of his extraordinary career than most top class footballers do in a lifetime, but then Whiteside was always something else.

He was the Bible reading kid who at 13 inspired the Northern Ireland schoolboy team to European Championship glory in 1979 and the young lad who made legendary Manchester United scout Bob Bishop chuckle when telling the story of how Whiteside had to be taken off in a trial match to give others a chance after smashing in SEVEN goals in the first 20 minutes. This Belfast boy was destined for greatness and while today he is revered as one of the toughest tackling and most fearless competitors to play the game, Whiteside was also a highly skilled technician, as comfortable with a subtle chip over the goalkeeper as smashing goals in with his hammer of a left foot, be it playing as a striker or in midfield.

A legend in Northern Ireland, he will forever be a huge hero to Manchester United fans who dubbed him the 'Shankill Skinhead' and look back with fondness on his breathtaking curler from outside the box, which won the 1985 FA Cup final against treble chasing Everton with the Red Devils down to 10 men following Kevin Moran's red card. Two years earlier he became the youngest player to score in a League Cup final with a brilliant goal in a 2-1 defeat to Liverpool and the youngest to score in an FA Cup final in a 4-0 replay success over Brighton. Whiteside loved Wembley saying he got more nervous playing snooker with his brother than playing in front of 100,000 spectators in the most famous stadium in the world.

Then again it seemed he was made for the big occasion from the start of his love affair with United, meeting the great Sir Matt Busby at Old Trafford when on trial as a 13-year-old and a week later finding out they wanted to sign him in another iconic building during a school trip to America. He told the UTD podcast: "One Monday I was at the Theatre of Dreams and the next Monday I was in the Oval Office with the President of the United States of America. It was 1978, Jimmy Carter was President. I came out of the Oval Office and my teacher pulled me aside to say my parents were on the phone. 'Manchester United want to sign you.' That's how I found out! What a week that was! Our school was over there because of the Troubles situation in Northern Ireland. We got invited to the White House. I was the school captain doing keepy-ups in the garden!"

Whiteside was just 16 when he first played for United in April 1982 and a few weeks later he was on the plane to Spain with the Northern Ireland squad for the World Cup finals after impressing manager Billy Bingham in a training camp, scoring a majestic goal that left goalkeeping star Pat Jennings amazed. Bingham said: "I had been thinking about perhaps using him as a substitute but we trained for a couple of weeks in Brighton and he was the outstanding player in all the practice games so I decided to start him in our first game against Yugoslavia."

Whiteside was 17 years and 41 days old and as he took to the pitch he became the youngest footballer to play in the World Cup finals, a record previously held by Brazilian icon Pele from 1958. The one time Boys Brigade member still holds the record and played in all five of Northern Ireland's games in the tournament with the freedom and fire he showed as a child on the streets of Belfast. Four years later, having won the British Championships and netted an historic winning goal in 1983 away to West Germany in a European Championship qualifier, which he described as his worst performance ever, he was back at the World Cup finals in Mexico scoring in a 1-1 draw against Algeria.

By that stage he had turned down a big money move to Italian giants AC Milan and an increasing number of unfortunate injuries were starting to take a toll. Whiteside enjoyed a beer and the company of good pals Bryan Robson and Paul McGrath and because of the drinking culture at the club he had some straight talking conversations with Sir Alex Ferguson, appointed United manager in 1986, though he insists he and the Scot had a good relationship, so much so that Ferguson helped the player negotiate a lucrative deal when he joined Everton in 1989.

Two years after moving to Goodison Park Whiteside was forced to retire at the age of 26 due to a knee injury with a host of memories and nine Northern Ireland goals from 38 internationals. Whiteside left school at 16 without qualifications but after finishing football went back to the classroom to study at the University of Salford and is now a qualified chiropodist and podiatrist. "I'm no academic. It was the toughest thing I've ever done going back to the classroom and sitting with kids who'd just done their A-levels," said Whiteside, who in recent times has worked in corporate hospitality at Old Trafford, where fans are still in awe of one of Belfast's finest.

ISABEL WOODS

CYCLING: RECORD BREAKING
QUEEN OF THE ROADS
B: 03/11/1928

Isabel Woods didn't have a bike as a child but became a history making cyclist breaking records on the roads of Ireland in the 1950s. A legend and Hall of Famer in her field, Isabel grew up during the Great Depression when money was scarce and it wasn't until she was 18 that she could afford to buy her first bike using savings she had accumulated from working since the age of 16.

Living in Belfast, she and her sister loved the countryside and would go touring together on their bikes. They joined the Trinity Harriers Club and when in 1949 Isabel finished second in her first race, the Ulster Ladies Road Club novice five mile time trial, she decided to buy a racing bike and from there went on to become one of the most celebrated and admired sportswomen of her era.

In the Mary Peters inspired book Passing the Torch, Woods explains that the then trainer of Irish League football club Glentoran, Bobby McGregor, helped her improve her fitness and soon she was winning a host of local races under her maiden name Clements and thinking about attempting to break long distance records.

Followed by an official timekeeper, what Isabel achieved in the 1950s was remarkable, doing it with an unwavering desire to set new benchmarks and fastest times which would inspire future generations and today Cycling Ireland lauds her as the most prolific record breaker in the history of road records in Ireland. At one stage she held eight records including in rides between Belfast and Dublin, Derry and Dublin and Enniskillen and Belfast plus for covering the most miles over a 24 hour period.

This was a lady breaking new ground across the island. There was the classic 386 mile End to End trek all over Ireland from Mizen Head in county Cork to Antrim's Fairhead in 1955 completing that journey in 23 hours and two minutes and on roads nowhere near as smooth or easy to navigate as they are these days. It wasn't until 2007 that Irish based Rose

Leith, born in Zimbabwe, set a new mark with Isabel there to meet her in a touching moment at the conclusion of an epic effort though in 1955 the course was understood to be 18 miles longer.

Approached to turn professional because she was viewed as one of the best riders around, Isabel preferred to remain an amateur and married to husband Peter she made the decision to focus on her family and their children rather than continue on her record breaking spree. Isabel wrote her autobiography 'Wheels of Change' in 2008 and will forever be treasured in the world of cycling for her long lasting feats of endurance and excellence and at a time when ambitions could be restricted she made people across Northern Ireland feel anything was possible.

THE FINAL SCORE

There you have it then. A ton of talent. Telling the stories of our sporting superstars it's clear humility and hard work are common features of the secrets behind their success. It's also a lesson to future generations with dreams of reaching the top in their chosen fields. Put the graft into your craft and don't lose the run of yourself when the good times come along.

By now you will have read about 100 of our sporting greats. Like I said at the start of the book there are many more and one of the toughest elements in putting it all together was deciding who to leave out.

I agonised over some decisions. Of course you have the obvious big hitters and I'd be surprised if everybody wouldn't select them in a list like this but the deeper I moved into the 100 the more testing the choices became.

I won't go through all of the names that missed out, because as previously stated I came up with 232 sports stars who could be considered for the top 100, but I believe it is worth pointing out some that were considered such as boxers Jimmy Warnock, Terry Milligan, Ryan Burnett, Eamonn Loughran, Brian Magee, Tommy Armour and Eddie 'Bunty' Doran, motorcyclists Tom Herron, Ryan Farquhar and Alastair Seeley, GAA players Brian Dooher, James McCartan Snr, James McCartan Jr, Sean Cavanagh, Jim McKeever, Iggy Jones, Henry Downey, Kieran McGeeney and Martin Clarke who became a hero in Aussie Rules, footballers Sammy McIlroy, Mal Donaghy, Derek Dougan, Terry Neill, Mickey Hamill, Keith Gillespie, Jimmy Nicholl, Gareth McAuley, Kyle Lafferty, Roy Carroll, Pat Rice and Julie Nelson, hockey players Violet McBride, Jenny Redpath and Eugene Magee, golfers Ronan Rafferty and Garth McGimpsey, triathlete Aileen Reid, jockeys Ray Cochrane and Tony Dobbin, rowers Holly Nixon and Joel Cassells, netball's Noleen Lennon, snowboarder Aimee Fuller, bowls star Jeremy Henry, Lisa Bradley and Lisa Kearney from judo, handball's Aisling Reilly, cricketers Kyle McCallan, Ivan Anderson and William

Porterfield, camogie's Mairead McAtamney and Jane Adams, athletes Philip Beattie, Martin Girvan and Janet Boyle, hurler Olcan McFetridge, Belfast Giants ice hockey legends Graeme Walton and Mark Morrison, motocross man Gordon Crockard, trials supremo Sammy Miller and a host of rugby players including Cecil Pedlow, Dick Milliken, Willie Anderson, Philip Matthews, Trevor Ringland, Keith Crossan, Blair Mayne, Andrew Trimble and David Irwin. I would loved to have included fantastic Ulster winger Tommy Bowe, a big favourite of mine, but with him being born in the South of Ireland and Ulster a club side he wasn't eligible. It's the same scenario for, say, South Africa born class act Ruan Pienaar.

If I were to re-write this book in five years I'm certain footballers Jonny Evans and Stuart Dallas would be in the top 100 and perhaps rugby's Jacob Stockdale and Iain Henderson, snooker's Mark Allen, hockey's Ayeisha McFerran and Katie Mullan, golf's Stephanie Meadow and MMA fighter Leah McCourt would join them because they still have much to achieve. There is even younger talent out there like Tom McKibbin who could take the golf world by storm in the future.

And if I re-wrote this book in a decade's time I believe more women would be included. There is a wonderful selection of outstanding women in the book who have inspired, influenced and achieved so much and it is brilliant to recognise their contribution though if we are being honest with ourselves opportunities for women in sport have not always been plentiful in Northern Ireland. Thankfully that is changing and I fully expect to see more sportswomen from here delivering at home and on the world stage in the years to come. I also look forward to seeing more of our men and women from ethic minorities shine.

You will have noticed that the 100 sports stars are in alphabetical order in the body of the book. Ranking them from 100 to 1 would have been nigh on impossible but I am willing to do my own personal countdown from 15 to 1 which is difficult enough.

I like the idea of giving a nod to the various sports we have excelled in and like the century of heroes my top 15 is open to debate. Why don't you try and name your top 15? Here's mine...

15. Paddy Hopkirk: To put into context what Paddy Hopkirk achieved when he famously won the Monte Carlo Rally in 1964 in his little Mini, it would be like Rory McIlroy winning the Masters at Augusta without a driver in his bag. One of sport's greatest triumphs.

14. Thelma Hopkins: A trailblazer who jumped into history by recording the first ever athletics world record in Ireland in the High Jump and became Northern Ireland's first female to win an Olympic medal. That's called leading the way. A hugely important person on the country's sporting spectrum.

13. Peter Canavan: Quite simply the best GAA player I've ever seen. I remember watching him years ago and this is not a trick of my memory but amid a 100 mile per hour game with tackles flying, Tyrone's All-Ireland hero was the only player on the pitch who had time on the ball. He made it with his awareness of space, knowhow and experience, playing the game at the pace he wanted to with everyone else caught up in the madness of it all. What a talent.

12. Carl Frampton: It shouldn't be underestimated how important boxing is across the communities in Northern Ireland. It's been our most successful sport and in the 21st century Frampton has been instrumental in flying the flag. His world title win over Leo Santa Cruz in America was one of our finest victories in his or any other sport and if he achieves his dream of becoming Ireland's first three weight world champion he would be higher on this list.

11. Jonathan Rea: This guy is one of the most impressive operators in world sport and we are lucky to call him ours. He has become a world champion winning machine and delivers with a humility and work ethic that have been hallmarks of many of the country's sporting greats. It's tough enough becoming champion of the world once but to keep doing it the way Rea has confirms he has one of the best mentalities around to go with all that riding ability.

10. Alex Higgins: The natural talent who could make a cue ball sit up and talk if he put his mind to it. While there was a sad end to his life, the Hurricane gave millions of us happiness when he was at a snooker table shuffling around the arena at lightning speed before potting balls that defied belief. All these years on when I see footage of Higgins winning the 1982 World Championship, it still makes me smile.

8. Steven Davis and Pat Jennings: All-time great Northern Ireland footballers adored for their selfless attitude to the team as much as their ability. The nation's most capped players who have inspired their sides in different generations to reach for the sky and reach the finals of major tournaments. A midfield maestro and goalkeeping giant, this dynamic duo stand tall.

7. **Sir Tony McCoy:** Another winning machine. The toughest of competitors who was at the top of his game for 20 years breaking so many records it became the norm. That's the thing about McCoy, he made the extraordinary appear ordinary because he was just so darned good. His medical history is one long list of injuries, and serious ones at that, but he kept coming back to be number one. He didn't wear a cape but he was a Superman in silks.

5. **Willie John McBride and Jack Kyle:** In the book the rugby players I've written about will be talked about for centuries such is the status of great men like Mike Gibson and Rory Best. Leading the way have been Willie John McBride and Jack Kyle. I can't separate them and I won't. Kyle inspired Ireland to their first Grand Slam and like the Lion King McBride had that wonderful quality to lift people on and off the field. Majestic, the pair of them.

4. **Lady Mary Peters:** Forever our Golden Girl and Northern Ireland's only Olympic champion in an individual sport. Not just our greatest female sports star but one of the best and most popular in the history of world sport. The 1972 success in the Munich Games was the stuff of dreams for Mary and it did the world of good for the rest of us. We have needed Mary Peters in our lives. Sporting legend for sure, but she is so much more than that. What a Lady.

3. **Joey Dunlop:** Joey is the most loved sporting hero of them all from this place. He had a modest, unassuming way about him that drew people to be on his side and when they saw him compete, giving it everything, they were desperate for him to succeed be it at the Isle of Man TT, where he created history, or elsewhere. If Mary will always be our Golden Girl, to the end of time we'll see five time World Champion Joey Dunlop as the King of the Roads.

2. **George Best:** When choosing this top 15, there were times I had Bestie at number one. The guy was a football genius and an artist who could paint everlasting images in your head and the town red within hours of each other. The goals, the glory, the fall from grace, Best's story is the most gripping tale of all. In the biggest sport and the world's game, the impact that he made is still being felt. He would be in the top 10 of anyone's

greatest ever footballer list and number one for many. Wow. Just wow. Hero to the heroes, boy, George, could you play.

1. Rory McIlroy: When you are working in sports journalism, every so often you will hear about the 'next big thing', a bright young talent who has the potential to go far. Some of them do well and make a fine career for themselves in their chosen sport and others fall off the radar and live their lives away from the spotlight. Then there's Rory McIlroy. Once upon a time the 'next big thing', he became the biggest thing, the best thing. What he has achieved from boy to man has been monumental becoming the world number one, claiming championships all over the globe and winning multiple major titles in a sport where it is crazily tough to win just one. In my view McIlroy isn't just Northern Ireland's greatest sports star, he's one of the greatest sports stars on the planet who constantly puts his place of birth on the map on a global scale. Revered all over the world, there's always a buzz when he swings into action, skips over the fairway and strides on to the green. Seeing McIlroy play live when he is in the zone is up there with watching Lionel Messi, Roger Federer and Usain Bolt in the flesh. I'm lucky to have experienced them all. He has that aura. He is that great. The Holywood star is box office, a mesmeric master who oozes class. Already viewed as one of the most gifted players in golf history, McIlroy has more to give. Much more. In this ton of talent, Rory tops my list of our sporting legends. Now it's your turn...

APPENDIX 1: LIST OF SOURCES

Arsenal FC
Aston Villa FC
Athletics NI
Athletics Weekly
Autocar
Autosport
balls.ie
Balmoral Golf Club
Banbridge Leader
BBC
BBC NI
BBC Radio Five Live
BBC Radio Ulster
Belfast Celtic Society
Belfast Live
Belfast Telegraph
Bellaghy Historical Society
Bestie
Best of Enemies
Bigredbookinfo
Birmingham Mail
Blessed
Boxing News
Box Nation
boxrec.com
British Athletics
British Bobsleigh Association
Britishhorseracing.com
British Rowing
BT Sport
Burnley FC
Celtic FC
Champions of Racing
Coleraine Chronicle
Coleraine Times
Commonwealth Games Federation
Conversations with my Father
Cool FM
cricketeurope.com
Cricket Ireland
cuetracker.net
Culture Northern Ireland
Cycling Ireland
Cycling Weekly
Daily Express
Daily Mail
Daily Mirror
Daily Record
Daily Telegraph
Derry Journal
Derry Track Club
devittinsurance.com
Dictionary of Ulster Biography
Disability Sport NI
Doncaster Rovers FC
Down Recorder
Dromore & District Local Historical
  Group Journal
Edmonton Journal
ESPN
espncricinfo.com
European Tour
Eurosport

Female Sports Forum
FIFA
GAA.ie
gbolympics.co.uk
Glentoran FC
Golf Monthly
gpracingstats.com
hockeymuseum.net
Harry Gregg Foundation
historickilkenny.com
Hockey Ireland
International Boxing Hall of Fame
International Football Hall of Fame
IRFU
Irish Athletic Boxing Association
Irish Bowls Association
Irish-boxing.com
Irishhealth.com
iomtt.com
Irish Examiner
Irish FA
Irish Independent
Irish News
Irish Squash
Irish Times
ITV
Just for the Thrill
Legends of Irish Boxing
Linfield FC
Lion for a Day
lionsrugby.com
Lisburn.com
Liverpool Echo
Liverpool FC
Mail on Sunday
Man and Ball
Manchester City FC
Manchester Evening News
Manchester United FC
Mary Peters Trust
Motogp.com
Motorcycle News
Motorsport.com
Motorsport Magazine
National Football Museum
Netball NI
Newry Reporter
News Letter
Newstalk
New York Times
NI Commonwealth Games Council
NIFG
NI Sports Forum
Northwest200.org
Olympic.org
Off the Ball
Observer
Olympic Federation of Ireland
Paralympic.org
Paralympics GB
Paralympics.ie
Passing the Torch

pgatour.com
premierleague.com
Punching Above their Weight: The Irish
  Olympic Boxing Story
Queen's University
Racing Post
racingtv.com
Radio Times
Rangers FC
Ring magazine
Ring TV
Road Racer It's in my Blood
RTE
Rugby World
Sky Sports
Spirit of '58
Sported
Sport NI
sportsjoe.ie
Spotlight on Football
Sunday Express
Sunday Independent
Sunday Life
Sunday Times
Talksport
Teamgb.com
the42.ie
The Guardian
The Herald
The Independent
The Little Book of Irish Boxing
The Making of Paddy Mo
The Open
The Road Racers
The Scotsman
The Times
The Ulster Cricketer
Tottenham FC
Transworld Sport
UEFA
UK Athletics
Ulster Gazette
Ulstergrandprix.net
Ulster GAA
Ulster Hockey
Ulster Rugby
Ulster Sports Museum
UTD podcast
UTV
Wartime NI
Watford FC
Watfordlegends.com
Wisden
World Athletics
Worldbowls.com
World Rally Championship
World Rugby
World Snooker
World Squash
World Superbikes
YouTube.

Appendix 2: Photo credits

Gerry Armstrong	Kelvin Boyes/Press Eye
Jim Baker	Kelvin Boyes/Press Eye
Paddy Barnes	William Cherry/Presseye
George Best	Belfast Telegraph Archives
Rory Best	Kelvin Boyes/Press Eye
Danny Blanchflower	Belfast Telegraph Archives
Ralph Bryans	Roy Harris
Mike Bull	Belfast Telegraph Archives
John Caldwell	Belfast Telegraph Archives
David Calvert	Stephen Hamilton/Presseye
Alan Campbell	William Cherry/Presseye
Peter Canavan	William Cherry/Presseye
Peter Chambers	William Cherry/Presseye
Richard Chambers	William Cherry/Presseye
Darren Clarke	Matt Mackey/Presseye
Michael Conlan	Jonathan Porter/PressEye
Fred Daly	Belfast Telegraph Archives
Steven Davis	William Cherry/Presseye
Robin Dixon	Belfast Telegraph Archives
Paddy Doherty	Belfast Telegraph Archives
Peter Doherty	Belfast Telegraph Archives
Joey Dunlop	Roy Harris
Michael Dunlop	Philip Magowan/Presseye
Robert Dunlop	Roy Harris
Richard Dunwoody	Darren Kidd/Presseye
Samuel Ferris	Public Domain
Stephen Ferris	Darren Kidd/Presseye
Bethany Firth	Declan Roughan/presseye
Carl Frampton	William Cherry/Presseye
Kelly Gallagher	Darren Kidd /Presseye.com
Mike Gibson	Belfast Telegraph Archives
Freddie Gilroy	Belfast Telegraph Archives
Harry Gregg	William Cherry/Presseye
Janet Grey	Jonathan Porter/Presseye
David Healy	William Cherry/Presseye
Anton Hegarty	Public Domain
Alex Higgins	Paul McCambridge/Presseye
Thelma Hopkins	Belfast Telegraph Archives
Paddy Hopkirk	Rallyretro.com
Wendy Houvenaghel	Ian MacNicol/Presseye
Aaron Hughes	William Cherry/Presseye
David Humphreys	Darren Kidd/Press Eye
Eddie Irvine	By Franmarjos - Own work, CC BY-SA 3.0, https://commons.wikimedia.org/w/index.php?curid=28401053
Martyn Irvine	Ian MacNicol/Presseye
Pat Jennings	Matt Mackey/Presseye
Margaret Johnston	Kelvin Boyes/Presseye
Jimmy Kirkwood	Darren Kidd /Presseye
Jack Kyle	Matt Mackey/Presseye
Maeve Kyle	Kelvin Boyes/Press Eye
Dermott Lennon	Mark Pearce/Presseye
Mickey Linden	Belfast Telegraph Archives
Ciara Mageean	Matt Mackey/Presseye
Stephen Martin	Darren Kidd /Presseye
Dave McAuley	Russell Pritchard/Presseye
Willie John McBride	Belfast Telegraph Archives
Phillip McCallen	Roy Harris
Shirley McCay	Rowland White/PressEye
Rhys McClenaghan	Sport NI
Billy McConnell	Rowland White/Press Eye
Oisin McConville	Russell Pritchard/Presseye

Jenna McCorkell	William Cherry/Presseye
Jim McCourt	Belfast Telegraph Archives
Sir Tony McCoy	Kelvin Boyes/Press Eye
Ray McCullough	Roy Harris
Wayne McCullough	William Cherry/Presseye
Graeme McDowell	Peter Morrison/PressEye
Barry McGuigan	Darren Kidd/Presseye
Jimmy McIlroy	Belfast Telegraph Archives
Rory McIlroy	Matt Mackey/Presseye
Michael McKillop	Darren Kidd /Presseye
Jimmy McLarnin	Belfast Telegraph Archives
John McNally	Belfast Telegraph Archives
Terence McNaughton	Presseye
Peter McParland	Belfast Telegraph Archives
Jackie McWilliams	Rowland White/Presseye
Jeremy McWilliams	Jonathan Porter/Presseye
Kris Meeke	Brian Little/Presseye
Syd Millar	Kelvin Boyes/Presseye
Rinty Monaghan	Belfast Telegraph Archives
Dermot Monteith	Belfast Telegraph Archives
Billy Murray	Billy Murray
Martin O'Neill	Belfast Telegraph Archives
Caroline O'Hanlon	Darren Kidd /Presseye
Sean O'Neill	Belfast Telegraph Archives
Bertie Peacock	Belfast Telegraph Archives
Madeline Perry	Darren Kidd /Presseye
Dame Mary Peters	Rowland White
Jonathan Rea	Kelvin Boyes/Press Eye
Brian Reid	Roy Harris
John Reid	Belfast Telegraph Archives
Hugh Russell	Belfast Telegraph Archives
Elisha Scott	Public Domain
Jason Smyth	Kelvin Boyes/Presseye
Paul Stirling	Rowland White/Presseye
Dennis Taylor	By John Dobson - Dennis Taylor Presentation Night, CC BY-SA 2.0, https://commons.wikimedia.org/w/index.php?curid=78892453
Anthony Tohill	Belfast Telegraph Archives
Colin Turkington	Darren Kidd/Presseye
John Watson	Esler Crawford collection c/o Rallyretro
Norman Whiteside	Belfast Telegraph Archives
Isabel Woods	Isabel Woods

223

Dear Reader,

I hope you have enjoyed this publication from Ballyhay Books, an imprint of Laurel Cottage Ltd. We publish an eclectic mix of books ranging from personal memoirs to authoritative books on local history, from sport to poultry, from photographs to fiction and from music to marine interests – but all with a distinctly local flavour.

To see details of these books, as well as the beautifully illustrated books of our sister imprint Cottage Publications, why not visit our website **www.cottage-publications.com** or telephone +44 (0)28 9188 8033.

Timothy & Johnston

BALLYHAY BOOKS